W9-DHG-513

MONTGOMERY COLLEGE LIBRARY
ROCKVILLE CAMPUS

WITHDRAWN FROM LIBRARY

1000
AB

SHAKESPEARE THE MAN

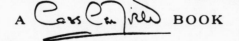

A Cass Canfield BOOK

Books by A. L. Rowse

Shakespeare's Sonnets

A modern edition, with prose-versions, and notes

The Elizabethan Age:

The England of Elizabeth

The Expansion of Elizabethan England

The Elizabethan Renaissance: The Life of the Society

The Elizabethan Renaissance: The Cultural Achievement

William Shakespeare

Christopher Marlowe: A Biography

Shakespeare's Southampton

Ralegh and the Throckmortons

Sir Richard Grenville of the Revenge

The Elizabethans and America

The Early Churchills

The Later Churchills

The Churchills

The English Spirit (*revised ed.*)

Times, Persons, Places (The English Past)

Tudor Cornwall

The Cornish in America

A Cornish Anthology

A Cornish Childhood

A Cornishman at Oxford

Poems Chiefly Cornish

Poems of Cornwall and America

Strange Encounter: Poems

SHAKESPEARE THE MAN

A. L. Rowse

La connaissance de l'homme est indispensable à qui veut approfondir la pensée et les intentions du poète.

André Billy on Appollinaire

HARPER & ROW, PUBLISHERS
New York, Evanston, San Francisco, London

SHAKESPEARE THE MAN. Copyright © 1973 by A. L. Rowse. All rights reserved. Printed in the United States of America. No part of this book may be used or reproduced in any manner whatsoever without written permission except in the case of brief quotations embodied in critical articles and reviews. For information address Harper & Row, Publishers, Inc., 10 East 53rd Street, New York, N.Y. 10022.

FIRST U.S. EDITION

ISBN: 0-06-013691-x

LIBRARY OF CONGRESS CATALOG CARD NUMBER: 72-10683

CONTENTS

TO
ALICE FAIRFAX-LUCY
OF CHARLECOTE
CUSTODIAN OF THE TRADITION
FOR THE YEARS OF FRIENDSHIP

LIST OF ILLUSTRATIONS

between pages 50 and 51

PREFACE

I HAD been intending at some time to follow my larger book *William Shakespeare* with a Portrait of the Man. The wholly unexpected discovery of the identity of his Dark Lady has made me advance the date. My intention was to concentrate on the biographical and correct the perspective, putting Shakespeare more into his proper world of the Elizabethan stage. This is what I have tried to do in this shorter book.

I did not think it likely that the Dark Lady would ever be discovered, still less discovered by me. And, indeed, I never set out to find her. All the attempts to put up some candidate by conjecture, and then seek to prove the case, were always so much waste of time – and pursuing a wrong method into the bargain, as I have said all along. There was this much to be said for my previous conviction – that there is nothing whatever about her in print.

To set out to look for her, as many have done – one would never find her that way. She was waiting for me all the time, as she had been waiting for centuries in the Bodleian, in the manuscript casebooks of Simon Forman, who knew almost everybody in Elizabethan London. I shall never forget my astonishment when I found who was waiting to be identified, or the date, 3 March 1972, when her identity forced itself upon me. (I need not say that, to follow Forman into his rabbit-warren, one needs to carry an Elizabethan *Who's Who* in one's head – without it, conjectures and speculations are valueless, as they all have been. Naturally, I have a feeling of fondness for the old reprobate, for what he has revealed to us, and propose to devote a book to him and his revelations.

The identity of the Dark Lady has constituted a prime problem in our literature and offered an acute challenge; for, without its solution, it has been difficult to write a biography of our greatest writer, at least one that was not two-dimensional. All prime discoveries have a certain simplicity, indeed obviousness, about them; but the consequences are immense. For the first time we can now write a three-dimensional biography of William Shakespeare.

The literary consequences are no less important. This problem was the last, and by far the most difficult, of the problems of the Sonnets to be solved. As I have said, I never thought it likely to be. But the discovery has triumphantly vindicated the answers I have put forward all along, and the method by which they were found: strict attention to chronology, the correlation of what Shakespeare tells us, of the topical references with historical circumstances at every point, the minute and precise corroboration of internal with external information. The discovery of the Dark Lady completely corroborates, and puts the coping-stone on, my previous findings.

I need hardly recapitulate these: the clear certainty that the Sonnets all belong to the same period, 1592 to the winter of 1594–5; the young Lord of the Sonnets, as of the Poems, the obvious person, Shakespeare's patron, Southampton; the Rival Poet, of course, Marlowe; 'Mr W. H.' – about whom so much nonsense has been written in hundreds of books, under the misapprehension that he was Shakespeare's young man – simply the publisher's dedicatee. It emerges still more clearly that the Sonnets are not at all homosexual in character, but are written fundamentally in the course of the duty owed by the poet to the patron – though recording so much else. A more original realisation is that the Sonnets offer a homogeneous and integrated work of art, belonging entirely to these years; one can only understand the story they tell – like another play, only Shakespeare's intimate personal drama – by reading them all straight through from beginning to end. (Few do – unless people do, they do not know what the Sonnets are telling us.)

The practical consequences are no less immense: it puts out of court all the existing editions of the Sonnets. It also puts out of court all the biographies of Shakespeare. For myself, I take comfort, and rather more than comfort, from the fact that my previous work on Shakespeare has been corroborated: it merely needed completion.

I realise all too well, from the uncomprehending way my previous work has been taken by the Shakespeare establishment, that it will take time before this new knowledge is absorbed. But Shakespeare scholarship has long reached a dead end, and scholars should be grateful for a new start, a new impulse.

In announcing these findings – except for the last, which clinches them all – I said that it would be found impossible to impugn the historian's account of the matter. Perhaps I should add now merely that it will be found quite impossible to impugn any of them, for they are the definitive answers. It should be encouraging to research to think that Elizabethan problems, which have awaited their answer for centuries, can still be resolved at this late date.

Since the approach in my previous book was more literary than dramatic, I should prefer it to be called *William Shakespeare: a Study*. I have incorporated material from it as convenient; but, for the convenience of the reader, I have minimised footnotes, giving only those references that are new. And I have provided a Comparative Chronology, so that the reader may see at a glance how Shakespeare's life and work related to the Elizabethan background, public, literary and personal.

My indebtedness for the new material in this book is to the Bodleian Library at Oxford. It is pleasantly ironical to think that complete and absolute corroboration was waiting all the time so close at hand: in the words of an uncompromising and great scholar, A. E. Housman, from 'the arsenals of the divine vengeance, if I may so describe the Bodleian Library.'

A. L. Rowse

All Souls College,
Oxford.

CHAPTER 1

Warwickshire Background

MUCH of the nonsense that has been written about William Shakespeare, in many languages, comes from ignorance of the Elizabethan age and its conditions. Such people think that we know hardly anything about him. This is a prime mistake: in fact, we know more about him than about any other dramatist of the time, with the exception of Ben Jonson, who lived rather later and had a longer life. Even with regard to him we know hardly anything about his early life, his family and origins. This is already a marked contrast with Shakespeare, about whose early life we know a great deal, for an Elizabethan.

In that age people were not much interested in the biographies of writers, especially mere dramatists, unless they were otherwise important. On the whole, we find biographies only of royal personages or grandees, of very literate or loquacious persons, bishops, academics, Puritans or Jesuit confessors. We know little or nothing of more fascinating people, like Robert Greene or Thomas Nashe, Webster, Tourneur or John Ford – let alone men of scientific genius such as Thomas Hariot or William Gilbert. What would we not give to know more about Christopher Marlowe! We are fortunate to know as much as we do about his contemporary, William Shakespeare.

Much of the confusion that has arisen with regard to him is, in part, quite unnecessary. It has arisen from even standard authorities – not only Victorians like Sir Sidney Lee, but Edwardians such as Sir Edmund Chambers and Professor Dover Wilson – leaving open questions that could have been settled, and adding to the confusion by superfluous conjectures (about 'Mr W. H.' notably). With an

Elizabethan, it is always better to stick to facts and known historical circumstance.

Perhaps one should add that a knowledge of the Elizabethan age in depth is advisable, if not indispensable. One cannot fully appreciate Dickens except in terms of the Victorian age; still less can one get Shakespeare right, or even understand the *nuances* of his language, unless we are immersed in the time in which he lived, and are familiar with its habits of thought, its values and modes of being. Of course, one can appreciate the plays, the drama, in all times and places – there is the universal element; and one can enjoy much of the poetry. But for what lies at the back of it, and for understanding the work in the round, one needs the dimension of time. And most of all with regard to the man.

Even with regard to the work, the historical sense is important and chronological order essential. How could one properly appreciate the work of Beethoven if one thought the last quartets came before the early piano sonatas? Or if one thought that *Samson Agonistes* came before *Comus*? People without historical sense, in the Augustan age, were apt to be misled by the First Folio of Shakespeare opening with *The Tempest*, his penultimate work, while the rest follow in no satisfactory order. Anyone who wants to study the development and unfolding of Shakespeare's genius should read his work in chronological order – plays, poems, sonnets, more plays. And yet, such is the strength of unimaginative and static conservatism that there is, even today, no such edition in all the world.

I have no prejudice against conservative tradition, when it is convincing and true to life; in fact, all my work on Shakespeare has been conservative and traditional. My new finds are in keeping – the last of them all, clinching the whole, the identity of the Dark Lady, in complete consistency, impossible to impugn because borne out by historical fact and based on chronological order and method.

This study of Shakespeare the Man will therefore be historical and factual. We have plenty of studies of the dramatist and poet, far too much writing about him by people with no sense of the age.

This study of his life – now that the facts regarding the most significant and formative years in his career have at last been brought to light – might be alternatively entitled Shakespeare the Elizabethan. For such will be its emphasis.

Warwickshire is the heart of England, and it was singularly appropriate that Shakespeare should have been born there in the Elizabethan age. The place and time, the very dates – born 1564, died 1616 – are significant: if he had been born twenty years earlier or later, his achievement would have been different, nothing like so rich and full. His career and work, what he made of his providential good fortune, provide a marvellous instance of the moment meeting with the man to express it. The age itself was an inspiration; everything was propitious to poetry, music, drama; after a hard apprenticeship and many set-backs, in the event he was unimaginably fortunate as a writer.

His native Warwickshire – revealingly reflected in his work as it is loyally in his life – lies before us in Dugdale's map as it was in Shakespeare's day. Already, in only the next generation, Dugdale noticed the distinction conferred on Stratford-upon-Avon in that 'it gave birth and sepulture to our late famous poet, William Shakespeare'. The county is lozenge-shaped, with the River Avon – an old Celtic word for river – running through the midst roughly dividing Arden from Feldon, the woodland country in the north, remains of ancient forest, from the open fields and pastures of the south.

There was something exciting to the imagination in the very situation of Stratford, on the threshold of the wooded Arden country, from which both Shakespeare's father and mother came – she, indeed, was born an Arden – to live in the lively, busy town. In his early works the free woodland is lovingly rendered: lovers wander off into it at leisure for refreshment and their own purposes. One recognises the landscape in *Venus and Adonis*, and Cotswold country to the south in the episode of coursing the hare. When the son came to write *As You Like It*, with several flecks of biographical interest in it, he did not hesitate to bring the Forest of Arden itself upon the stage. Warwickshire is given a good show in several of his plays, from the early *Henry VI* trilogy to old Justice Shallow in his Cotswold garden and Falstaff recruiting there in *Henry IV*.

All round about the county there was the vivacious, very individual, often violent life of the time, of which we have evidences in the documents and those other documents, the tombs in the churches and the houses that remain. Shakespeare was an historically minded, backward-looking man, much interested in the memorials of a previous past, as by its chronicles and its folklore. In English history he was especially drawn to the excitements, the melodramatic chops and changes of the century before, of the wars in France and the conflict between Lancaster and York. Not far away at Warwick, in the chapel of the parish church, lay the magnificent figure of Richard Beauchamp, the Earl, who had borne great sway in France from his castle at Rouen. There is his image still, in copper and gilt, the coloured enamels and coats of arms, hands together in prayer, the fixed stare of eternity upon the noble masculine features – enough to make the past live to any boy of imagination. In Shakespeare's maturity there came into the chapel the two Dudley earls, whom the youth would have seen about the county: the splendid Leicester, first and last in the affections of the Queen, and his elder brother Ambrose, whose widow consoled her last years.

Elizabeth had granted the castle at Warwick to the genial Ambrose; but he had no children, and King James gave it to Fulke Greville, Philip Sidney's friend. In Shakespeare's later years Greville was engaged in reconstructing the castle and making it more livable, while writing his sombre dramas. Just up over the hill to the north-west of Stratford, through pleasant elmy pastures, lay Alcester – still with a number of Elizabethan houses by the church; in that lay Fulke Greville's father, in armour and ruff, a leading figure in the county in William Shakespeare's growing days. Not far up the road was Coughton Court of the Catholic Throckmortons, where waited the women of the family for news of their menfolk involved in Gunpowder Plot in 1605.

To Leicester the Queen – more generous than people know –

granted beautiful Kenilworth. For her celebrated visit of 1575 he added on the grand lodgings we now see in ruins, to house her and the Court. The most sumptuous entertainments of the reign were laid on for her there – it was Leicester's last bid to capture her in marriage, and something of a crisis in their personal relations seems to have arisen. The men of Coventry came to present their pageants, their 'storial show' in the courtyard; the puritanically inclined City corporation were endeavouring to suppress the traditional mysteries, but this did not weigh with a cultivated queen, who bade them perform and rewarded them. In her the Shakespearian drama had a good friend; in fact, her support was decisive. Without her the Lord Mayor and Corporation of London would certainly have suppressed the theatres – a glory of the town to visiting foreigners.

In Shakespeare's time Kenilworth Castle had a large lake on the south side, upon which took place the water-pageants. Several thousand people from the neighbourhood crowded to catch a glimpse of the Queen and enjoy the shows. There is no reason why Shakespeare's father, then an alderman of Stratford, should not have brought along his clever boy of eleven, with the wide-open eyes to take it all in. Nor – with our better knowledge of the way in which contemporary events were absorbed into his experience to reappear in his work – is there any reason why there should not be a reminiscence in Cupid aiming his shaft

> At a fair vestal, thronèd by the west . . .

and missing; for

> the imperial votaress passed on,
> In maiden meditation, fancy-free.

Would it be fanciful to suppose that Warwickshire knew something of what transpired during that memorable visit? The countryside usually knows.

The Queen had passed close to Stratford three years before, in

1572; the town contributed loyally to the expenses of such a number, as in 1566, when twenty oxen had been consumed. In 1572 – shortly before the horror of the Massacre of St Bartholomew – she halted at Sir Thomas Lucy's at neighbouring Charlecote. (A fifteenth-century Lucy is given a good mention in *Henry VI.*) Shakespeare would recognise Charlecote still, not so greatly changed in spite of Victorian interference; the gatehouse remains as it was, with pretty diaper pattern in the brick. And there are still the three Sir Thomas Lucys he knew laid out on their tombs in the chapel.

Coming close to the town, there is Clopton House on the slope to the north; though a good deal altered, the core of the house belongs to the sixteenth century with its Renaissance porch added at the time. The Cloptons up there remained Catholics; at the time of Gunpowder Plot the house was rented by one of the conspirators. In the later fifteenth century Sir Hugh Clopton had been Stratford's great man, and he was still very much present to a youth of imagination. For he had built the Gild Chapel into which townsfolk and scholars from the school next door crowded for services, and the fine bridge that carried across the Avon the road which led south to Oxford and London, and fame. He had also built the finest house in the town, New Place, which success in the theatre in London eventually enabled the former schoolboy to buy.

If one has the eye to look below the surface of the hideous accumulations of the population-explosion of our time – though it is rapidly requiring the techniques of archaeology to do so – it is surprising how much remains. Now within the borough boundaries is the old manor-house of Alveston, with Elizabethan wing. In 1603, when Shakespeare was acquiring property in and around the town, Nicholas Lane bought the house, whose odd effigy with padded sleeves is up-ended in the truncated shut-up church. It was his nephew, John Lane, who was cited to the Consistory Court at Worcester for slandering Shakespeare's daughter, Susanna.

The house where Shakespeare's wife, Anne Hathaway, was brought up remains in the village of Shottery: still recognisable under its thatched roof, in their day it was known as Hewlands Farm. Now practically a suburb of the borough, it was then approached across the wheat fields and the rye, a pleasant walk for an ardent youth.

> It was a lover and his lass,
>   With a hey, and a ho, and a hey nonnino,
> That o'er the green cornfield did pass,
>   In the spring time, the only pretty ring time,
> When birds do sing, hey ding a ding, ding;
> Sweet lovers love the spring.
>
> Between the acres of the rye,
>   With a hey, and a ho, and a hey nonnino,
> These pretty country folks would lie,
>   In the spring time, the only pretty ring time,
> When birds do sing, hey ding a ding, ding;
> Sweet lovers love the spring.

On the Elizabethan stage such a song would be accompanied by appropriate, suggestive gestures; but it was at harvest-time, at the end of August 1582, that William Shakespeare's first child was conceived hereabouts, when he was passing eighteen.

Or we may take the road up and out to Wilmcote, on a little ridge to the north-east, whence we see the blue sickle of the Cotswolds on the south-west horizon. In the village is the Tudor house now known as Mary Arden's, for it belonged to Shakespeare's grandparents, the Ardens, whence his mother married John Shakespeare. The Ardens were superior folk, probably related to the Arden gentry of Park Hall in north Warwickshire.

Perhaps, after all, it is in the churches that things are least changed – like his own, with its noble spire reflected in the Avon that washes the churchyard wall. At Snitterfield, whence his father married Mary Arden and to which his grandfather came in the reign of Henry VIII, the old church still has its fine stalls of the time, just before the Reformation, the font in which many of the family were baptised. At Rowington is the church where earlier

Shakespeares were buried, still with its Elizabethan altar-table, oak chests and alms-box. Aston Cantlow has more woodwork from the Forest of Arden – oak pulpit, chests, a candelabrum; and here Shakespeare's parents would have been married, for it was Mary Arden's parish.

And so down again into the lush water-meadows of the Avon – hardly a couple of miles across is Clifford Chambers, beloved of that other Warwickshire poet, Michael Drayton. (It is endearing to think how closely the age brought into association, and how fruitfully, those three Warwickshire men: William Shakespeare, Michael Drayton and Holinshed the chronicler.) As Shakespeare used to come back to Stratford every summer, from London or touring the country, so Drayton used to spend the summers with his friends the Rainsfords at moated Clifford Chambers. The charming old half-timbered house was burned down this century, but Sir Henry and his wife – whom Drayton celebrated in his cool sonnets, *Idea's Mirror* – remain upon their monument in church, kneeling face to face.

Drayton also was an Arden man by origin, brought up at Polesworth, by the River Anker in the north of the county. He was not a family man, but a bachelor, more of a solitary, a bookish fellow. A voluminous and a good poet, he had no success with his plays and made no money. But he, at least, was without envy of his fellow countryman (the Elizabethans used the word to mean from the same county) in that quarrelsome age, and Shakespeare's good nature was not one to attract spite for long. Drayton paid him the compliment of drawing upon *A Midsummer Night's Dream* in his exquisite poem *Nymphidia* – both full of Warwickshire folk- and fairy-lore. It is an old tradition, which there is no need to reject, that the two countrymen would foregather in summer.

A small county from the Anker in the north to Barton-on-the-Heath in the south – where Shakespeare's uncle and aunt lived, Edmund and Joan Lambert, and the creation of his early fancy, Christopher Sly, 'old Sly's son of Barton Heath' – but, with its cathedral city of Coventry, its grand castles like Warwick and Kenilworth, with their splendid denizens and the comings and goings of Queen and Court, the numerous manor-houses of Grevilles, Throckmortons, Comptons, Lucys, the busy little towns like Stratford with their intimate teeming life, the churches and schools, the vivid, variegated inhabitants: it made a full world for the imagination to feed upon.

CHAPTER 2

A Stratford Family

IF Shakespeare could return to Stratford, he would find his native town still very recognisable – remarkably so, considering the hideous destruction and reconstruction general in our time. We still approach it from the south over Hugh Clopton's strained and tottering bridge; on the left the open space used for archery in Shakespeare's day, now presided over by the *genius loci.* The towering Theatre is all that is new in that direction; behind it, on the exquisite curve of the river, the tapering spire known all over the world, in the shadow of which he and his family lie.

Ahead of us is Bridge Street, now double in width, for a row of houses used to run down the middle. There, conveniently placed at the entrance to the town, were the three chief inns, the Swan, the Bear, the Angel – only the last remains, much translated. In 1583 we find the Earl of Warwick staying at the Swan, which had a Protestant inflexion, while the Bear had a Catholic flavour. At the top, at the intersection of High Street with Henley Street stood the market-cross in Catholic days; in Shakespeare's, it was replaced by a covered structure, under which his father had his standing with the other glovers on market days – the eldest boy would have helped here.

A half-turn to the right takes us along Henley Street to the house where he was born, not so much changed inside. One of these two small houses was the glover's shop, the other the family home. At the back a wing extends into a pretty garden, now filled with the son's favourite flower, roses. It would have made a cosy little home to bring his wife to, if somewhat cramped in the Elizabethan manner, when people lived their briefer lives more gregariously, more intensely. The living-room still has its open fireplace of brick and stone, raftered ceiling and flagged floor; at the back the kitchen with open hearth; upstairs the big family bedroom dominating the house, the place of birth and death.

An admirable old custodian of the place writes: 'it gathers memories and fancies. Shadows and weird noises are in the rafters, the wind is in the chimney, crickets are on the hearth, through the casement windows shines the moon, from without comes the 'to-whit, to-whoo' of the owl.' It must have been a fine place for owls: there were a thousand elms in and about the town in 1582, the small houses bowered in trees and birdsong, the upper end of Henley Street open country, orchards and a grove of ash and elm. Here was Shakespeare's home, until in 1597 he was able to buy New Place, the grandest house in the town: a significant gesture – much in keeping with what Robert Greene wrote about him. He did not occupy this house much till closer to retirement, however; most of the year he would be away, in London or on tour.

Round about were the little homes of the people he knew as boy and youth – as later he came to know the better-off residents at the other end of town, remembering a number of them in his will. For he was essentially a family man, a good townsman, with a sense of community – in contrast to Christopher Marlowe, and unlike Ben Jonson. Next door in Henley Street lived an unrespectable tailor, in spite of being a Wedgwood. Alderman Whately, draper, was very respectable, though there were skeletons in his cupboard in the shape of his brothers, two fugitive Catholic priests. In his garden he had beehives, 'wax, honey and other things in the apple-chamber' – how delightfully it must have smelt! There are still Whateleys in Stratford. A few doors away was another glover, Gilbert Bradley, for whom Shakespeare's brother would have been named.

A stream flowed across the street into Rother Market, thence by New Place down Chapel Lane to the river. Below the stream was Hornby's smithy. When Shakespeare came to write *King John* – with its touching reflection of grief for his only boy, who died young – he remembered also:

> I saw a smith stand with his hammer, thus,
> The whilst his iron did on the anvil cool,
> With open mouth swallowing a tailor's news;
> Who, with his shears and measure in his hand,
> Standing on slippers, which his nimble haste
> Had falsely thrust upon contrary feet. . . .

Evidently a familiar scene in Henley Street.

Down at the bottom in High Street lived the more prosperous shopkeepers and principal burgesses. Adrian Quiney, mercer, was a close colleague of John Shakespeare on the town-council, until the decline of the glover's affairs. In the next generation Thomas Quiney was to marry William Shakespeare's daughter Judith. Here too lived another mercer, his friend Henry Walker, whose son William was the poet's godson, to whom he left a gold sovereign. Here also were Hamnet and Judith Sadler, after whom his twins were named. Philip Rogers, the apothecary, sold liquorice, aniseed, and the new specifics coming from America, sassafras, guaiacum and 'tobecka'. Two grander houses that remain with decorative timber-work are Tudor House and Harvard House, so called because the daughter of the man who built it became the mother of the founder of Harvard College, Massachusetts.

Or from Henley Street we could follow the stream into the Rother (i.e. cattle) Market:

> It is the pasture lards the rother's sides.

Here remains part of Abraham Sturley's house, plaster ceilings and friezes within. Most fascinating, within the White Swan hotel, is an Elizabethan fresco, scenes from the Book of Tobit, all in colour with swags of fruit and texts. The rich brewer who owned this house objected to his daughter's marriage: to the offspring of the marriage, a young William, perhaps a godson, Shakespeare left 26*s* 8*d* for a ring to remember him by.

Down the lane is the Gild Chapel with its grey stone tower and in the precincts behind the Gild-hall, where the council-meetings so often attended by Alderman Shakespeare were held; also the grammar school attended by his sons, almshouses, and homes for schoolmaster and vicar. Across from the Chapel, with its clanging bell – the interior robbed of its richness by the sad Reformation – was New Place: a five-gabled house built back from the street with a little court before it, barns and garden at the back. This was the successful dramatist's home in his later years: nothing left of it but foundations, cellar-walls, the two wells. Rebuilt in the eighteenth century, it was then pulled down by its occupant, a clergyman already irritated by sightseers and quarrelling with the corporation.

Adjoining it along the street is the fine house of Thomas Nash, first husband of the poet's granddaughter; next, the house of Julian Shaw who witnessed his will. Then came that of the Reynolds family – now part of the Shakespeare Hotel: again, he left William Reynolds *26s 8d* to buy a ring in remembrance of him. In front of the Chapel was another market-cross, where country butchers sold their meat. From New Place Shakespeare could look out on it all – 'the vulgar sort of market-men . . . at wakes and wassails, meetings, markets, fairs'. The ringing of the market-bell from the Chapel told them when time was up.

We follow the road down which they were carried at the beginning to baptism in church, and at the end for burial.

> Now it is the time of night
> That the graves all gaping wide,
> Everyone lets forth his sprite,
> In the churchway paths to glide.

As one goes up the churchway path to the porch, the way they all came and went and came again, one has the sense that it is haunted. In his time there was a charnel-house in the graveyard, like that in *Romeo and Juliet*. I have always loved the little page in that play, who felt as many a Stratford boy must have done:

> I am almost afraid to stand alone
> Here in the churchyard; yet I will adventure.

An Elizabethan *revenant* would have no difficulty in recognising the familiar interior: the high nave, the clerestory, the chancel that beckons one up to it. At the back is the broken bowl of the medieval font in which he and all the family were christened. Up beneath the pulpit was the New Place pew; on the other side the former Cloptons in all the glory of their painted tombs. After the Reformation the chancel was boarded off; in winter the wind rustled in the roofs:

When all aloud the wind doth blow,
  And coughing drowns the parson's saw. . . .

And so into the chancel, the original stalls of the medieval college of priests, which was dissolved at the Reformation; Shakespeare eventually purchased a moiety of the tithes which had been part of the endowment. Within the sanctuary – in sanctuary at last – Shakespeare and his family are gathered, his bust looking blandly down on the unending procession from all parts of the world.

It was within his lifetime that Stratford became a self-governing borough: before, it had been subject to the see of Worcester. Some vestige of its earlier status may have remained in the title of 'bailiff' the head of the corporation held, instead of the more usual 'mayor' – a position to which John Shakespeare attained in the year 1569, when his eldest boy was five. The town-council consisted of fourteen aldermen and fourteen burgesses, with a permanent officer in the town-clerk. In 1603, the year of the Queen's death, Shakespeare's cousin, Thomas Greene, a lawyer of Middle Temple, got the office. He was succeeded by Francis Collins, an active Stratford attorney, who wrote the playwright's will, was made an overseer of it and was left twenty marks. One sees how loyally Shakespeare kept up his connections with his native town and how naturally and in what neighbourly fashion he made part of its life, though his work and fame were elsewhere

The town had its proper complement of officers, from ale-tasters and bread-weighers upwards: we can watch the upward progress of the municipally minded glover through them, to his ultimate embarrassment by having neglected his own business for the town's. It is pleasant to think that it still possesses the bailiff's, now mayor's, privy seal presented by Richard Quiney in 1592 (just when Alderman Shakespeare's son was starting upon the Sonnets). Sir Thomas Lucy took a helpful interest in the town's well-being, and from 1576 Stratford shared a recorder with Warwick, who was succeeded by Sir Fulke Greville, and he in turn by his more famous son, the poet, from 1606 to 1628.

The town lived chiefly by marketing for the country round about and by trade, its principal business being malting, with which it served quite a large area, as far as Lancashire and into Wales: plenty of Welsh folk came to and fro, to be observed. One-third of the more substantial householders were invested in malt, Shakespeare among them: at one time he held ten quarters at New Place.

There was increasing activity in organising the crafts and trades, the aim being to bring all the members of a craft into one company, to control apprenticeship and – improbably, as it may seem today – to uphold standards of craftsmanship. First came the bakers, followed by smiths and weavers; then came those in the building trade, masons, joiners, carpenters, to form one joint company. The individualistic glovers came last: there were not many of them, only seven or eight, but several of them were to the fore on the corporation, Alderman Shakespeare notably. Altogether it made a good scene upon which to observe a Bottom the weaver, Quince the carpenter, Snug the joiner, a bellows-mender and the rest of them.

The vivacity of life in the little community was much increased by religious dissension: this was reflected on the corporation, in the changes of vicars and schoolmasters, as among the surrounding gentry. The Marian priest was succeeded by Protestant vicar Bretchgirdle, who baptised the burgess's son William. He left a useful collection of books to the school: Cooper's Latin dictionary – of which the schoolboy made traceable use – Virgil and Cicero's *Offices*, Erasmus and the Psalms in English metre, with singing-books and school texts. He was succeeded by schoolmaster Smart, whose place was taken by Bretchgirdle's pupil Brownsword, wh won fame as a schoolmaster and was mentioned by Francis Mere for his Latin poems, as Shakespeare for his English. Vicars an schoolmasters lived in proximity in the Chapel precinct. Some o them had Catholic leanings. Simon Hunt was master from 157 to 1575, when William was a young schoolboy; but Hunt left fo Douai and ended up in Rome. Another Oxford man, Thoma Jenkins, was master (1575–9) during the boy's chief schoolyears. A Lancashire Oxonian, Alexander Aspinall, lasted there a long time 1582 to 1624. He had the sense to marry a well-to-do widow wit a wool-business, so he engaged in trade, buying and selling malt and became burgess, alderman, headborough of the ward Shake speare lived in.

The tradition is that the poet wrote the posy for him when h went a-wooing, with the offer of a pair of gloves:

> The gift is small:
> The will is all:
> Alexander Aspinall.

I am the more inclined to believe it, for it has the naughty play o the word 'will' of which Shakespeare was exceedingly fond. Ther is no reason why Shakespeare's father should not have provided th gloves.

At the church-end of the town, in the secularised College, live John Combe, who had done well out of church properties – fron whom the successful playwright bought a large slice of the bes land, just over a hundred acres, in Old Stratford. Later Shakespear made a larger purchase, of tithes at Welcombe, Bishopton an villages round about. This John Combe remembered Shakespear in his will with a bequest of £5, along with others of their friends to Francis Collins, who drew up Combe's will too, £10; 20*s* t Henry Walker, and large sums to young tradesfolk and the poor Combe has a grand tomb in the church, made – like Shakespeare' later, perhaps following this example – by the Southwark worksho of the Johnsons (or Janssens). The two friends are placed near by o the north side of the chancel. Combe had made his money by lending out at interest: hence the rhyme fastened on his monument:

> Ten in the hundred the Devil* allows,
> But Combe will have twelve he swears and avows.
> If anyone asks who lies in this tomb,
> 'Oh,' quoth the Devil, ''tis my John a Combe.'

And, of course, people ascribed the verses to the local poet.

In the year of his birth, 1564, the worst visitation of plague during Elizabeth's reign reached Stratford. 'Hic incipit pestis', wrote Vicar Bretchgirdle in the church register in July, and for the rest of the year it raged. Whole households perished; one-sixth of the population was wiped out – a near chance for a child in the cradle in Henley Street. The father attended council meetings in the Gild garden – which he had secured for their use when chamberlain – for fear of infection; there amid the orchard-trees they voted money towards the relief of poor sufferers.

Stratford has preserved a very full series of town documents, so that we can trace the impact of national events upon the little community, and the part played locally by Alderman Shakespeare from many references to him. In the stormy summer of Armada year, 1588, the Avon rose so high that three men were marooned on the bridge. The gentry of the county were called upon to furnish a hundred light horsemen for the army under Leicester's command at Tilbury. The town sent up its contingent of soldiers; we have the payments recorded for coat and conduct money, for swords, daggers, girdles, etc., out of the armoury – kept in the council-chamber with the great chest containing the moneys. We recall the reminiscence of 'An old rusty sword ta'en out of the town armoury'.

That we know so much about Shakespeare's family background

* The Devil in this case was Parliament, which by statute limited interest to ten per cent.

is mainly due to his father's prominence in town life, and to th
son's exceptional attachment to his native place. Where othe
fellows made money out of the London theatres, they usuall
invested it in London property – or not far away, as Edward Alleyn
invested his in the manor of Dulwich. William Shakespeare wa
exceptional in his fidelity to his birthplace: he invested practicall
all his gains in Stratford property – with only one acquisition i
London, a house within Blackfriars, a useful lodging for the theatr
there in winter. We shall see that there were reasons for this attach
ment, though really to a countryman it needs no explanation
Shakespeare was determined to cut a figure as an independen
gentleman, in the town where his father had once been prominen
and then lost face with his affairs becoming embarrassed.

Shakespeare was a fairly common name in the villages north o
the Avon. The grandfather, Richard, took a farm in Snitterfield i
Henry VIII's reign: he rented it from Robert Arden of Wilmcote
Arden was of superior standing and stock, something betwee
yeoman and gentleman; for in the inventory of his house we fin
not only solid oak furniture, copper pans, brass pots and candle
sticks, but no less than eleven painted cloths – five in the chambe
below, two in the hall, four in the bedrooms. One did not have tha
sort of thing in an ordinary Elizabethan farmhouse. He left
number of daughters. Joan married Edmund Lambert of Barton
on-the-Heath; Margaret married Alexander Webbe of Bearley
The youngest daughter Mary, as yet unmarried, was left 'all my
land in Wilmcote called Asby's and the crop upon the ground'
and £6 13*s* 4*d* before the division of the goods among the daughters
She was made an executor of the will.

With this generous provision, she was now free to marry wher
she liked; shortly after proving the will, she married her tenan
Richard Shakespeare's son, John. This is where William Shakespear
got his emphasis upon gentility from – and, in fact, the characteristics of it in his behaviour, which marked him off from all th
other theatre-folk, many of whom were decidedly ungentlemanly
in their behaviour. Nor is it superfluous to point out that some socia
disparity between parents has an effect in sharpening the socia

awareness and sensibilities of a clever, observant child – D. H. Lawrence offers a case in point.

John Shakespeare would have been born in the later 1530s, and was brought up in the parish of Snitterfield where there was no school. So that he never learned to write; that was not a necessary accomplishment in the Elizabethan age, when many people could conduct business and read who could not write. John's father had friends in Stratford who had confidence in him, for a clothier bequeathed him 'my four oxen which are now in his keeping'. And he apprenticed his son in the town. John was already a householder in Henley Street before he married, active in the exchanges of town-life in the court of record. He brought a suit over a deal in barley against Henry Field – whose son subsequently went to London, to become a well-known printer in Blackfriars. It was he who printed Shakespeare's early poems.

In 1557 Mary Arden married John Shakespeare; immediately he became ale-taster of the borough, the first step in an active career of twenty years in its affairs. The dowry his wife brought him, land as well as ready money, advanced his status and gave him the wherewithal for a municipal career. He became a burgess on the council, in 1558 and 1559 one of its four constables. From 1561 to 1565 he was chamberlain, overseeing the accounts and approving them with his mark, a pair of glover's compasses. In 1565 he was made an alderman: henceforth it was 'Master' Shakespeare who, in his black, furred gown – such as we see on brasses – went with his fellow-aldermen in procession to church on Sundays or on public business about the streets. Such was the status of the father the children grew up with: he had initiative, public spirit and, as we shall see, aspirations that went beyond his status. In this his son followed him with more success.

In 1561 John Shakespeare's father died, leaving goods valued at £38 17*s*, evidently a respectable yeoman. Alexander Webbe took over the farm at Snitterfield; his son bought up various properties, including one of Mary Arden's, and did well. An uncle, Henry Shakespeare, died there, with money in his coffers, corn and hay in his barn. They were all inching their way up.

In Henley Street the children were arriving. In 1558 a first child Joan, who died; in 1562 a second, called Margaret after an Arde aunt. In 1564 a son, William, christened in Stratford church o 26 April – and this was usually a few days after birth: so that S George's day, on which he died, by custom is celebrated as hi birthday. In 1566 a second son, Gilbert: he became a haberdashe and, remaining a bachelor, made himself useful in taking seisin o his elder brother's purchase of land while busy away. A secon Joan, named again for an Arden aunt, was born in 1569; this on survived her eldest brother, who left her the old home in Henle Street – hers were the only descendants of the family to surviv to the eighteenth century: the Harts. Another girl was given a Arden name, Anne, but died young. There was another boy Richard, of whom we hear nothing: he was not old when he died To complete the family there was Edmund, born in 1580, wh followed his brother into the profession of player.

Meanwhile John Shakespeare rose to chief place as Bailiff of th town in the critical year of the Northern Rebellion, 1569, whic added excitement and a great deal of work. He and his deputy wer escorted from their houses to the Gild-hall by the serjeants carryin their maces, and so on their perambulations on market-days, beatin the bounds at Rogation-tide, to and from church on Sundays an feast-days. The Bailiff presided as a J.P. at the court of record, a well as over the town-council; he had to look after the tow properties, seal leases, execute the orders from the central govern ment in this year of crisis. He had a busy time of it. When his yea as Bailiff was over he was elected chief alderman and deputy t the new Bailiff, Adrian Quiney (pronounced 'Queenie'). Togethe they had to go up to London on the town's affairs, matters a variance with the Earl of Warwick, lord of the manor.

In London the Alderman took the opportunity to recover a deb from a Banbury glover, while himself was sued for a debt by former steward of Stratford. He did not pay up, for in 1578 he wa sued again. In Stratford he bought two more houses, one of whic he leased to a William Burbage – a Warwickshire name. A fe years later Burbage was released from the agreement and was to g back the money he had already paid. He seems never to have got it. John Shakespeare stood surety for an acquaintance at Shottery, Richard Hathaway, for two debts which were paid when harvest came in. In several instances Alderman Shakespeare was willing, good fellow, to stand surety for other people's debts, in one instance having to pay the forfeit. One gets the impression of his being easy-going about money matters, and there is no doubt that he neglected his own business for the town's. And he had large ideas; for, just before his fall – in the way that sometimes happens – in 1575–6 he took steps to apply to the Heralds' College for the grant of a coat-of-arms. Mary Arden's husband would be an armigerous gentleman.

It is not difficult to see why it did not come off. From his election as Bailiff up to the end of 1576 he attended every meeting of the town-council without fail. After that, never again – except for one particular occasion – in all the years of his life. His brethren of the corporation went out of their way to be lenient to him: they reduced his rate of tax for equipping soldiers from the town, they remitted his fines for absence from meetings, they let him off poor-rates. It was not until ten years of non-attendance had passed that at last they elected another alderman in his place. This forbearance and special treatment show their sense that he had sacrificed himself for the town. The day came when he had to absent himself from church for fear of process for debt being served on him. No longer processing in state with this former colleagues, the borough's most active townsman was forced into entire withdrawal. We find him selling off bits of his wife's property. His prosperity had ended; family affairs, local standing taken a downward turn from 1577.

At this time the Alderman's eldest son was a sharp and observant lad of thirteen. Is it to be supposed that the blow and its consequences went unnoticed by his mother's son, as much of an Arden as a Shakespeare? One thing we can be quite certain about; in later years he was careful and provident about money.

CHAPTER 3

Education

HERE, again, much misunderstanding of Shakespeare has arisen – in this case across the centuries – on the score of his education, by people who do not know the facts and circumstances of Elizabethan school-life. In fact, he had the regular grammar-school education of the day – much the same as Christopher Marlowe had contemporaneously at King's School, Canterbury. Grammar-school education was almost entirely in Latin, and the school at Stratford was taught mostly by M.A.s from Oxford. Dr Johnson in the eighteenth century, with no particular knowledge of Elizabethan conditions, testified, 'I always said Shakespeare had Latin enough to grammaticise his English.' Though he was to go further than anyone in his exploitation of language, in both a romantic as well as a classical sense, this was the foundation.

In our day a much fuller knowledge of the process of Elizabethan education has been built up. In fact, the process is more fully illustrated, commented upon, guyed, the schoolmasters and pedagogues laughed at, phrases and tags, whole lines remembered and rather nostalgically cited upon occasion, by Shakespeare than by any other dramatist of the time. We shall see that there was good reason for this.

However, he did not go on to the university. With his father's affairs in the way they were, was there any reason why he should? – his schooling was probably cut short, though it proved sufficient for his purposes. Christopher Marlowe went on to Cambridge with a scholarship, and stayed there for some five years. He emerged an intellectual, interested in intellectual issues and abstract ideas for their own sake; an astonishingly original and inspired genius, he was not so good a dramatist.

William Shakespeare, too, was an intellectual – in the best sense, not the pejorative: he was a naturally clever schoolboy, who picked up things quickly as he went along. There was his instinctive sense of language from the first, his early interest in all going on around him, particularly nature and the facts of nature, the life of the countryside. But ideas are not ends in themselves with him; intellectual issues are not the stuff of his plays: they arise out of the conflicts and collisions, the subtleties, the comedy and tragedy of life itself. His knowledge of human beings, of the human condition, has never been surpassed. He would not have been improved by going to the university.

His was the university of life – more exacting, more deeply informative. Though he had a perfectly adequate foundation from school, like any man of genius he was fundamentally self-educated.

In Elizabethan days grammar-school education was much the same all over the country, based on Lily's Latin grammar (he was grandfather of the dramatist, John Lyly). At Stratford there was some elementary teaching, prior to the grammar-school, for which one had to be able to read and write before one entered. Elementary school was for the 'petties' to learn their ABC, their numbers and the salutary truths of the Catechism, grace before and after meals, the psalms in metre. (After the Reformation there was a nation to bring up the right way.) Shakespeare reflects all this, with several references to the Absey book, its rows of letters beginning with a cross – hence 'Christ-cross row' for the first row of the alphabet; reading by rote before one could spell, the catechism form of blunt question and answer. All this, naturally, in earlier plays.

Much more interesting, and memorably reflected, is the grammar school. A boy entered at about seven. Contemporary books tell us what was, ideally, expected. He was to say his morning prayers, bid his parents 'Good morrow', take his satchel of books and be in his place, while the Chapel bell rang, by six in summer, seven in winter. One thinks of those early hours, the streets of Stratford cold and dark, and

> the whining schoolboy, with his satchel
> And shining morning face, creeping like snail
> Unwillingly to school.

Morning and afternoon, school opened and closed with a reading from the Bible, a psalm sung, and prayers – no wonder these are more quoted in the Plays than any other works.

Latin grammar and the classics are well to the fore, exposed in regular school order. The schoolboy memorised his Lily – quotations and references appear in all his earlier work: Sir Toby Belch and Sir Andrew Aguecheek, staying up late at night, both laugh at the familiar tag about getting out of bed early: 'Not to be abed after midnight is to be up betimes, and *diluculo surgere*, thou know'st.' *The Merry Wives of Windsor* has a whole parody of a Latin lesson from Lily, given by the Welsh curate, Sir Hugh Evans, garnished with Welsh mispronunciations and bawdy innuendoes.

At seven the boy would have entered the school about 1571, to spend the first three years in the lower school under the usher. Simon Hunt, *in animo Catholicus*, was then master; the boy would get the better part of his education from the next master, Thomas Jenkins, from 1575 to 1579; he sounds Welsh. Both were Oxford men, with degrees, equipped for the job. Among the pupils was Richard Field, the tanner's boy; a couple of years older than William, he too made a successful career in London, in his case by a sensible marriage – he married the widow of Vautrollier the printer and carried on the business.

Since the boys were supposed to converse in Latin, they began with phrase-books, and easy texts from Aesop and Cato. (The wonderfully imaginative Quatercentenary Exhibition at Stratford in 1964 had a revealing collection of these, now rare, contemporary schoolbooks.) *Love's Labour's Lost* has a parody of such discourse with schoolmaster Holofernes, Nathaniel and Don Armado, sticking to their tags and trying to converse in them. A good deal of Shakespeare's folk-lore about animals is remembered from Aesop. The boys began poetry with Mantuan, a Renaissance Christian, perhaps more suitable than the pagan Virgil. So Holofernes quotes Mantuan:

> Fauste, precor gelida quando pecus omne sub umbra
> Ruminat. . . .

and sighs, 'Ah, good old Mantuan! . . . Old Mantuan, old Mantuan! who understandeth thee not, loves thee not.' It is Shakespeare, not only remembering his schooldays but, as in all the early plays, making the most of what he had learned.

The boys began Latin comedy with passages from Terence and Plautus, and these provided models for Shakespeare's first comedies, naturally enough. Another popular Renaissance text was Palingenius's *Zodiacus Vitae*; this was remembered to provide at least two famous speeches on the Ages of Man, intertwined with Shakespeare's own experience:

> All the world's a stage,
> And all the men and women merely players:
> They have their exits and their entrances;
> And one man in his time plays many parts,
> His acts being seven ages.

Towards the end of his career, with *The Tempest*, the memory of what he had imbibed in learning the Zodiac of Life bore fruit in Prospero's farewell to his art – how unfailingly appropriate, and touching, that it should go back to early schooldays!

In the upper school he went on to Ovid. This was the love of his life among Latin poets – as it was with Marlowe and most of the Elizabethans; for they made a cult of Love, in one form or another. The impression Ovid made Shakespeare carried with him all his days. Along with the Bible and the Prayer Book, Ovid makes the most constant refrain. The story of Lucrece comes from Ovid's *Fasti*; but the *Metamorphoses* provided the bulk of his classical mythology. He used it both in the original and in Golding's popular translation: subjects, themes, characters, phrases come out of Ovid.

When he challenged attention as a poet with his first published poem, *Venus and Adonis*, he did so with a couplet from Ovid. People recognised a similarity and spoke of his poetry as that of an English Ovid.

Though he drew upon all the books, it was the first book of the *Metamorphoses* with which he was most familiar. Similarly with the Bible; the *first* book in the Old Testament, the *first* Gospel in the New. This must indicate something in his education – can it be that his schooldays were cut short? In any case, his mind was not that of a scholar, pursuing these things as ends in themselves, but that of a poet fastening instinctively onto the phrases. Words had a fascination for him and a life of their own in his unconscious. No poet was ever more fortunate in this respect: his unconscious worked for him day and night, whatever his conscious mind was up to, so that the images and phrases tumbled out of a cornucopia, without trouble – almost always appropriately, but occasionally with an odd effect, as Ben Jonson noted. Ovid's phrase *rudis indigesta moles* tickled the schoolboy's fancy: it pops out several times in early plays. King John's reign was 'indigest . . . so shapeless and so rude', Richard III was 'a heap . . . foul indigested lump'. A collocation of words caught him at school, like Quintilian's *universis . . . largitur*: out it comes, years later, as 'largess universal'. It is the words themselves that play tricks in such a mind, dance like fire-flies before the eyes.

The plain fact is that he had a fabulous aural memory, conscious and unconscious, the foundation of which was laid at school. All Elizabethan education cultivated and relied on the memory, to an extent we scarcely realise today, when softer opinions prevail.

Then there were Elizabethan modes and methods, important in his intellectual development. One graduated to logic and rhetoric: the part this played is plainly discernible, and the dramatist made the fullest use of it, particularly in the earlier plays. There are the text-book tricks turned to dramatic purpose, the sentence-by-sentence question and answer, statement and rejoinder line by line, passages of wearisome antiphony to our ears, hair-splitting about words. This was drilled into one at school, and Elizabethans liked that sort of thing. It turned out extremely useful for a young playwright, who could fill in the interstices of action with these exchanges when life had not as yet provided him with the experience for content; for comedy, they were very much to the point, seasoned with his well-tempered wit.

Even more useful was the schooling in rhetoric, so important to Elizabethans – and to which he took naturally. He developed a lordly way with words, and used them with a swagger. The textbook methods are easily recognisable: the high, low and medium styles; the use of epithet and synonym for varying – while he caricatures pedagogues in Holofernes for too much varying, without taste or sense. There is the business of narration, comparison, amplification to carry one on. The text-book used was Aphthonius, where the example adduced is the story of Venus and Adonis: while the very next example is that of Pyramus and Thisbe, parodied in the play put on by Bottom and his fellows. Much of the banter of Shakespeare's clowns is in accordance with the formulas of school-rhetoric, playing with them and turning them inside out.

Shakespeare rated invention, in its technical sense, at the highest, for these things were not ends in themselves to him, as they were to a schoolman: they all came in handy to the overriding artistic intentions of the poet and dramatist. Nor must we forget the set oration, which set a model for the famous soliloquies and formal speeches of the plays. Such orations were a feature of public life, the Queen herself a star-performer. Such a performance is clearly described:

> As, after some oration fairly spoke
> By a belovèd prince, there doth appear
> Among the buzzing pleasèd multitude. . . .

Little enough history was read in schools, almost entirely for moralising purposes, the lessons taught by experience, the consequences of good and ill courses, the comparisons to be made. Sallust and Caesar were the chief authorities – Vicar Bretchgirdle left his

Sallust to the school – supplemented by some Livy. Shakespeare knew Caesar and Livy's version of the Lucrece story. He had a marvellous capacity from the outset for making a little go a long way; his real historical reading came later – he was very much a reading man, and he read quickly – with Holinshed's Chronicles, the second edition, of 1587 and North's Plutarch. His attitude towards history is the Elizabethan one, inculcated at school, of a series of moral examples; though, to the dramatist, the drama is the thing, the excitement of conflict, the collisions of wills and personalities, events flowing from character. Thus good and evil find their reward: the bad are not allowed to get away with it. In the plays dealing with the Wars of the Roses, the trilogy of *Henry VI* and *Richard III*, as again with *Richard II* or *King John*, there is not only the drama: the plays are held together by the moral, the results of good or bad kingship, the duties of authority as well of obedience, the fearful results of the breakdown of government, anarchy, the unleashing of passions, the infection of cruelty.

These lessons are as much enforced in the Roman plays, *Julius Caesar* and *Coriolanus*, as in the English. Altogether it is surprising in a writer whose natural bent was for comedy, as Dr Johnson saw, that he should have turned out the most historically minded of dramatists. Nearly a half of his output is devoted to history of one kind or another: ten plays on the pageant of English history from *King John* to *Henry VIII*, four plays on Roman history, two on the pre-history of Britain, with *Cymbeline* and *King Lear*, which had virtually the status of history with Elizabethans. And this is not to mention *Hamlet* and *Macbeth*, which had a chronicle basis.

However, all this came from later reading; it was the attitude to history as morality that came from school, from Church, from society as a whole.

Hardly less important than his education at school, for an Elizabethan boy, was that which he received from the Church, from its services from earliest childhood, catechising, teaching, sermons, singing the psalms, prayers; for regular attendance at church was obligatory for the family, not only for schoolboys, whose school-prayers were additional. Nor is this any the less fully reflected throughout the Plays. Altogether there are allusions to forty books of the Bible, including the Apocrypha. The story of the primal curse upon Cain gripped his imagination – he refers to it not less than twenty-five times. Other stories held his mind with hardly less tenacity. It has been estimated that his Biblical indebtedness is five times that of Peele or Marlowe, greater than that of any contemporary dramatist.

In the first instance, there was the regular attendance at church from childhood on. This was unavoidable in a small town like Stratford, or in a country parish; it could be avoided more easily in the back alleys of London where literary Bohemia congregated, such as Robert Greene or Marlowe or Peele. They were townsmen, and they were not family men; William Shakespeare was a countryman, or an inhabitant of a country town, and he was a family man with family obligations. Moreover, he was a conforming man, too sensible and sceptical to stick his neck out and get into trouble – in marked contrast to Marlowe, who asked for trouble with his aggressive heterodoxy, and Ben Jonson who got into it by a spell of Catholicism.

Shakespeare's numerous phrases from the Bible show that up to 1596–7 those from the Bishop's Bible predominate, which was used in church. After that readings from the Genevan version are more numerous, and he evidently possessed a copy at home. Above all, he quoted the Psalms, or echoed their phrasing, always in the Prayer Book version, and this is what he would have heard Sunday by Sunday in church. When he quotes the Commandments, he does so in the Prayer Book form, and phrases abound from most of its services. Prince Henry sees 'a good amendment of life' in Falstaff; Falstaff bids Bardolph, 'Do thou amend your face, and I'll amend my life.' The phrase comes at Morning and Evening Prayer, in the Litany and the Communion Service. The phrase from the Litany, 'O God, we have heard with our ears' has struck others oddly besides Sir Hugh Evans: 'What phrase is this, "He hears with ear"? Why, it is affectations' (a Welshman is speaking).

We gather from the evidence that for Shakespeare, as for

Protestants generally, there were only two sacraments: Baptism and Holy Communion – not a trace of Catholic teaching, nor had he any knowledge of the Vulgate. He was a conforming member of the Church into which he had been baptised, in which he was brought up and married, his children reared and in whose arms he was buried at the last.

A regular feature in those days was a reading from the *Book of Homilies* when, as was often the case, there was no sermon. There are references both to the custom and to individual homilies that made their impression. That against Swearing and Perjury came to mind several times at junctures in the Plays. Still more important is the impact of the political homilies, those on Obedience, Disobedience and Wilful Rebellion. His political views were in accord with what he heard enforced in church all his life. He expressed them with notable consistency; there is no doubt that he held them with conviction and urged them in his plays with greater force than any other dramatist. A man with a strong sense of community, a neighbourly man, he had a deeper sense of political and social responsibility than any – all the more because cleverer, more sceptical and more humane.

With these thoughts we approach the adult Shakespeare: it is unlikely that the grammar-school boy, though boys matured earlier then, plumbed their full significance. Nevertheless, the magnificent phrases would reverberate in the mind, to achieve their own expression in time. 'Almighty God hath created and appointed all things in heaven, earth and waters, in a most perfect order.' This becomes:

> The heavens themselves, the planets and this centre
> Observe degree, priority and place,
> Insisture, course, proportion, season, form,
> Office and custom, in all line of order. . . .

But, warns the homily, 'Take away kings, rulers, princes, magistrates, judges and such estates of God's order . . . no man shall sleep in his own house or bed unkilled, no man shall keep his wife, children and possession in quietness', etc. This becomes, in *Troilus and Cressida*, after the Essex Rebellion:

> Take but degree away, untune that string,
> And, hark, what discord follows!

The homilist brought home the consequences of rebellion with the image: 'the brother to seek and often to work the death of his brother, the son of his father'. This seized upon the mind of the dramatist in one of his early plays, *3 Henry VI*, which has a scene:

> *Alarum. Enter a son that hath killed his father,*
> *at one door; and a father that hath killed his son,*
> *at another door.*

Students of the subject conclude that it is not likely that young William was grounded in the Bible at home; there is no interest in doctrine, no position taken. He was grounded in school and at church, and read the Genevan Bible later. It was the most familiar and popular book of the day – especially the Genevan Bible, with its handy size and low price – this was the one to buy for later reading at home. Then, too, the language of Bible and Prayer Book was contemporary, and made all the more fresh an impact – where for us the effect is the opposite; it has the charm of the archaic, with mnemonic echoes, and lulls the mind, where they were stimulated and compelled. The Bible provided the foundation of popular culture, for everybody had to go to church. It is impossible to exaggerate the importance of this grounding in childhood and youth: for the adult writer Bible and Prayer Book formed the most constant and continuing influence.

Home influences were otherwise, but played their part. We can see what kind of youth he was from hints as to his choices and preferences in his writings, though we must watch for corroboration from external evidence. After all, a writer writes about his own experience, and willy-nilly betrays himself in his work.

There was the environment of his father's respectable trade as glover and wool-dealer – after all, the famous dramatist was not above dealing in malt. As whittawer John Shakespeare tawed (dressed) the white skins of deer, sheep, goats, but not those of cattle and swine, which would fall to a tanner, such as Richard Field's father. John Aubrey thought that Shakespeare's father was a butcher; he was not so far out, for a whittawer would take a hand in killing the animals. Aubrey adds, 'I have been told heretofore by some of the neighbours that when he was a boy he exercised his father's trade, but when he killed a calf he would do it in a high style and make a speech.' Nothing improbable in that: it would, in fact, be rather like him.

The son refers to most kinds of skin that were dealt with at Stratford, and he knew their specific uses – neat's (cow's) leather for shoes, sheep's leather for bridles, sow's skin for tinkers' bags. Noticeable is his interest in deer and deerskin, i.e. cheveril, on account of its softness and flexibility used for the best gloves. He has several references to cheveril. He knew well that the deer's skin was the perquisite of the keeper, and tells us that Slender had 'a great round beard like a glover's paring-knife'.

Studies of his imagery have been revealing. His 'sensitiveness about the quality, freshness and cleanliness of food developed rather late – possibly after experience of more delicate fare than at Stratford'. He has an unusually large number of images from kitchen occupations – washing and scouring, dusting and sweeping, sewing, patching, mending, above all removing spots and stains. One sees the close quarters he lived in in the house in Henley Street until he was well past the middle of his life.

But the house had a garden, and Stratford was full of gardens and trees, fruit and flowers. The poet has innumerable references to and images from the processes of growth in the garden. Beyond that were the out-of-door sports of the town, the pastures outside, or up on the Cotswolds. Archery at the town-butts by the bridge was a favourite; there is an obvious autobiographical note in this –

In my schooldays, when I had lost one shaft,

I shot his fellow of the self-same flight
The self-same way with more advisèd watch,
To find the other forth, and by adventuring both
I oft found both. . . .

Bowling was a superior game, for the middle and upper classes, and this Shakespeare favoured most: a score of images from bowls, besides other references – more than thrice those from any other game – betray him.

Out in the stubbles, on the heaths to the north of the town, there was coursing the hare; *Venus and Adonis* has a full-length inset of coursing poor Wat, vivid and sympathetic, by one very familiar with the sport. Further afield there was chasing the deer, which had an irresistible appeal to sporting young sparks in the Elizabethan countryside. Deer-poaching was regarded as fair game, by Oxford students on Shotover as by Cambridge dons in rural retreat in Staffordshire.* Shakespeare's earlier writings have a perfect fixation on hunting the deer – numerous descriptions, of deer and hounds too, all by one who knew the points of the chase. There is the hound that 'runs counter and yet draws dry-foot well', or the observation,

coward dogs
Most spend their mouths when what they seem to threaten
Runs far before them.

Like a good sportsman, his sympathy is yet with the hunted animal:

the poor frighted deer that stands at gaze,
Wildly determining which way to fly. . . .

Most suspicious is the expert comment,

What, hast not thou full often struck a doe,
And borne her cleanly by the keeper's nose?

* See my *The Elizabethan Renaissance: the Life of the Society* (1971) p. 149.

There is always something in an early and tenacious tradition. there is no reason why the early Stratford tale, that the young Shakespeare incurred Sir Thomas Lucy's displeasure for poaching his deer, should not be true.

Back in town there were dramatic entertainments for a schoolboy to take part in or watch, mummings, the regular St George's play performed all over England, pageants, disguisings. Plays were presented by the towns-folk at Whitsuntide:

> . . . at Pentecost,
> When all our pageants of delight were played,
> Our youth got me to play the woman's part,
> And I was trimmed in Madam Julia's gown,
> Which servèd me as fit, by all men's judgments,
> As if the garment had been made for me. . . .
> And at that time I made her weep agood,
> For I did play a lamentable part. . . .

Then there were the professional players visiting the town, small troupes under the protection of some grandee, or else they might be brought under the heading of 'vagabonds' to which a parliamentary statute consigned them. The profession was gradually taking shape, but it would be some years before it became established – the career of Shakespeare and his fellows being an important factor in its becoming so. In the 1570s the Earl of Worcester's men and Leicester's were most to the fore. Leicester's, led by James Burbage, came to Stratford in 1573, 1576 and 1587; the Earl of Warwick's in 1575, and Worcester's six times between 1569 and 1587. In addition, there were visits by Lord Berkeley's, Lord Strange's, Lord Derby's, the Countess of Essex's, the Earl of Essex's, Lord Chandos's, the Queen's. There were usually two or three troupes a year. Observe that in 1587 there were five.

By then Worcester's men already had Edward Alleyn as their star, and Marlowe, with *Tamburlaine* a success of that year, to write for them. The Queen's Men had been reorganised in 1583, with twelve of the best players drawn from other troupes, including the leading clown, Tarleton. This reorganisation marked a new departure; the troupes were on the way to becoming companies. When the Queen's Men came to Stratford in the year 1587, they were lacking an actor, who had been killed by one of his fellows on the way. Some of Leicester's players were also missing: they had accompanied him to the Netherlands and then went on to amuse the King of Denmark at Elsinore.

On Leicester's death in Armada year, 1588, his company broke up; three of its leading men, Kemp, Bryan and Pope, joined that of Lord Strange. When we reflect that both Burbage and Kemp had been Leicester's men, and that they and Pope became associates for years with Shakespeare in the Lord Chamberlain's Company, remembering also Leicester's close connection with the county, we do not have to look far for a possible channel of recruitment for a promising young man from Stratford. At least there were possibilities opening here, when prospects were not at all inviting at home.

For Alderman Shakespeare's affairs were going downhill. Already in debt to his brother-in-law Lambert, in 1578 he mortgaged to him, for £40 ready cash, a house and fifty-six acres in Wilmcote, part of his wife's inheritance. John Shakespeare was unable to repay the money; this led to a family quarrel and a lawsuit in which William's name was joined as his father's heir. Ten years later the father offered to repay the £40, which was refused because now the property would fetch a higher rent. Notice that this was in 1587, when William was recouping the family fortunes in London; this part of the Arden inheritance was never recovered.

In that year 1578 a further considerable section of Mary Arden's property, some eighty-six acres in Wilmcote, was conveyed to a Webbe relative for a term of years, for ready cash evidently needed. Next year they sold their share of the Arden property in Snitterfield. In 1580 John Shakespeare was fined £20, a considerable sum, in Queen's Bench for not appearing to find surety for keeping the peace, another £20 as a pledge for a Nottingham hatmaker; two others were fined £20 for forfeiting their pledges on the Alderman's behalf. He was in serious trouble: two years later he petitioned for surety of the peace against four men who had threatened him, evidently creditors. In spite of that his easy-going, good nature led him to come to others' aid. In 1586 he went surety for his brother Henry, for which he was sued by Nicholas Lane and was driven to obtain bail from a fellow-alderman. The same year he gave bail at Coventry for a Stratford tinker, a Welshman who welshed on him, and John Shakespeare forfeited his £10. He never paid the debt and damages recovered against him by William Burbage in 1589. He failed to appear in court in April 1592, when the judges ordered the sheriff to execute the judgment against him. In that year Master Shakespeare's name appears on the Warwickshire J.P.s' list of those open to fine for not attending church: in his case it was 'for fear of process for debt'. What a sad contrast from the blithe days when he sat in his alderman's gown in the front pew and processed through the streets with the town's officers before him!

It is not to be supposed that this improvidence, obviously the result of neglect of business for municipal self-importance – and in a family that was proud of its Arden connection, the inheritance now whittled away – was without its effect on the son and heir, as much an Arden as he was a Shakespeare.

Unfortunately, he himself with his 'sportive blood' – his own word for it – was adding to the family difficulties and equipping himself with a millstone round his neck. At the end of August 1582, at the mature age of eighteen, he got Anne Hathaway with child, a woman more than eight years older than himself – a disparity more significant in those days when people aged earlier. Her father, Richard Hathaway, was an old acquaintance of the Alderman, who with his usual good nature had stood surety for a debt of Hathaway's before this. Hathaway died in September 1581, leaving Anne, his eldest daughter, a small dowry of 10 marks (£6 13*s* 4*d*); she had no property of her own, unlike Mary Arden. But Anne was of respectable parentage, and her young lover was always a gentleman.

When she was three months gone with child, William with two

friends of hers rode to the diocesan court at Worcester for a licence to marry. As a minor, he had to have the consent of his parents and Anne had to have a couple of sureties on her behalf. There was some need to hurry, for Advent was about to begin, when there was a close season for marriages, and in spring another, until April when Anne would be eight months pregnant. So they were married, after calling the banns only once, on 30 November or 1 December 1582.

The adult Shakespeare had plenty of reason to regret his hasty and disadvantageous marriage – a Christopher Marlowe, for obvious reasons, never embarrassed himself with such *impedimenta*. But, with characteristic good nature, William Shakespeare never expressed it: a normal family man, he was all in favour of marrying and giving in marriage. In this, as in so many respects, like ordinary folk – one reason why his work has always appealed to them – he writes enthusiastically of the marriage-bed and marriage night, if in his case he had anticipated it:

> O, let me clip [embrace] ye
> In arms as sound as when I wooed, in heart
> As merry as when our nuptial day was done,
> And tapers burned to bedward!

Back to Henley Street they went, to live under his parents' roof, where their first child was born, and baptised by vicar Barton at church on festive Trinity Sunday, 26 May 1583. Twenty months later, twins were born, and baptised Hamnet and Judith, 2 February 1585, after the godparents, neighbours Hamnet and Judith Sadler. Here was a family to provide for, a wife and three children, when the husband was not yet twenty-one and his father's affairs were embarrassed.

How are we to suppose that the young man contributed to the upkeep of the family? No doubt he helped in his father's shop and with his business as wool-dealer. We find later he is knowledgeable about the ways of shepherds and sheep-shearing feasts, and how many pounds go into a tod of wool, besides the headlands that should be sown with red wheat, the greyhounds outrun on Cotswold and 'how a yoke of bullocks at Stamford Fair?'

John Aubrey picked up the information from the family of Christopher Beeston, one of the company at the Globe, that Shakespeare 'had been in his younger days a schoolmaster in the country'. There is no reason to reject this: it is rather corroborated by his marked use of schoolmasters and pedagogues and their ways as comic material in several of his plays. There is a further indication: it is significant that his earliest efforts in comedy and tragedy, *The Comedy of Errors* and *Titus Andronicus*, are the one Plautine and the other Senecan; and Plautus and Seneca were the school-models for comedy and tragedy respectively. Such an occupation would have given time to store up the reading that went into his work and is quite exceptional for a non-university man. For all that Robert Greene was to fling at him later, as a mere actor, an outsider, William Shakespeare was closer to the university wits than was to the liking of that Cambridge M.A. and competed with them on their level – much to Greene's annoyance.

There was no future, however, in being an usher in the country. One fine day in the later 1580s – the year 1587 was specially inviting, with five companies visiting Stratford, Leicester's below strength and the Queen's wanting a man – he took the road to London.

CHAPTER 4

The Player Becomes Playwright

OF the world's greatest dramatists only Shakespeare and Molière were primarily actors, and this is made evident in their work. Ben Jonson was an actor in early life, but Aubrey tells us – what we can well believe – that he was better at instructing than at acting. There was an essential didacticism about him, in contrast to Shakespeare's smooth actor's flexibility. In our time we have come to appreciate once more how effective the plays of Marlowe are, and two of them were among the greatest favourites with Elizabethans, *Tamburlaine* and *Dr Faustus*. But Marlowe was not an actor, and his plays do not have the professional facility of his rival, who was a professional player. Marlowe's are the rugged and inspired works of a poet who was also an intellectual. Nothing flexible about him, either: he held by what he believed, or did not believe; he enforced his heterodoxy about religion, and about sex, into whatever company he came. Both he and Ben Jonson were of rather lower social status than that by which William Shakespeare set such store, and regarded himself as belonging to: they were decidedly not gentlemen.

That Shakespeare was an actor is obvious all through his work, from his comments on the profession from the inside, all the way from the revealing autobiographical sentiments of the Sonnets to the most illuminating dramatic criticism of the age in Hamlet's instructions to the players. Images drawn from his profession are frequent, numerous phrases as well as extended comments on it; whole dramatic episodes are inset into the plays, such as the parody of the country tradesmen's performance in *A Midsummer Night's Dream*, the play inserted into *Hamlet*, the masques in *The Tempest* and *Pericles*, all the references in choruses, prologues and epilogues. William Shakespeare in the end was a complete man of the theatre: player, dramatist, producer, part-owner, sharer of profits. A perfect Johannes Factotum, as Robert Greene said.

The stage and the players are commented upon from almost every angle (except that of business, which he kept to himself). He was a good actor, as we know from John Aubrey, and he had the appearance and personality for it – 'a handsome well-shaped man, very good company, and of a very ready and pleasant smooth wit'. There were the mobile, flexible features we know so well, the sexy nose and sensuous lips, the large luminous eyes and dome of a cranium. The tradition is that he played 'kingly' parts, and old Adam in *As You Like It.* He was not the star of the company; that was Burbage for tragic parts, Will Kemp and later Robert Armin for the comic. As time went on, writing plays became more important than acting – though we know that he played in Ben Jonson's *Every Man in His Humour* later, for we have, exceptionally, a list of the performers.

Poor players were familiar enough – 'dull actors' who had forgot their part and were 'out, even to a full disgrace'. Or there is the

> unperfect actor on the stage
> Who with his fear is put besides his part,
> Or some fierce thing replete with too much rage,
> Whose strength's abundance weakens his own heart. . . .

Or, again, there is the

> strutting player, whose conceit
> Lies in his hamstring, and doth think it rich
> To hear the wooden dialogue and sound
> 'Twixt his stretched footing and the scaffoldage. . . .

Earlier Elizabethan acting was more declamatory and rhetorical, stomping about the stage – such a part as Tamburlaine lent itself to that.

> O, there be players that I have seen play, and heard others praise, and that highly, not to speak it profanely, that–neither having the accent of Christians, nor the gait of Christian, pagan, nor man–have so strutted and bellowed that I have thought some of nature's journeymen had made men and not made them well, they imitated humanity so abominably.

As for clowns and their habit of gagging, this offended Shakespeare's artistic conscience:

> And let those that play your clowns speak no more than is set down for them; for there be of them that will themselves laugh, to set on some quantity of barren spectators to laugh too; though, in the meantime, some necessary question of the play be then to be considered. That's villainous, and shows a most pitiful ambition in the fool that uses it.

This is strong language, but Shakespeare makes a strong disjunction, as all intelligent people do: what makes

> the unskilful laugh, cannot but make the judicious grieve; the censure of the which one must in your allowance o'erweigh a whole theatre of others.

He describes the contrasting reactions of the audience to an excellent actor and an indifferent one:

> As in a theatre the eyes of men,
> After a well-graced actor leaves the stage,
> Are idly bent on him that enters next,
> Thinking his prattle to be tedious. . . .

Through the mouth of Hamlet Shakespeare tells us how an actor should perform his part, expresses his own aims in acting and what the stage should be:

> Speak the speech, I pray you, as I pronounced it to you, trippingly

on the tongue; but if you mouth it, as many of your players do, I had as lief the town-crier spoke my lines.

He goes on to instruct as to gesture:

> Nor do not saw the air too much with your hand, thus, but use all gently; for in the very torrent. . . of passion, you must acquire and beget a temperance that may give it smoothness.

Yet, one must not be so smooth as to be tame:

> suit the action to the word, the word to the action; with this special observance, that you o'erstep not the modesty of nature. . . .

His whole conception of acting is summed up in a sentence:

> the purpose of playing, whose end, both at the first and now, was and is, to hold, as 'twere, the mirror up to nature. . . .

We can conclude from this that Shakespeare's direction in the theatre, not only in his writing but in acting and producing, was away from the earlier crudity, the prating and orating, towards an altogether subtler and more natural style. And that was in keeping with his nature.

His nature was not only mimetic, but full of sympathy of heart. We hear it in such a phrase as

> a poor player
> That struts and frets his hour upon the stage. . . .

When Bottom the Weaver and his rude mechanicals ultimately get through their appalling performance before the Court of Athens, Hippolyta says, 'This is the silliest stuff that ever I heard.' Then comes that charming note of sympathy, which makes it up to the poor fellows who have done their best:

> The best in this kind are but shadows; and the worst are no worse, if imagination amend them.

He frequently thought of the theatre, this wooden O, as a mirror of the world, and the players as shadows of reality. At the very end of the *Dream*:

> If we shadows have offended,
> Think but this, and all is mended,
> That you have but slumbered here
> While these visions did appear. . . .
> Gentles, do not reprehend:
> If you pardon, we will mend. . . .

One notices, too, the player's constant wooing of the audience, his own agreeable nature – in contrast to Ben Jonson's tendency to insult it, express his contempt for it, the patronising self-sufficiency of

> My God! 'tis good, and if you like't, you may.

This is very unlike Shakespeare's prologues:

> But pardon, gentles all,
> The flat unraisèd spirits that have dared
> On this unworthy scaffold to bring forth
> So great an object: can this cockpit hold
> The vasty fields of France? or may we cram
> Within this wooden O the very casques
> That did affright the air at Agincourt?

The wooden O was Burbage's Globe, and *Henry V* the play with which it opened:

> Admit me Chorus to this history;
> Who prologue-like your humble patience pray,
> Gently to hear, kindly to judge, our play.

This is William Shakespeare speaking, and it looks pretty certain that he himself played the part of Chorus, for at the end the Epilogue says, with the same propitiatory note of apology:

Thus far, with rough and all-unable pen,
Our bending author hath pursued the story . . .

One sees him bowing to the audience (no wonder he was always more popular than Ben Jonson!). He concludes with an autobiographical reference to the three parts of *Henry VI*, with which he had originally stepped into public acclaim:

Which oft our stage hath shown; and, for their sake,
In your fair minds let this acceptance take.

So much for the public, reconciling himself to the trade by which he must needs live. But, earlier, he had resented the necessity, who would have preferred to be known as gentleman and poet. In the Sonnets, which are autobiography throughout, he tells us ruefully,

Alas, 'tis true I have gone here and there
And made myself a motley to the view,
Gored mine own thoughts, sold cheap what is most dear. . . .

In the next sonnet his resentment at the necessity he was under, to earn his living this way, is made quite explicit: he girds at Fortune

That did not better for my life provide
Than public means which public manners breeds.
Thence comes it that my name receives a brand,
And almost thence my nature is subdued
To what it works in, like the dyer's hand.

Indeed, he had been maligned for the shifts he was put to, to earn a living, by one of the best known, if most disreputable, of London intellectuals, the envious Greene. He appeals to his young patron, Southampton,

Your love and pity doth the impression fill
Which vulgar scandal stamped upon my brow;

For what care I who calls me well or ill,
So you *o'er-green* my bad, my good allow?

In the end, as he achieved success and prosperity in his profession, and even a certain social status – for the profession itself was going up and achieving respectability, largely as the result of the work of such as he and Edward Alleyn, Burbage, Heming and Condell, good citizens, some of them even taking out coats-of-arms – he became reconciled. The players, who earlier had not been much better than vagabonds and, in Shakespeare's experience, had often enough been shown into the kitchen, Hamlet commands to be 'well bestowed':

> Do you hear, let them be well used; for they are the abstract and brief chronicles of the time. After your death you were better have a bad epitaph than their ill report while you live.

And the purpose of playing has become 'to show the very age and body of the time his form and pressure'.

He had found his genius – with reluctance and sometimes resentment, after misfortune and setbacks and some insults – to be after all on the stage, in the theatre: even his genius as a poet flourished better and found greater scope and power there.

All this was far off from the harsh beginnings, the hard apprenticeship he endured. Not for him the easy success Marlowe had with *Tamburlaine* on coming down from Cambridge, while George Peele was writing plays when still at Christ Church. Will Davenant said that he had held horses outside the theatre before he got a posting within. That sounds like romancing, perhaps a wish to exaggerate his early trials before eventual success. But there is nothing impossible in it; he was a good judge of horse-flesh, an out-of-doors fellow (unlike Marlowe) with an instinctive sympathy with horses – witness Roan Barbary and the Sonnets. It is part of the tradition, however, that emphasises the difficulties of his early career, corroborated by himself.

There could not be, in the long run, a more propitious moment for a young man to set out on such a London career than in the year or so before the Armada. The inspiration of patriotism, the surge of self-confidence, the thrill of pride in a youthful and ardent people are expressed in a hundred ways: in the poems and books they wrote, the ships they built, and the names they gave them; in the incitements they urged, the sense of inferiority passing over into the realisation that they were catching up, the boastfulness natural with such achievements, the defeat of the Armada, the daring confrontation with the empire of Spain; the exploits of the seamen, the oceans penetrated, in which the flag of St George had been shown for the first time; in the heroes of the age, such men as Drake and Grenville, or Philip Sidney, the unparalleled figure of the Queen herself; in the possibilities of the language, the future they foresaw for it, as to which they were not wrong.

So much of what they began – that rainbow-arc of achievement over the next centuries – is now at an end. We have witnessed its sad ending in our time.

Of the martial activity and excitement of these years (like that of 1940–5, to those of us who remember it) Shakespeare was a spectator like any other, and enjoyed the fun. Just outside Bishopsgate, where we hear of him lodging early on – near the theatres out in the fields of Shoreditch – lay the open space of Artillery Yard where the gunners of the Tower did their weekly practice. At Mile End the armed bands of the City did their training: 'I remember at Mile End Green . . . there was a little quiver fellow, and 'a would manage you his piece thus; and 'a would about and about, and come you in and come you in. "Rah, tah, tah," would 'a say; "Bounce", would 'a say; and away again would 'a go, and again would 'a come.'

All this would be with appropriate bawdy gestures on the stage – 'Come you in,' indeed, and how the little quiver fellow managed his piece! Shakespeare is the bawdiest of Elizabethan dramatists, with the natural bawdy of the highly sexed normal heterosexual, possibly the sexiest writer in the language – to anyone who knows the full possibilities of innuendo in contemporary usage. Here is the salty element that, in part, helps to preserve him, the rude fun and enjoyment.

The mood of national pride and self-confidence – popular through and through – provided one of the impulses carrying the theatre, and with it Shakespeare, upwards into the 1590s. Shakespeare was its most responsive register, even exponent, in his first plays on English history. He caught the mood and made himself its mouthpiece, as Nashe corroborates; there was a *panache* about him that fitted the time. From then on, there never has been a time when he has not been popular, in the deeper as well as in the more obvious sense.

First, there came his apprenticeship in the theatre as a player and, along with that, as a reader of the new literature coming forth at last, in the 1580s – after a long winter – in brilliant promise. Here also we can learn a good deal, by reading back from what appears in his work. He had a lot of leeway to make up, as a young country fellow who had not had the advantage of a London background like Thomas Lodge, a Lord Mayor's son, or Thomas Kyd, educated like Spenser at Merchant Taylors'; or of years at the university like Lyly and Peele, Greene and Marlowe and Nashe. Shakespeare was an outsider and a provincial: the fact that he ultimately went beyond them all showed his innately greater capacity for development, but also his artistic determination, usually so little realised. The *Sonnets* show that he was very conscious of his handicap compared with them.

In London he had one Stratford contact of importance to him. Richard Field was also an ambitious young fellow, a couple of years senior; having married Vautrollier's widow, he was now comfortably established in his printing business in Blackfriars. He printed his fellow-townsman's first works, his two narrative poems in 1593 and 1594; the proofs were very well corrected, and no doubt the poet was in and out of Blackfriars. For we can tell that he was particularly familiar with the excellent productions of Field's press.

The first of them was Puttenham's *Arte of English Poesie*, 1589.

This was the finest and most comprehensive of Elizabethan works of literary criticism. It is evident that the poet-to-be read it but, more remarkably, how closely it chimed with his own attitude, tone and temper. It influenced him and must have helped to build him up; on the other hand, it agreed with his own instinctive preferences, both with regard to language and writing.

The language itself was in a most interesting condition, pregnant with possibilities and about to give birth.* It was a moment of extreme flexibility and expansiveness, of readiness to experiment; though the direction it would take was fairly indicated, it was not wholly settled. A large share in the way it went was taken by the blossoming theatre, and the largest share in that was to be contributed by Puttenham's teachable young scholar. Lyly was writing, 'it is a world to see how Englishmen desire to hear finer speech than the language will allow'. All the writers of the time co-operated to expand its capabilities, but it was the time itself and its needs – the English at large – who supplied the driving force.

Puttenham was no theorist, any more than Shakespeare, about metrics or language: no nonsense about hexameters which appealed to pedants like Abraham Fraunce and Gabriel Harvey. With Puttenham, Shakespeare followed, more subtly, the instinct of the language, with its own nature dictating the rhythms. Spoken English falls naturally into iambic pentameter, and this is the norm throughout Shakespeare's work. We can see in his early work how fascinated he was by the new mint of words, and by verbal play – as Nashe was among prose-writers – which was to reach a crest with *Love's Labour's Lost.* In 1591 another courtier, Sir John Harington, wished Puttenham's book to be a model for the printing of his translation of Ariosto. Here was another author, the bawdy wit of *A Metamorphosis of Ajax*, with whose mind the apprentice Shakespeare was in sympathy – and we know that Harington knew *The Taming of the Shrew*.

A number of other works issuing from Field's shop were made use of by the budding dramatist: several pamphlets dealt with

* See my *The Elizabethan Renaissance: The Cultural Achievement* (1972) ch. II, 'Language, Literature and Society'.

French affairs, in which names to the fore in *Love's Labour's Lost* appear – Navarre, Longueville, Mayenne, Biron. In 1592 Field published a translation of Du Bartas' *Divine Weeks and Works*, which has left its trace on Shakespeare. His Italian phrases are all traceable to the *Campo de Fior*, a handbook for learning Italian and French. Field printed a number of the school-texts familiar to the poet – Ovid, Cicero, Manutius, Plutarch. Timothy Bright's *Treatise on Melancholy* had been taken over from Vautrollier – it was drawn upon later for *Hamlet*, or else was remembered from early association with the shop in Blackfriars.

This was an aristocratic precinct within the confines of the former friary, the great church having been pulled down. Here lived the Dowager Lady Russell, aunt of Robert Cecil and the Bacons, of whom we know so much from her letters to them. There were also a number of foreigners serving luxury trades, goldsmiths, jewellers and Vautrollier's printing press. There was also an intermittent connection with the theatre, since Sir Thomas Cawarden, Queen Mary's Master of the Revels, had moved in. In the 1580s the Children of the Chapel were using the old frater as a theatre: here Lyly produced his plays under the patronage of the Earl of Oxford. In the 1590s these premises were leased by the first Lord Hunsdon, first cousin to the Queen and her Lord Chamberlain, and the second Lord Hunsdon had his house here. In 1600 the Children of the Chapel resumed playing here; in 1608 the partners in the Globe – now the King's Men, formerly the Lord Chamberlain's – took over the Blackfriars for a winter playing-house. Ben Jonson lived here at one time, and later Shakespeare bought himself a house within the precinct.

One way and another Blackfriars was familiar ground, and played a part in his life and career.

These same years, the later 1580s, saw a development of theatre – companies, theatres, players and playwrights – reach a crest and achieve the form by which it became a supreme moment in the world's drama. By 1600 foreign visitors regarded the London theatre as a chief glory of the nation. What was it that made the drama, hitherto rather pedestrian, become poetical? What brought about the fusion of drama at such a high level, with increasing tension and power?

The answer cannot be given only in literary terms, but in terms of the society, which was both musical and poetical; at any rate it gave voice to music and poetry at every level. Something of what poetry meant to them may be heard, and felt along the nerves, in the lines Marlowe was writing at that moment:

If all the pens that ever poets held
Had fed the feelings of their masters' thoughts,
And every sweetness that inspired their hearts,
Their minds and muses on admirèd themes;
If all the heavenly quintessence they still
From their immortal flowers of poesy,
Wherein as in a mirror we perceive
The highest reaches of a human wit;
If these had made one poem's period,
And all combined in beauty's worthiness,
Yet should there hover in their restless heads
One thought, one grace, one wonder, at the least,
Which into words no virtue can digest.

In that marvellous passage we see what poetry could mean in that time – and also what Marlowe meant to the poets. From first to last, Marlowe was a more important influence than any other on his junior, who, in three or four years, would be echoing this same passage, along with another still more popular in the theatre:

Is it not passing brave to be a king
And ride in triumph through Persepolis?

In *3 Henry VI* Shakespeare wrote:

How sweet a thing it is to wear a crown
Within whose circuit is Elysium
And all that poets feign of bliss and joy.

Portrait of Shakespeare by Droeshout in First Folio

Shakespeare's birthplace

The school quadrangle at Stratford

Mary Arden's house at Wilmcote

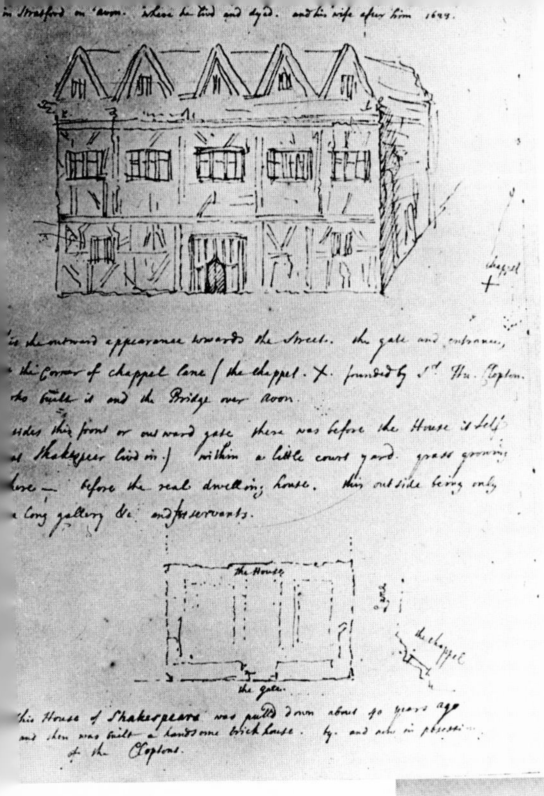

New Place at Stratford, Shakespeare's later home, from Vertue's sketch

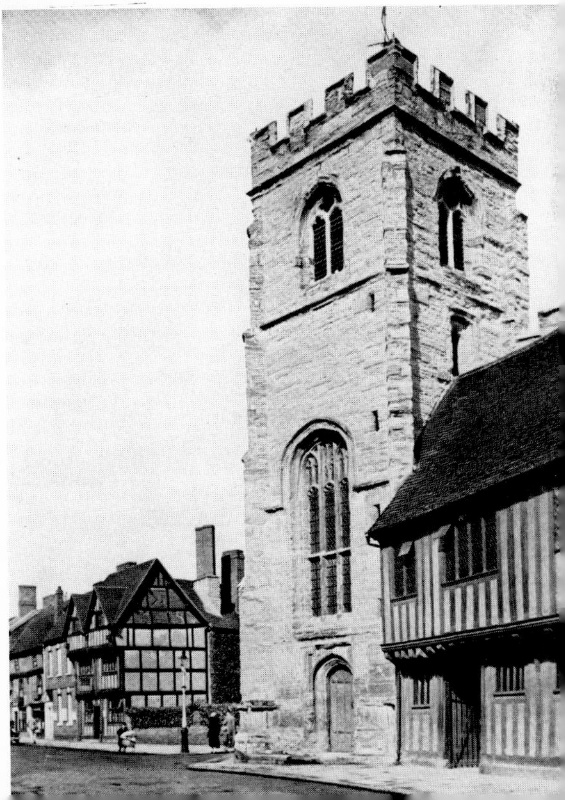

The Gild Chapel and the site of New Place

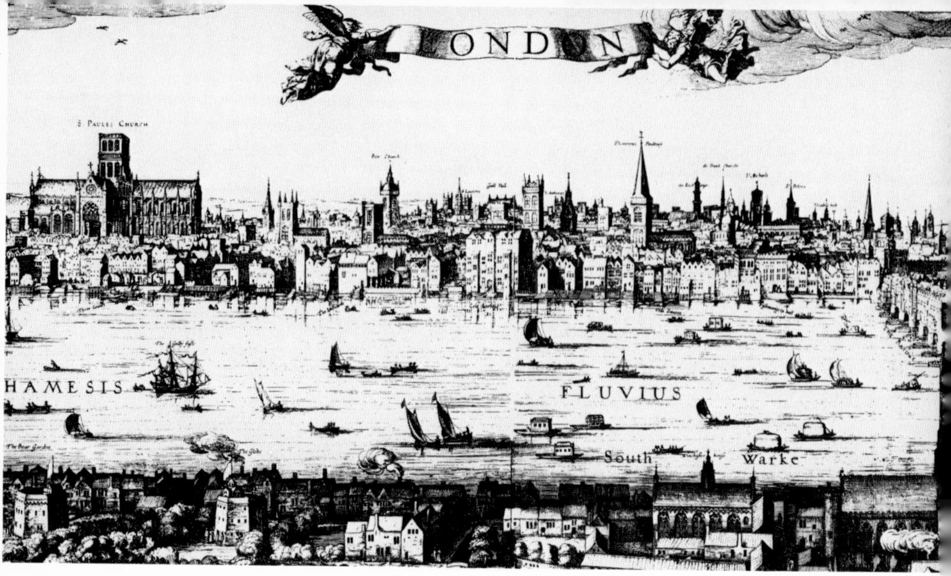

Bankside at the time of Shakespeare's death

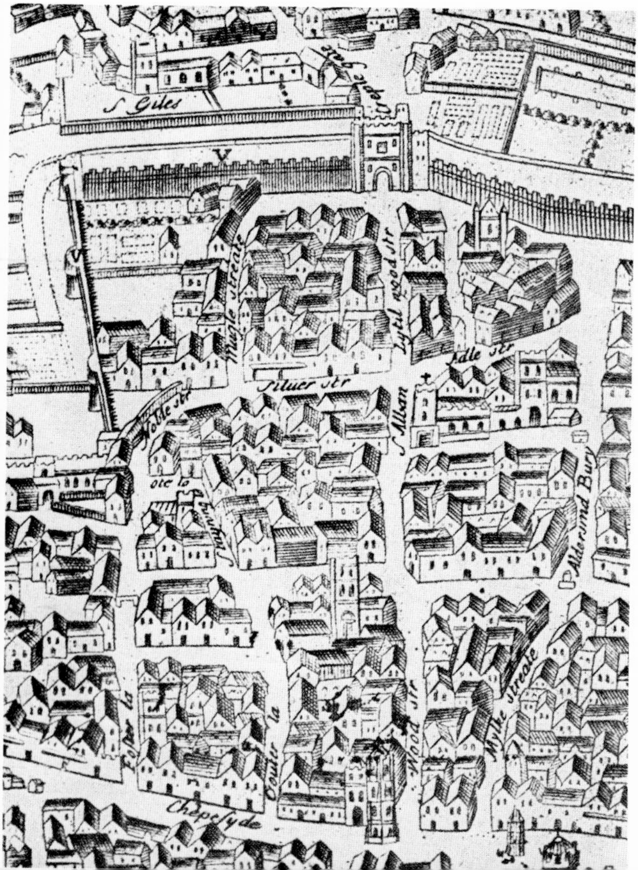

Where Shakespeare lodged with the Mountjoys *from Aggas map, c.* 1560

The house at the corner of Silver Street and Monkswell (Mugle) Street

Ben Jonson

Richard Burbage

The Earl of Essex

An Elizabethan player

Southampton as a young man

Southampton at the period of the sonnets

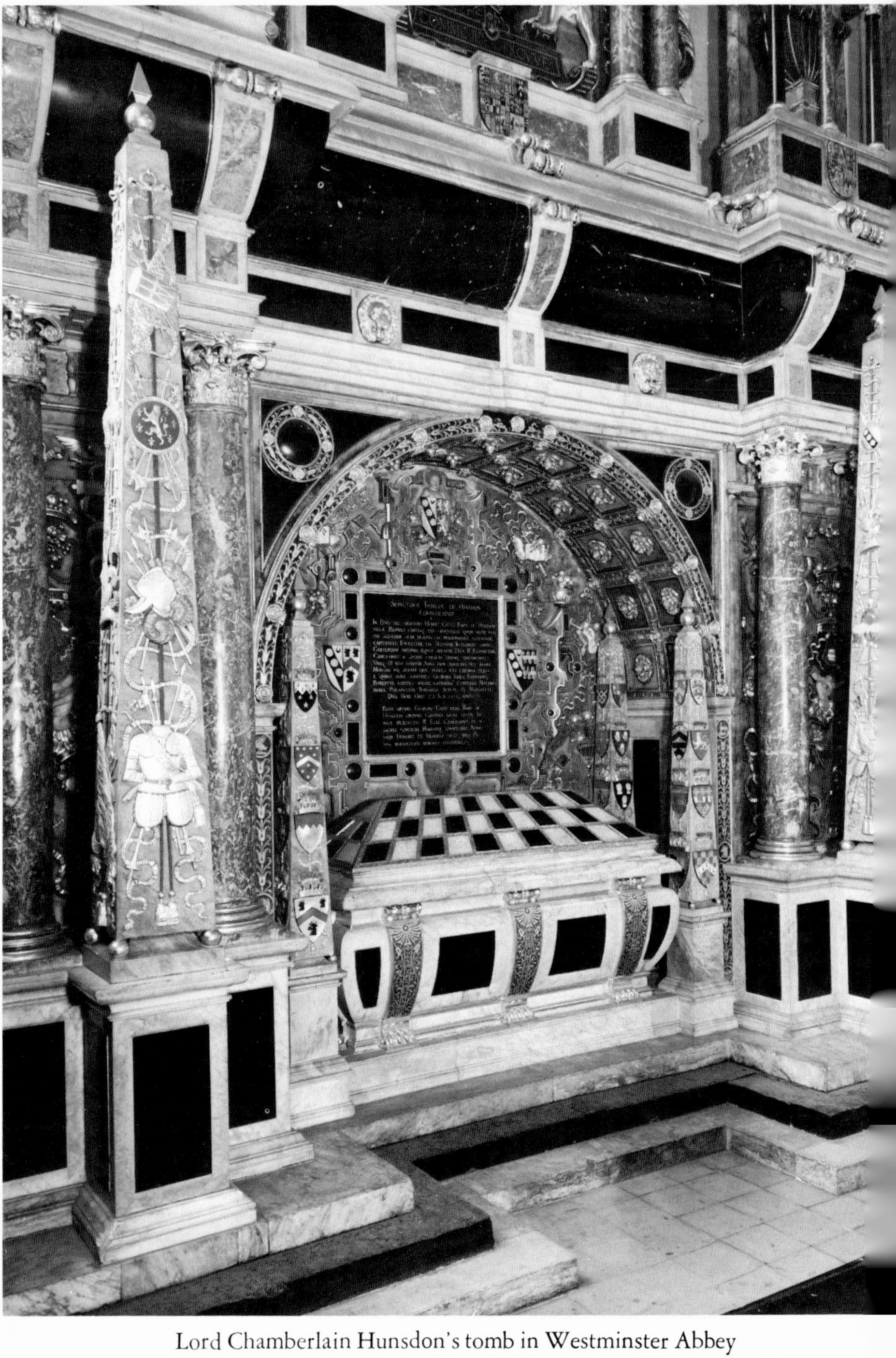

Lord Chamberlain Hunsdon's tomb in Westminster Abbey

Grant of 1596

Shakespeare's Arms, impaled (with revision) 1599

Shakespeare's coat-of-arms

A lady at the virginals

William Lanier consults Forman

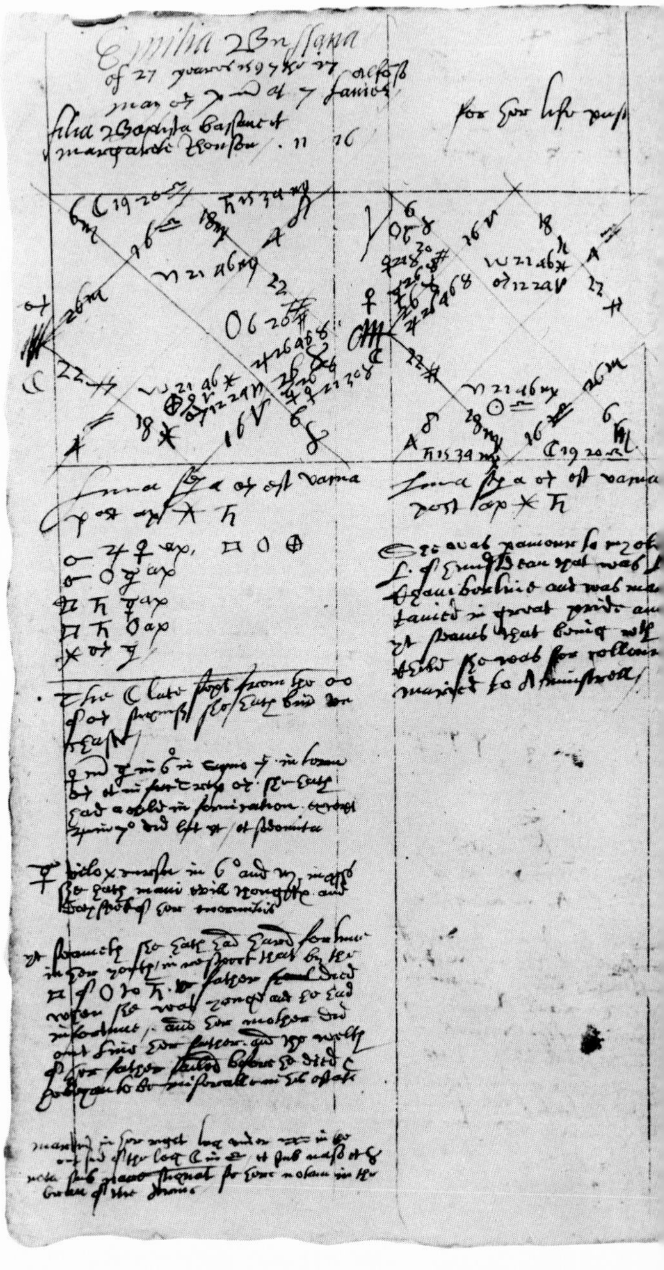

Emilia Bassano consults Forman for her life past

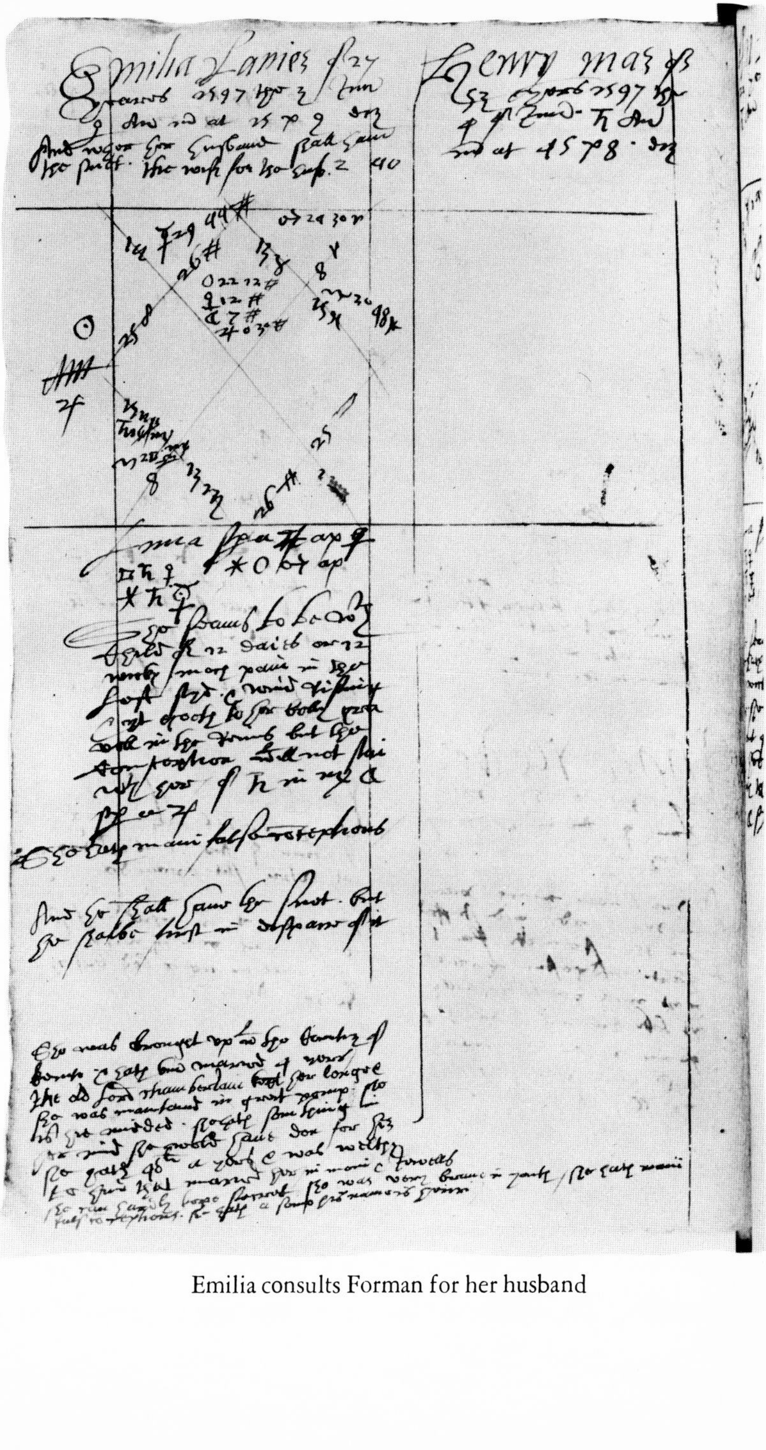

Emilia consults Forman for her husband

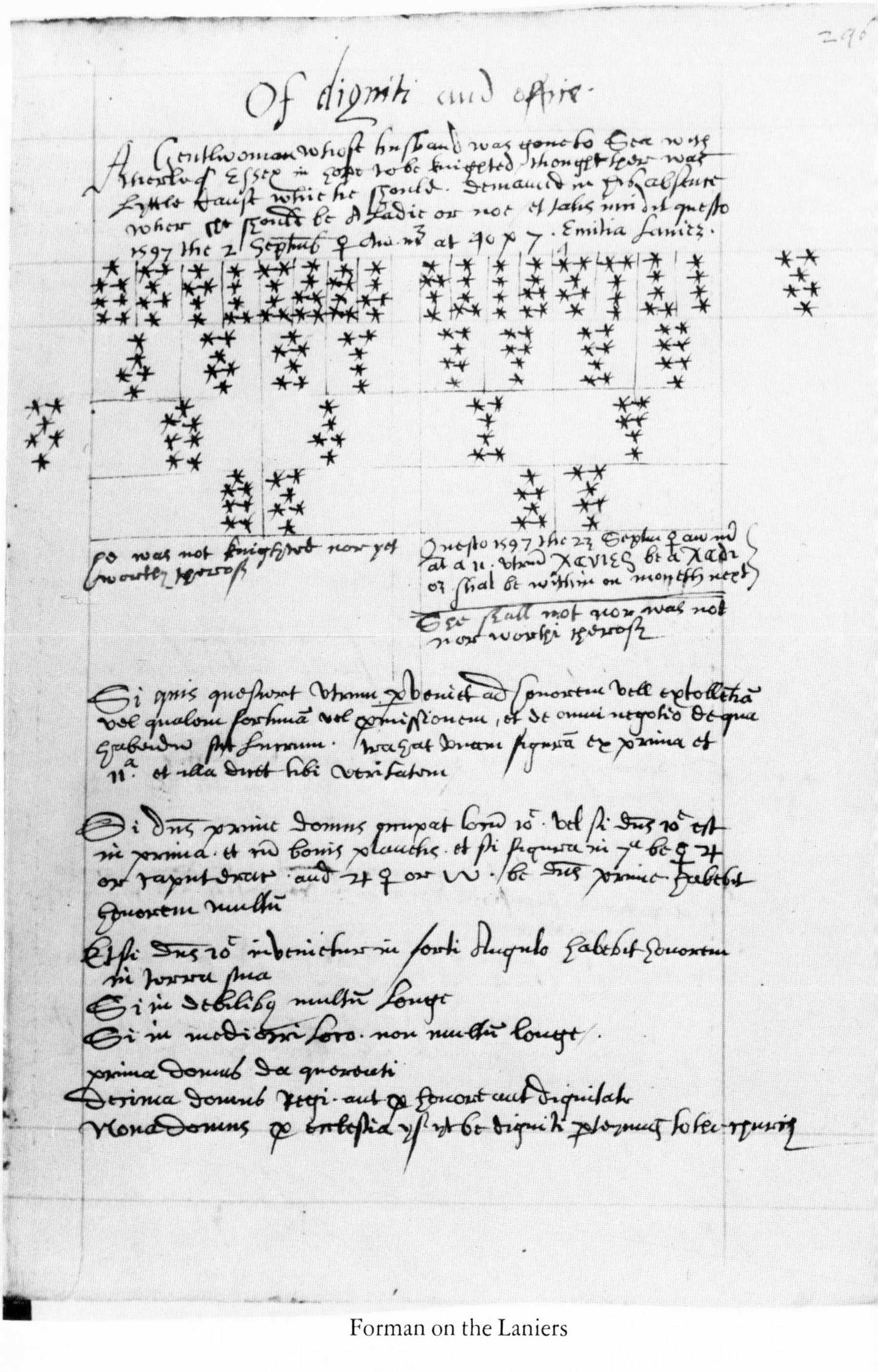
Of digniti and offic.

A Gentlewoman whose husband was gone to Sea with the Erle of Essex in hope to be knighted though there was little cause whie he should. Demanded ... whether she should be a Ladie or not ...

1597 the 2 Septemb ... Emilia Lanier.

he was not knighted nor yet ... worse thereof

Questio 1597 the 23 Septem ... at a 11 ... Emilia Lanier be a Ladi or shal be within on month next

she shall not nor was not nor worse thereof

[illegible]

Forman on the Laniers

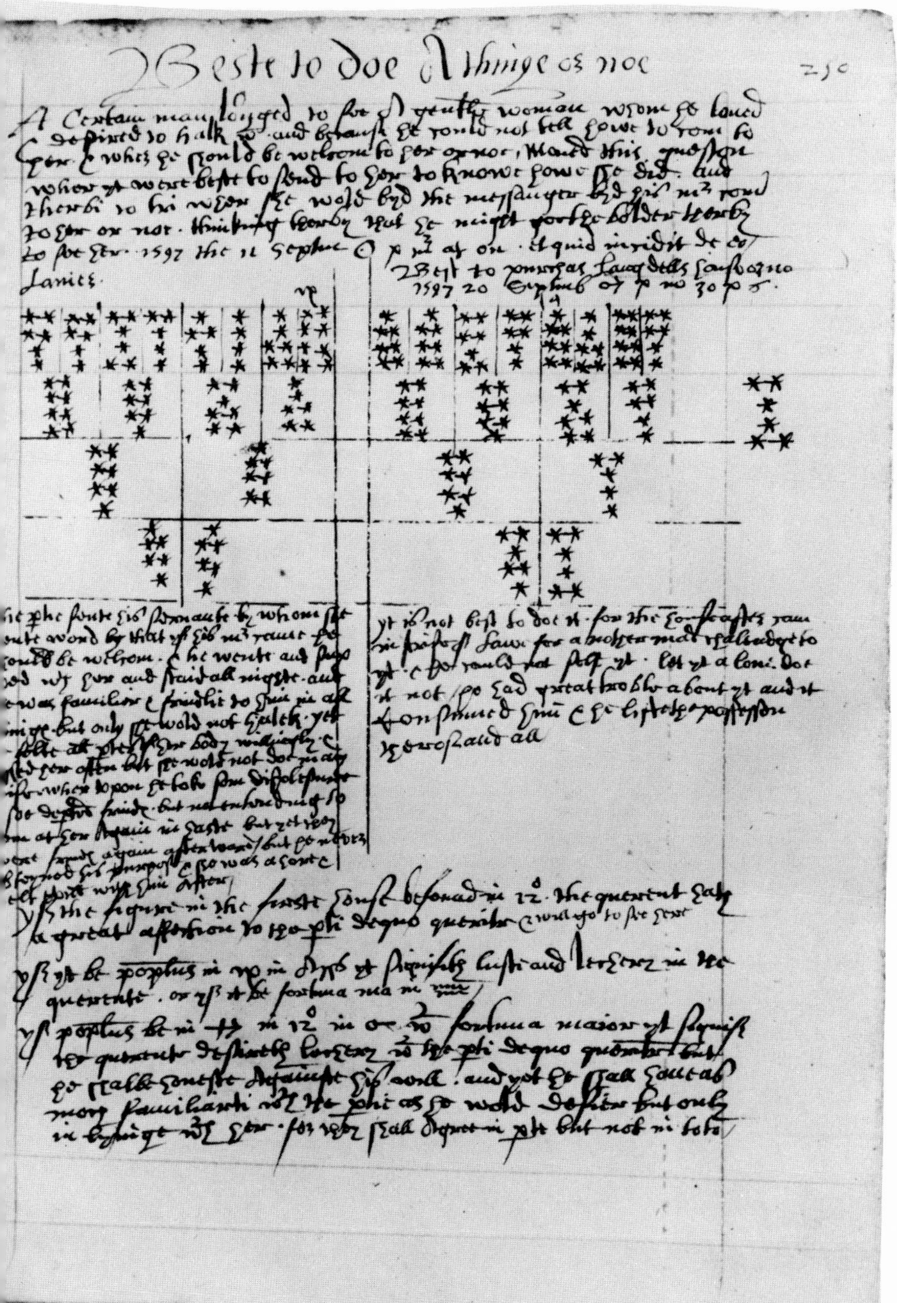

Forman visits Mrs. Lanier

Enter Tamora pleadinge for her sonnes
goinge to execution

Tam: Stay Romane bretheren gratious Conquerors
Victorious Titus rue the teares I shed
A mothers teares in passion of her sonnes
And if thy sonnes were ever deare to thee
Oh thinke my sonnes to bee as deare to mee
Suffizeth not that wee are brought to Roome
To beautify thy triumphes and returne
Captiue to thee and to thy Romane yoake
But must my sonnes be slaughtered in the streetes
for valiant doinges in there Cuntryes cause
Oh if to fight for kinge and Common weale
Were piety in thine it is in these
Andronicus staine not thy tombe wth blood
Wilt thou drawe neere the nature of the Gods
Drawe neere them then in being mercifull
Sweete mercy is nobilityes true badge
Thrice noble Titus spare my first borne sonne

Titus: Patient your selfe madame for dy hee must
Aaron do you likewise prepare your selfe
And now at last repent your wicked life

Aron: Ah now I curse the day and yet I thinke
ffew comes within the compasse of ~~your~~ my curse
Wherein I did not some notorious ill
As kill a man or els devise his death
Ravish a mayd or plott the way to do it
Acuse some innocent and forsweare my selfe
Set deadly enmity betweene too freendes
Make poore mens cattell breake theire neckes
Set fire on barnes and haystackes in the night
And bid the owners quench them wth their teares
Oft have I digd vp dead men from their graves
And set them vpright at their deere frendes dore
Even almost when theire sorrowes was forgott
And on their brestes as on the barke of trees
Have wth my knife carved in Romane letters
Let not your sorrowe dy though I am dead
Tut I have done a thousand dreadfull thinges
As willingly as one would kill a fly
And nothing greives mee hartily indeede
for that I cannot doo ten thousand more &c

Henricus Peacham
Anno m° q° q° q°

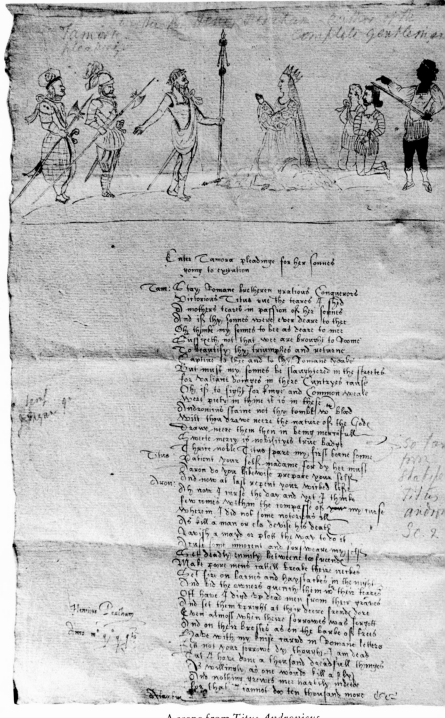

A scene from *Titus Andronicus*

The Swan Theatre

Shakespeare's monument in Stratford church

In a scene or two later he follows suit with

Now are they but one lamp, one light, one sun.

In short, Marlowe's historic achievement was to marry great poetry to the drama; his was the originating genius. William Shakespeare never forgot him: in his penultimate, valedictory play, *The Tempest*, he is still echoing Marlowe's phrases.

A decisive step had been taken, on the threshold of the 1580s, with the building of the first permanent theatres, out beyond the City walls and City authorities, in the fields of Shoreditch: the Theatre and the Curtain. Hence it is that many of the earlier theatre folk lived in that area – actors like Tarleton, most famous of clowns, the Burbages, Marlowe and his friend Thomas Watson, Shakespeare in nearby Bishopsgate; and not only theatre people but Court-musicians like the Italian Bassanos, a numerous clan.

A further decisive step came in 1583 with the formation of the Queen's Company: in place of small troupes, a company of twelve of the best selected players, sponsored by her Council at her command. *There* was a reply to the City authorities always trying to clamp down on the naughty stage. The Queen's Men held the lead until Tarleton's death in 1588; Leicester died the same year, when his company came to an end. Thus new formations, new possibilities, were opening up just when Shakespeare came to London. The company that took the lead now was the Lord Admiral's, with Edward Alleyn as its star, Philip Henslowe as entrepreneur, Marlowe to write for it.

It looked as if the future was with it; and, indeed, it had a most distinguished future. But eventually there came into being a combination that went beyond it: that of the Burbages with Shakespeare to write for it, the Lord Chamberlain's Men, formed in 1594, after the fearful havoc wrought by the plague years of 1592 and 1593. The letters exchanged between Henslowe and his stepson-in-law, Alleyn, give us a vivid impression of the effects of the plague on the theatre-folk. Even so, luck was with the Burbages; for Marlowe was killed in 1593, and Alleyn, greatest of tragic actors, withdrew from the stage. Henslowe was not by origin a theatre-man, the theatre was only one among his interests. Whereas James Burbage, who built the Theatre and eventually removed it to build the Globe on the South Bank, was a full-time theatre man and had been one of Leicester's players.

His son Richard became the leading actor in the Lord Chamberlain's Company. He makes a dramatic appearance in real life a few years before, in 1590, in a brawl about the profits. Evidence was given in a court-case that he had appeared with a broomstick in hand: '"Huh! they come for a moiety. But," quoth he, holding up the said broomstaff, "I have, I think, delivered him a moiety with this," and sent them packing.' This was the good fellow – a talented painter too – with whom William Shakespeare spent the whole of his professional life, the twenty-two years from 1594 to 1616, and to whom he left money in his will for a mourning-ring to remember him by.

These years between 1588 and 1594 are full of shifts and changes in the theatre-world, compounded and made dangerous for the players, threatening life as well as livelihood, by an exceptional visitation of plague running high two years in succession in 1592 and 1593. This is one reason for the shifts and changes of the companies and what makes it difficult to trace their individual histories with certainty. One company, Pembroke's – taking its name from Henry, the second Earl, not William, the third Earl – ventured a country tour in 1593, and came back broken. The family of a well-known actor, Robert Browne – who later made his career in Germany – was wiped out. A young bricklayer, Benjamin Jonson, did not help Henslowe by killing one of his best actors, quarrelsome Gabriel Spencer.

Already before this time of crisis for the theatre and all those who lived by it, by 1592 the outsider, the player turned playwright, was at last establishing himself and becoming well known for his plays. His earliest plays were written for Pembroke's Men; but intermediately the men who become his lasting associates in the Lord Chamberlain's Company – Richard Burbage, Augustine Phillips, John Heming, Thomas Pope, George Bryan, William

Sly – are to be found together in that of Ferdinando, Lord Strange. He died in 1594, leaving these men free to make another combination, with William Shakespeare both to play and to write for them.

One thing we can be sure about, which has not been sufficiently emphasised, the player-poet was very much of a reading man – one might almost say bookish, except for its pejorative overtone: for him life was more important than books. But he was a quick and avid reader, especially of the fascinating books at last beginning to tumble out of English presses. As the result of his independent reading, he was coming abreast of the university wits dominating the literary scene; in fact, he was tending to approximate to them, almost as if he had been to the university himself; he was making himself capable of competing with them on something like equal terms.

Two books coming out in the late 1580s were of continuing importance to him. In 1587 came out the second, and much enlarged, edition of Holinshed's chronicle history of England, of which Shakespeare made such splendid use for the rest of his life. It opened up for him a new world of his country's past, untaught at school; it provided him not only with material, but inspiration: it fed that love of his country which was an abiding theme, along with a deep concern that things should go well under proper direction. This countryman had a far more responsible attitude towards society than any other dramatist, let alone foot-loose London intellectuals without roots. A family man, with a stable background, eventually a man of property, he was from the first concerned with social order, the disasters consequent upon bad or feeble government (Richard II, Henry VI), the chaos and cruelty that are concomitant with social breakdown; the necessity of order and obedience, everybody according to his proper function. This theme was reinforced by his reading of Hall's Chronicle, the whole moral of which was the ending of the feud between Lancaster and York in the Tudor dynasty.

A second work – of poetic rather than dramatic importance to him – was Spenser's *Faerie Queene*, the first three books of which were published in December 1589. His reading of this was reflected immediately all through the three *Henry VI* plays, written 1590–1.

Sidney's *Arcadia* and his poems provided another continuing influence; both Sidney and Samuel Daniel are echoed in the Sonnets. Daniel's *Civil Wars* suggested material somewhat later for *Richard II*; his *Complaint of Rosamond*, of 1592, is imitated by what we must take to be the player-poet's first piece, his prentice-work, 'A Lover's Complaint'. A passage in *The Rape of Lucrece* was inspired by a poem of Marlowe's friend, Thomas Watson. Altogether a strongly literary quality pervades his early work, and this has a special significance. For it is a different inflexion from his true nature, as it subsequently developed, with its powerful individuality and strongly marked idiom. One has the paradox that one notices also with Elgar – that, in spite of being a magpie, picking up bits and pieces from everywhere, the work that emerges has its own unmistakable personality and accent.

One gets the impression of a young man, much on his own, having to pick up his education from books and make the most of what he can get. Not for him the intellectual companionship of the university wits – of the Oxford group from which Peele, Lyly and Lodge came, or the Cambridge circles of Spenser and Harvey, or Greene, Marlowe and Nashe. He was too young and unknown to be taken up by Sidney and the *cognoscenti* of Leicester House. He was an outsider, but a great one for making the most of every opportunity. Needs must.

A grand patriotic opportunity, with historic reverberations, opened up with the new campaigns undertaken in France to come to the aid of Henry of Navarre, the Protestant champion hard pressed by the Catholic League and Spain. Particularly in Normandy, with its age-old memories of campaigning there, the stout masculine tune of the fifteenth century we still sing:

Our King went forth to Normandy. . . .

Now, in 1591, it was the gallant young Essex, favourite of both Queen and people, who was to lead the return to France, with chivalrous rather than predatory intentions.

Normandy brought back a surge of memories to the English – of Agincourt and Henry V, a hero to the Elizabethans, of the Hundred Years' War, Crécy and Poitiers, and brave Talbot. It was this surge of patriotic feeling that the *Henry VI* plays seized on and expressed, and won for their player-author the popular acclaim at last which Marlowe had won at once with *Tamburlaine*. Nashe, Marlowe's friend, whom Shakespeare knew, expressed it, when Talbot once more walked the stage. 'How it would have joyed brave Talbot, the terror of the French, to think that after he had lain two hundred years in his tomb, he should triumph again on the stage and have his bones embalmed with the tears of ten thousand spectators at least – at several times – who, in the tragedian that represents his person, imagine they behold him fresh bleeding.'

This was the triumph enjoyed by the player who was also a playwright that aroused the anger and apprehension of an envious senior, the best-known literary journalist in London: Robert Greene.

The newcomer had by this time not only the *Henry VI* plays to his credit but *Titus Andronicus*. These four plays are clearly the work of an 'inexperienced dramatist' – they are the works of his apprenticeship, though they all bear evidence of great promise, capabilities of future fulfilment. They are much influenced by his school-reading of Seneca – Newton's translation of the Roman tragedies had been coming out at intervals – but still more verbally, by Marlowe. With *The Taming of the Shrew*, however, Shakespeare achieves his own authentic voice, and it is redolent of the Cotswolds. One can see that the ingenuous author is a countryman, a provincial. Dr Johnson, whose criticism has the force that comes from a mind on a level with what he is criticising, observed that Shakespeare's natural bent was for comedy; he had to work towards tragedy.

But even in the barbaric classicism of *Titus Andronicus*, where he was not himself but imitating someone else, the countryman – contrary to the nature of the play and its horrors – breaks through. It is as if he were writing with the meads of Stratford around him, or certainly in mind:

One hour's storm will drown the fragrant meads. . .

as meadows, yet not dry,
With miry slime left on them by a flood.

And hunting the deer – somewhat improbably, amid all the shedding of human blood – is not far away in his thoughts:

The hunt is up, the morn is bright and grey,
The fields are fragrant and the woods are green:
Uncouple here and let us make a bay. . . .

Or

Seeking to hide herself, as doth the deer
That hath received some unrecuring wound.

It is in this early play that we have the reminiscence of the deer-poacher carrying the deer by the keeper's nose.

The Taming of the Shrew begins with a return from hunting and a good deal of knowledgeable talk about the hounds. Even more to the point is the Stratford background at the beginning. Christopher Sly is Old Sly's son of Barton-on-the-Heath, where Shakespeare's Arden aunt, Joan Lambert, lived. Marian Hacket is the 'fat ale-wife of Wincot' – which must be the old pronunciation of Mary Arden's Wilmcote. Among the names are

Stephen Sly and old John Naps of Greet

– and, believe it or not, editors of Shakespeare have been pedantic enough to retain the Folio misprint 'Greece' for the familiar place near home!

There are other reflections from the poet's early life: plenty of school touches and tags about. When a character quotes Terence he quotes it not from the original but as it appears in Lily's grammar. Schoolmastering appears, with the suitors getting through to the lady they are after as teachers, one to instruct her in Latin, the other in fingering on the lute – with bawdy suggestions of fingering, of course. Again, the imitative player turned playwright is greatly indebted for material to an earlier Elizabethan writer, George Gascoigne, whose *Supposes* he read up for his play.

Again *3 Henry VI* has a hunt:

> Under this thick-grown brake we'll shroud ourselves;
> For through this laund anon the deer will come;
> And in this covert will we make our stand,
> Culling the principal of all the deer.

No budding dramatist was so much addicted to the hunt – it is something special to this one – certainly not those townees, Marlowe, Kyd, Greene. These historical chronicle plays are, in fact, full of the country and country sports: we have falconry, snaring woodcock and taking conies in the net, foxes at work, greyhounds

> Having the fearful flying hare in sight

– not long before the familiar long insert of coursing the hare in *Venus and Adonis*. A real writer does not disguise himself in his work: the young Shakespeare peeps out at us again and again.

Not least is the way Warwickshire is brought forward into the picture. Sir William Lucy of Charlecote, who was sheriff in Henry VI's reign, is brought on in two or three scenes in the first of these plays. In the third, the loyal dramatist goes out of his way to bring the opposing Lancastrians to 'a plain in Warwickshire', 'a camp near Warwick'. Not only do Warwick and Coventry appear as in the history-books but small places like Dunsmore, Southam and Daintry, the old pronunciation of Daventry. The player turned playwright was an adept at making the most of what he knew.

He is recognisable thus early in the grandiloquent way he has with language, stretching the bow to the utmost. Though rather naïve – in contrast to the mature artistic control of Marlowe – they are effective, high-sounding terms that would bombast out well on the stage: 'rehearse the method of my pen', 'particularities and petty sounds', grand words like 'intermissive', 'sequestration', 'exigent', 'my words effectual' and so on.

An admirable old student familiar with West Midlands speech has shown from the dramatist's spellings that this is how he spoke. An Elizabethan historian can corroborate that this would be so. Disparities of speech were then much wider, local dialects stronger, the patterns stronger and more diversified. Grandees at Court spoke with the accents of the region they came from (as did Lord Curzon up to our day). Sir Walter Ralegh 'spake broad Devonshire to his dying day' – we can hear it in his peculiar spellings.

So too with William Shakespeare, who said 'woonder' for 'wonder', 'woone' for 'won', 'smoother' for 'smother', 'smoake' for smoke, 'sturre' for 'stir'. West Midlands speech inverts the 'u' sound from southern usage: Shakespeare said 'kuckoo' for cuckoo, i.e. cookoo. Other vowel-sounds were stronger, especially the long *a*: he said 'auncient' and 'inchaunt' and 'awnser'. The sound 'er' was pronounced more broadly 'ar' then, as we still do with 'serjeant' and 'clerk'. Consonant sounds were more emphatic, as we can see in spellings like 'shedde', 'kisse', 'mistresse', 'chidde', 'starre', 'jarre' – the *r* being rolled. Altogether his pronunciation, with its provincial tones, had a stronger, broader, more masculine sound, and would be better suited to dramatic declamation than our etiolated speech.

Another theme that is announced in these plays is Shakespeare's insistent concern with gentility that runs all through his work, from beginning to end. When it is insisted upon over and over we may conclude that it is important for the author. Here it is:

> Let him that is a true-born gentleman
> And stands upon the honour of his birth. . . .

This goes along with a friendly contempt for the common people, which evidently did not go against the grain with those who flocked to see the plays: they recognised the truth, along with the good nature, of the presentation. Their humours and absurdities provided him with some of his most characteristic material: he understood them through and through.

Much of this is recognisable in the first public notice we have of the dramatist who had achieved marked popularity with the *Henry VI* plays, all the more noteworthy because they were written by a mere player. This was quite exceptional. Neither Marlowe nor Kyd, Lyly nor Peele, Greene nor Nashe, Watson, Lodge was an actor. This was what infuriated Robert Greene in his last illness, who warned his fellows – pure writers, university bred – against the competition of this player who could turn his hand to anything, in words so bitter that there must have been something personal behind them, some acute disappointment, to account for the malice.

Robert Greene was six years older, the most talked-about figure in the popular reaches of London literary life. A Cambridge man, like Marlowe and Nashe, he took his M.A. at both universities, a fact which he blazoned on all his books. He was prolific and versatile, pouring out prose romances, pamphlets in the vein of social realism, poems of considerable charm, and eventually plays. Here he was less successful. He attempted to imitate the triumphs of his junior, Marlowe: that of *Tamburlaine* with an *Alphonsus*, a poor play, and of *Dr Faustus* with *Friar Bacon and Friar Bungay*, rather better but no great success. He wrote, or collaborated in, four or five plays; but he is not remembered by them. Now, at thirty-seven, he was in his last illness and another junior – a complete outsider to them all – was coming up fast.

The envious attack which Greene launched against the newcomer is famous; but there is an earlier passage which has been taken little notice of and yet would seem to indicate personal contact between the actor and the well-known writer. Roberto, i.e. Greene, falls in with a countryman, i.e. a provincial, who turns out to be a player, the profession which, according to Greene, was 'to get by scholars their whole living'. This already expresses the resentment of a university man reduced to penning plays at the behest of mere actors. 'What is your profession?' said Roberto. 'Truly, sir, I am a player.' 'A player!' quoth Roberto, 'I took you rather for a gentleman of great living; for, if by outward habit men should be censured [estimated], I tell you you would be taken for a substantial man.' This is rather snide. 'So I am, where I dwell,' quoth the player, 'reputed able at my proper cost to build a windmill. What though the world once went hard with me, when I was fain to carry my playing-fardel a footback? *Tempora mutantur:* I know you know the meaning of it better than I. But thus I construe it: it is otherwise now, for my very share in playing apparel will not be sold for £200.' 'Truly,' said Roberto, 'it is strange that you should so prosper in that vain practice, for that it seems to me your voice is nothing gracious.' But the player is quite self-confident, rather pleased with himself: 'I can serve to make a pretty speech, for I was a country author, passing at a moral . . . and for seven years was absolute interpreter of the puppets.'

The episode ends with the player engaging Roberto, poet and scholar, to pen plays, 'for which you shall be well paid'. Roberto '*perceiving no remedy*, thought best, *in respect of his present necessity*, to try his wit and went with him willingly: who lodged him at the town's end in a house of retail'.

We know that the whole thing was autobiographical on Greene's part; but who was the player with a provincial accent who gave himself the airs of a gentleman? It was just seven years since the birth of Shakespeare's twins at Stratford. 'For seven years . . . absolute interpreter of the puppets' would seem to indicate an apprenticeship of that duration at acting. There is ill-feeling, a sense of humiliation, in this passage at the writer and scholar being hired by the player. But real bitterness bursts out in his attack on Shakespeare openly, for by parodying a line in the last part of *Henry VI* Greene identifies him:

> O tiger's heart wrapt in a woman's hide!

becomes

> Tiger's heart wrapt in a *player's* hide.

What had happened between them?

For the dying Greene proceeded to warn his friends the writers – Marlowe, Peele, Nashe – against the players, who had made use of him, Greene, more than any of them. Yet

> is it not strange that I, to whom they all have been beholding [obligated], is it not like that you to whom they all have been beholding, shall – were ye in that case as I am now – be both at once of them forsaken?

Then comes the particular warning against that one of the players who was ready to take *their* place by writing the plays too:

> Yea, trustt hem not: for there is an upstart crow, beautified with our feathers, that with his
>
> Tiger's heart wrapt in a player's hide
>
> supposes he is as well able to bombast out a blank verse as the best of you: and, being an absolute Johannes Factotum, is in his own conceit the only Shake-scene in a country.

Having spat out his venom, Greene thereupon died. There was a rumpus, for both Marlowe and Shakespeare protested. Marlowe had been recognisably referred to as both atheist and Machiavellian. Henry Chettle, who had published the tract upon Greene's death, did not apologise to Marlowe, replying merely that he had cut out another charge which, 'had it been true, yet to publish it had been intolerable'. This was clearly a reference to Marlowe's well-known homosexuality. 'With neither of them that take offence was I acquainted,' wrote Chettle, 'and with one of them I care not if I never be.'

His response to Shakespeare was quite different; Chettle had evidently received a formal call from him in the interval, and thereupon published a complete apology:

> The other, whom at that time I did not so much spare as since I wish I had. . . . That I did not I am as sorry as if the original fault had been

my fault: because myself have seen his demeanour no less civil than he excellent in the quality he professes. Besides, divers of worship have reported his uprightness of dealing, which argues his honesty, and his facetious grace in writing that approves his art.

This is the most handsome apology that I know in the Elizabethan age. They all read Latin and would know that 'facetious' was the compliment Cicero had applied to Plautus. There is a tribute to the player's bearing being as gentlemanly as he was excellent in his profession. Moreover, gentlemen of position had spoken for him and his upright dealing – as Ben Jonson later: 'he was indeed honest, and of an open and free nature'.

He had indeed arrived.

CHAPTER 5

The Poet Finds a Patron

THE decisive period in Shakespeare's life and career, in the development of his art with the opportunities opening before him, came with his finding a patron in 1592 and the intense, inspiring and inspired three years that followed. Things would have taken a very different course if it had not been for this providential good fortune. There might have been disaster, as with those other poets who perished in these years with their work unfinished: Greene himself, Watson, Kyd, Peele, Marlowe. For plague struck the theatre-folk and independent, exposed writers a cruel blow; this was dangerous enough in itself, but things took an even more serious turn in 1593 when the visitation, quite exceptionally, raged for a second year in succession.

Shakespeare made the acquaintance of Southampton in the winter of 1591–2, when the young Earl had just come of age at eighteen and the poet was twenty-seven. We do not have to look far to see what attracted the young peer's attention. For him, too, the Normandy campaign was an experience, his first taste of campaigning. In January or February of 1591 he had slipped across the Channel, without licence or permission, to serve under Essex, the leader of his order. For him Southampton conceived a passionate devotion that led him ultimately to the Tower, and a narrow escape from the scaffold.

Now, in March 1591 in Dieppe, the seventeen-year-old youth offered himself to Essex 'to be disposed of by your commandment', expressed himself exceedingly proud if he might win Essex's favour, which he would endeavour to deserve. 'In the meantime wishing your fortune may ever prove answerable to the greatness of your own mind.' In the event, Essex's fortune did not: he lost his only brother, 'the half-arch of my house'. But Southampton returned safe and sound, to take something of that brother's part in the Earl's fortunes. The younger peer had two overriding desires: to win glory in the war, either on land or at sea; to shine in the reflected glory of the arts, literature, drama, painting – he came to be painted more frequently than any, except those more famous peers, Leicester and Essex.

He was intelligent and aspiring, well educated by the care of his guardian, Lord Treasurer Burghley, who sent him to his own college at Cambridge, St John's, for four years, 1585–9. He had been left an orphan by his father's early death, when the boy was only eight and had succeeded to the peerage conferred by Henry VIII upon his Lord Chancellor, Thomas Wriothesley.* In spite of this patronage, the second Southampton, named for the King, remained an obstinate Catholic and endangered the family by his perverse support of Mary Queen of Scots, for which he fetched up in the Tower. He had made his charming wife – of the Catholic Montagu family – most unhappy and a confounded nuisance of himself. There was a strain of wilfulness in the son as in the father. The family needed protection and the Lord Treasurer was willing to give it.

It was important to provide for the marriage of the heir to such an inheritance. The youth was the last of the family; it was his prime duty to provide for its continuance. Lord Burghley had a suitable granddaughter, Lady Elizabeth Vere – daughter of the gifted and erratic Earl of Oxford; before attaining his majority the boy had promised to marry her.

Born on 6 October 1573 he came of age on 6 October 1591, but would not carry out his promise. A number of people took a hand in trying to persuade him to do his duty – his mother, the Countess, who was anxious to see him settled; Lord Burghley, who wanted to see his ward settled and his granddaughter provided for; the youth's grandfather, Lord Montagu, upon whom Lord Burghley

* The proper pronunciation of the family name was Risley.

brought pressure. All to no avail: the young Earl did not wish to marry at all. He wanted to be free, to follow Essex anywhere; to follow his own desires and interests, perhaps to find his own nature and fulfil it his own way. As he ultimately did, by the way of adversity, which he brought upon himself, self-willed, loyal to his friends, generous to a fault. For his nature was golden; he was always popular and beloved.

He was also as beautiful as a woman: Renaissance people admired that and had a passionate cult of youth – one has only to think of Italian portraits of young men, as appreciative of their beauty as of women. From Hilliard's miniature of him at this time we see the long gold tresses falling over the left shoulder, the fair complexion and eyes – with a residual masculine stare in them. Perfectly arched eyebrows, aquiline nose and sensitive, not sensual, lips complete the picture of a young aristocrat, a rising star in the firmament now coming into public notice. Young for his age, with something of delayed adolescence about him, he was not yet sexually directed. As yet unresponsive to women, he was attractive to men and women alike – again the Renaissance saw a doubling, an enrichment, of nature in that: nothing of Victorian disapproval, a disqualification in perception from understanding the subtle and complex relations that ensued.

All these characteristics, the personality and circumstances, are crystal-clear throughout the Sonnets that Shakespeare wrote in the course of his duty to the young Lord upon being accepted as his poet. Indeed they are obvious and the personality recognisable in the first poem Shakespeare wrote for him, 'A Lover's Complaint.' It is a charming pastoral invention, with a country background, as it might be the Cotswolds, and with a literary flavouring of both Spenser and Chaucer. But the young man of the tale –

> His qualities were beauteous as his form,
> For maiden-tongued he was, and thereof free. . . .

Again,

> That he did in the general bosom reign

Of young, of old; and sexes both enchanted. . . .

So many have, that never touched his hand,
Sweetly supposed them mistress of his heart. . .

Actually, the young man had not yet given his heart to anyone (except possibly Essex): he was rather, at this age, in love with himself.

It is visibly Southampton – odd that people should not have perceived that: all the more so since the poem fetched up ultimately with the *cache* of the Sonnets and was published along with them, by Thorpe, in 1609.

It is still more extraordinary that people should not perceive that the Sonnets are sonnets of duty from the poet to his patron, from beginning to end, obvious throughout and evident in many of the sonnets individually. The failure to realise this comes from picking out a sonnet here or there, instead of reading them right through consecutively for the story they reveal. When one does that, one sees that the poet–patron relationship is fundamental, the basis of the whole thing. Further – to make a more original point, which creative writers can appreciate – Shakespeare saw in the relationship a subject and characteristically seized upon the artistic, no less than the personal, opportunity. As the Sonnets unfold one sees that they have a homogeneous development, an artistic integration towards which Shakespeare was working, consciously and unconsciously (so like him): which he held in his mind like the development of a drama. The Sonnets, to a reader who understands such things, are not disparate objects, but a whole work of art; the drama was his own personal one.

Now for the story they tell, perfectly clear, like the poet himself 'open and free' – though the key was lost for so long.

Shakespeare, a normal family man, always in favour of marrying and giving in marriage – with a more than normal responsiveness to women, their nature and functions – was very willing to lend his pen to persuade the young Lord, politely, sympathetically, with proper deference, to marry. This would not be disagreeable to his anxious mother, the Countess, who receives an initial tribute:

> Thou art thy mother's glass, and she in thee
> Calls back the lovely April of her prime.

His own beauty called upon him to reproduce himself:

> Look in thy glass, and tell the face thou viewest
> Now is the time that face should form another. . . .

Nor would that be disagreeable to a rather narcissistic, young Renaissance peer accustomed to flattery on every hand. Shakespeare's approach is more serious, like that of a highly responsive tutor to a fascinating but fatherless youth:

> Dear my love, you know
> You had a father: let your son say so.

The poet-tutor tells him it is his duty to shore up his house, instead of selfishly

> Seeking that beauteous roof to ruinate
> Which to repair should be thy chief desire.

The tone becomes warmer as the acquaintance progresses, but to catch the exact *timbre* requires an intimate familiarity with the usage and language of the time. This was a poet-playwright of inferior station writing to a beautiful youth of exalted rank, who was pleased to extend his patronage to Shakespeare, where others – Nashe, for example – were rejected. The high-flown language was in keeping, the terms of endearment not going beyond the bounds of affection and decorum. For, make no mistake about this, Shakespeare's interest in the youth is not at all sexual – as Marlowe's or Bacon's might well have been: that was clean contrary to Shakespeare's highly heterosexual nature. In case there should be any mistake about it, he has made it quite clear in so many words: Nature, in forming the youth, had

> by addition me of thee defeated,
> By adding one thing to my purpose nothing.

That thing is named in broad Elizabethan fashion:

> But since she *pricked* thee out for women's pleasure,
> Mine be thy love, and thy love's use their treasure.

So far as sex is concerned the women can have him – whether this choice was agreeable to the young man we are not told. Shakespeare responds to his colouring and complexion, eyes and expression, quite unlike Marlowe's more vibrant response to youthful muscles and torso, thighs and other things. Shakespeare's real response was to Southampton's golden nature as yet unsullied, its transparent purity, with its generous impulses and spontaneous affection – everyone witnessed to these qualities in him: like his mother, not his perverse and difficult father.

And what reason Shakespeare had to be grateful! – this relationship was the chance of a life-time, the entry into a cultivated and sophisticated society to which his own nature responded with alacrity and enthusiasm. After all, was he not himself a gentleman, born an Arden, with the instinctive courtesy and tact observable in all his work? Students of his imagery have noticed the increasing refinement reflected in his senses upon his contact with this aristocratic household and circle. John Florio was an intimate of it, the Earl's Italian tutor; but he was a household servant, and his dedication of a *World of Words* to his master bears obsequious witness to it. Shakespeare remained on an independent footing, though 'beholding' to his lord – to use Robert Greene's phrase.

This is made perfectly clear in the sonnet that ends the first phase of the relationship, Sonnet 26, an envoi which accompanied the first batch of poems to the patron:

> Lord of my love, to whom in vassalage

Thy merit hath my duty strongly knit,
To thee I send this written ambassage,
To witness duty, not to show my wit:
Duty so great. . . .

Shakespeare fulfils his duty as the accepted poet of his young patron, and does not fail in it through the ups and downs, the complications and stresses, that ensue in the course of the developing relationship. The other side of the relationship implied a degree of support, for which the player-poet is deeply grateful, with the closing of the theatres, his means of livelihood, and the worsening of his situation in the second year of plague, 1593.

Underneath everything the deepest reason a writer can have for gratitude is inspiration, and this the relationship supplied in abundance, opening up new contacts, new channels of experience, new countries of the mind to explore. With acting in abeyance, writing poured forth in a tumult of creation in these inspired years, poems, sonnets, plays. One sees the pent-up inspiration in spate, hitherto held back by the ill-chances of life, a too-early marriage with its obligations, his father's embarrassed affairs, his own long apprenticeship. It is observable what a part friendship plays in the works of these years, in *The Two Gentlemen of Verona*, *Love's Labour's Lost*, *Romeo and Juliet*, *The Merchant of Venice*, no less than in the Sonnets, and witnessed to by the dedications of *Venus and Adonis* and *Lucrece* to the patron.

I do not propose in this book to discuss the plays, merely to note what evidences they bear upon their author's biography. *The Comedy of Errors* is the shortest of the comedies and so would serve for an afternoon or evening performance in some great house or at Court. Written out of his school-reading of Plautus and therefore very early, the new contacts gained it performance both at Gray's Inn and at Court during the Christmas festivities of 1594. But notice that this was after the formation of the Lord Chamberlain's Company, which performed it: it was probably written at least a couple of years before. Shakespeare's reading of Hakluyt is reflected in it, and the *Principal Navigations* had appeared in 1589.

The Two Gentlemen of Verona reflects more the influence of John Lyly's witty and artificial Court-comedies. But the character of Lance and his dog gives us one of those transcripts from below-stairs life at which Shakespeare was already unsurpassed. *The Taming of the Shrew* again was performed by the Chamberlain's Men at the Newington Butts theatre in June 1594, immediately upon their coming together. These plays were by then arrows already in his quiver, along with the *Henry VI* plays and *Titus Andronicus*. We have observed the Cotswold background of the *Shrew*, the hunting and the hounds, the falconry and the bowls; but there is a new note of social sophistication:

> burn sweet wood to make the lodging sweet. . . .
> Let one attend him with a silver basin
> Full of rose-water and bestrewed with flowers;
> Another bear the ewer, the third a diaper,
> And say, 'Will't please your lordship cool your hands?'

After the 'written ambassage' of Sonnet 26 Shakespeare departed from London for the country, and absence, as is the way with poets, heightened his feelings and gave them an edge: he fell in love with the idea of being in love – another reason for gratitude to the inspirer. Henceforth one can follow, sonnet by sonnet, the motions of his mind, and sometimes the movement of his body, with greater intimacy than in any other of the contemporary sonnet-sequences. (Even than Philip Sidney's, the only ones to come in the same class, though his consciousness of his high station and the public expectations of him imposed a certain reserve.) Nothing of this with the gentlemanly Shakespeare, who was, however, no aristocrat: his only control is that of art. In the end there is nothing that he does not say: this gives the Sonnets their power and makes them the greater work, though Sidney was the originator.

Shakespeare often wrote his sonnets in pairs, the theme of the first answered or given a new turn in the second – a good way of increasing these offerings of duty, in which we find him sometimes, as he says, labouring for invention. His native facility triumphs, even when he has not much to say; later on, as the relationship developed and complications intervened, there was plenty. Before this, early on, we find Shakespeare lamenting his lot, expressing his resentment at his ill-fortune, his station and circumstances in life: it is a theme he returns to again and again:

> Wishing me like to one more rich in hope,
> Featured like him, like him with friends possess'd,
> Desiring this man's art, and that man's scope,
> With what I most enjoy contented least. . . .

That looks like a revealing reference to his profession as an actor: he must have enjoyed his talent, while resenting the necessity to live by it and the station in life to which it consigned him.

In the next, we find him recalling the memory of old friends now dead, consoled only by the new friendship and what he owes to it. Southampton was 'endearèd with all hearts' – he had the gift for popularity which his leader, Essex, also could command. The poet had the consolation of sharing in his elevation:

> And by a part of all thy glory live.

Thus he could take proper pride in his devotion, while disclaiming pride in his poems:

> And though they be outstripped by every pen,
> Reserve them for my love, not for their rhyme.

Southampton had the feeling and the taste to reserve them, to keep them – to come forth many years later, after his mother's death and her bequest of her goods and chattels to her third husband, Sir William Harvey.

We are still in the year 1592, for Sonnet 25 has a transparent reference to the fall of Sir Walter Ralegh from the Queen's favour, for his intrigue, and secret marriage with her maid-of-honour, Elizabeth Throckmorton, which made a sensation in the early summer of this year.

Great princes' favourites their fair leaves spread
But as the marigold at the sun's eye,
And in themselves their pride lies burièd,
For at a frown they in their glory die.

Ralegh's pride was notorious, a prime characteristic, but the lines that follow pin-point him in a thumb-nail sketch:

The painful warrior famousèd for fight

– in Elizabethan English 'painful' means painstaking, and Ralegh was as industrious as he was arrogant –

After a thousand victories once foiled,
Is from the book of honour razèd quite,
And all the rest forgot for which he toiled.

That is just what Ralegh himself said: 'Once amiss, all is lost; and Robert Cecil wrote of him at this moment, 'he can toil terribly'.

These comments would be bandied about – Shakespeare could easily hear them from Southampton. While Ralegh was in the Tower, the Court progressed to Oxford, where the young Earl was incorporated as M.A. – he was already a Cambridge M.A. We do not know whether the poet was in attendance on his patron – conveniently on the road to Stratford; but it seems likely, for shortly after, in *A Midsummer Night's Dream*, we have a skit on the dons' reception of the Queen:

Where I have come, great clerks have purposèd
To greet me with premeditated welcomes;
Where I have seen them shiver and look pale,
Make periods in the midst of sentences,
Throttle their practised accent in their fears
And in conclusion dumbly have broke off. . . .

With the intermission from acting, Shakespeare occupied himself with what he regarded as his true vocation, the writing of poetry. With the long narrative poem he was preparing to present officially to his patron, *Venus and Adonis*, he meant to stake his claim for public recognition as a poet. 'A Lover's Complaint' was a private piece for his patron – hence its being put away with the Sonnets, to fetch up later: a prentice-work like a first picture deposited at the Academy by way of qualification. That the theme of *Venus and Adonis* was running in his mind we can see from references all over his work at the time. For, with his prolific fertility, his facility and speed in writing, the theme spills over into sonnets and plays from the main work upon which he was engaged.

A group of sonnets about Adonis and Venus under her name of Cytherea was got hold of by Jaggard and published with others in *The Passionate Pilgrim*. We can be as grateful as Thorpe was later to his Mr W. H., for otherwise they might have been lost. They must have been among the 'sugared sonnets' which, Francis Meres noted, were handed around among his private friends. Some of the Southampton sonnets could have been too, though by no means all of them, nor the sequence as a whole: they revealed too intimate a story of personal relations. They certainly could not have been published at the time. But naughty poems, suitably camouflaged, were just what such a youthful Elizabethan circle – not sage Poloniuses, like Lord Burghley – would enjoy.

In Sonnet 41 Shakespeare makes a direct application to Southampton – now under siege by the Dark Lady – of Venus's complaint to Adonis in the poem. Venus says,

> Art thou a woman's son and canst not feel
> What 'tis to love? how want of love tormenteth?

In the Sonnet Shakespeare says, excusing him:

> And when a woman woos, what woman's son
> Will sourly leave her till she have prevailed?

We see that the Southampton theme is the theme of *Venus and*

Adonis, that of the handsome youth who will not, as yet, respond to the love of women.

Here we will not go into the content of the poem, its sparkling naughtiness, its comic passages, the scintillating freshness of it all – even if too long – the country descriptions, coursing the hare, the brakes, the deer; we must confine ourselves to the biographical. The poem was printed by Shakespeare's Stratford friend, Richard Field, and came out in April 1593, 'to be sold at the sign of the White Greyhound in Paul's Churchyard'. It bore upon the title-page the bold, almost arrogant, contention from Ovid:

> Vilia miretur vulgus; mihi flavus Apollo
> Pocula Castalia plena ministret aqua.

Let the populace admire base things, but let Apollo minister to me cups filled with water from the purest spring. Or, as Ben Jonson rendered it, still more arrogantly, later:

> Kneel hinds to trash: me let bright Phoebus swell
> With cups full flowing from the Muses' well.

No Elizabethan fell for any humbug about popular taste.

The dedication to Southampton is phrased with courtly deference: 'Right Honourable, I know not how I shall offend in dedicating my unpolished lines to your Lordship. . . . Only, if your Honour seem but pleased, I account myself highly praised.' The Earl's poet promises to take advantage of all idle hours, to present him with some 'graver labour' later on. Meanwhile, 'I leave it to your honourable survey, and your Honour to your heart's content, which I wish may always answer your own wish, and the world's hopeful expectation. Your Honour's in all duty, William Shakespeare.'

How much we wish we had Southampton's response to it, but his private correspondence – which would have included letters from Shakespeare – disappeared with the end of the male line, the destruction of Southampton House, and the dismantling and unroofing of Titchfield.

The poem had a growing success with the public as time went on: ten or eleven editions in his own lifetime, twenty before the odious Civil War struck at culture. *Venus and Adonis* made its appeal to the cultivated, to the Court and fashionable society; it found its audience especially among the young men of the Inns of Court and the universities, who found it stimulating. At Cambridge a few years later, the young men in their skit, the *Parnassus* plays, say, 'O sweet Master Shakespeare! I'll have his picture in my study at the Court.' There follow verses imitating the poem, with 'Let this duncified world esteem of Spenser and Chaucer, I'll worship sweet Master Shakespeare, and to honour him will lay his *Venus and Adonis* under my pillow.' A discriminating don, Spenser's friend, Gabriel Harvey, reports: 'the younger sort takes much delight in Shakespeare's *Venus and Adonis*; but his *Lucrece* and his tragedy of *Hamlet, Prince of Denmark*, have it in them to please the wiser sort'.

This recognition from the university – he was never offered a degree, however – came several years later. But, by 1593, he had arrived as a poet.

Other poets, too, were anxious for the patronage of the generous young peer. Peele paid tribute to him in *The Honour of the Garter*, and shortly disappeared:

> Gentle Wriothesley, Southampton's star,
> I wish all fortune that in Cynthia's eye,
> Cynthia, the glory of the western world,
> With all the stars in her fair firmament –
> Bright may he rise and shine immortally.

Alas, he found no fortune in her eye – nor did he conduct himself in such a way as to win her favour. Young Nashe – the 'tender Juvenal' of *Love's Labour's Lost* – tried to gain the Earl's patronage by dedicating *The Unfortunate Traveller* to him, without permission 'A dear lover and cherisher you are, as well of the lovers of poets as of the poets themselves.' He did not succeed in pushing his way in and dropped the dedication in the next edition.

A more formidable competitor now appeared, and was welcomed. This was Marlowe. Up to this time, and to the day of his death, he had the lead over Shakespeare, both as a poet and as a dramatist. After all, *Dr Faustus* remained the most popular Elizabethan play, *Tamburlaine* was hardly less so; and the poet of *Hero and Leander* was a more accomplished artist than the poet of *Venus and Adonis*. But William Shakespeare had come in from outside; only a couple of months junior to Marlowe, he had not had Marlowe's early start or precocious success, nor had he had Marlowe's more finished education at a university. Every reference of Shakespeare to Marlowe courteously acknowledges his intellectual and artistic superiority: he is referred to, a little ruefully, as one of the learned; he is that 'able spirit', that 'worthier pen'; his is that 'polished form of well-refinèd pen' – quite true, Marlowe was up to his death the better artist.

It is now quite clear that Marlowe's *Hero and Leander* was written in friendly rivalry with *Venus and Adonis*, and that the beautiful young Earl was described for Leander as much as for Adonis, and equally recognisably in the Sonnets.* Here he is described by Marlowe:

> Some swore he was a maid in man's attire,
> For in his looks were all that men desire . . .
> And such as knew he was a man would say,
> 'Leander, thou art made for amorous play:
> Why art thou not in love – and loved of all?
> Though thou be fair, yet be not thine own thrall.'

It is the very language of the Sonnets. And so is the person. Leander is no dark, close-cropped Greek; he is fair, with very white skin and the long uncut tresses that single out Southampton in his early portraits:

* Douglas Bush says of *Hero and Leander*, 'we must assume that Shakespeare had early knowledge of it, since both *Venus and Adonis* (1593), and *Lucrece* (1594) contain many obvious parallels' (*Mythology and the Renaissance Tradition in English Poetry* pp. 122–3). But, of course. What is most obvious, however, is the overriding parallelism of *Hero and Leander* with *Venus and Adonis*.

His dangling tresses that were never shorn,
Had they been cut and unto Colchos borne,
Would have allured the vent'rous youth of Greece
To hazard more than for the Golden Fleece.

Marlowe begins his poem with a salute to the rival theme: Hero's sleeves are embroidered with a grove,

Where Venus in her naked glory strove
To please the careless and disdainful eyes
Of proud Adonis that before her lies.

There are comparable passages on similar themes – those on the proud, curvetting horse, on Narcissus, the use of gold and usury. Marlowe also enjoins the use of one's treasure, not hoarding it like a miser:

being put to loan
In time it will return us two for one.

It is the theme of the early Sonnets, recommending Southampton to spend, not hoard, his treasure. The parallels between the two poems have often been noticed, without people realising what they signify. It has always been supposed that Shakespeare was the debtor; but, in fact, he had finished his poem and got it out, when Marlowe was only half-way through his at the time he was killed on 30 May 1593.

It is inspiriting to scholars to think that even at this late day we can correct errors and mistaken assumptions about long-dead Elizabethans. Up to quite recently it was held that Marlowe was socially superior, simply because he was a university-man and Shakespeare was not. We now know that the reverse was the case. Marlowe was the son of a feckless Canterbury cobbler, brought up in a household of unrespectable, blaspheming daughters. Having the luck to go to King's School there, he got Archbishop Parker's scholarship to Corpus Christi College, Cambridge. From his conduct he was no gentleman, though his friends loved him for the genius he was. Drayton wrote that he

> Had in time those brave translunary things
> That our first poets had . . .

and that his 'raptures were all air and fire'. Drayton has a more modest estimate of his fellow-Warwickshireman.

This being the contemporary preference, is it any wonder that Shakespeare grew more and more alarmed at the challenge to his position with his patron?

The story of this brief rivalry is told in a few Sonnets, 79 to 86: they are all, except the last, in the present tense and relate to the early months of 1593. The theatrical troupes were still hard hit by the effects of plague and were still more smitten when it returned that summer. These were the months in which Ned Alleyn went on tour for a living, writing home urgent letters to his wife how to take precautions against plague: this did not prevent it from entering Henslowe's house. Shakespeare was evidently not touring at this time but writing.

He was aware that his own verse was traditional and conservative, nor was he in sympathy with the innovations and new-fangled words of experimenters like Donne, the new men coming up. They might capture his patron's ear:

> Why is my verse so barren of new pride,
> So far from variation or quick change?
> Why with the time do I not glance aside
> To new-found methods and to compounds strange?

This was not his way, he answered simply, and he proposed to continue in the path he had marked out in simple duty and love for the friend to whom he owed so much. His devotion was now so well recognised

> As every alien pen hath got my use
> And under thee their poesy disperse.

He turns this, with his usual facetious grace, to compliment by saying that it is the inspiration of Southampton himself that has

> added feathers to the learned's wing
> And given grace a double majesty.

Hitherto, Shakespeare has been sole in his patron's favour, but now his muse – of which Southampton may tire, wishing for something new – 'doth give another place'. With characteristic courtesy he allows.

> I grant, sweet love, thy lovely argument
> Deserves the travail of a worthier pen. . . .

Well, now the young patron has received him, for Shakespeare describes him as 'thy poet'. The next Sonnet, 80, reveals that the situation was serious,

> Knowing a better spirit doth use your name,
> And in the praise thereof spends all his might,
> To make me tongue-tied, speaking of your fame!

Shakespeare's hope is that, since the Earl's worth (we may add, generosity) is boundless as the ocean, it would bear up both poets,

> My saucy bark, inferior far to his . . .
> The humble as the proudest sail.
> Your shallowest help will hold me up afloat . . .

while the other could ride upon the main, 'the soundless deep'. On the other hand, if Southampton withdrew his support, Shakespeare might well be cast away:

> Or, being wrecked, I am a worthless boat,
> He of tall building and of goodly pride.
> Then if he thrive and I be cast away,
> The worst was this: my love was my decay.

Shakespeare consistently claims that he had only his love to offer i.e. his affection. We may well ask, what more had Marlowe? In Shakespeare's view it was not love but flattery that others had to offer. Southampton might be looking for

> Some fresher stamp of the time-bettering days.
> And do so, love; yet when they have devised
> What strainèd touches rhetoric can lend,
> Thou truly fair wert truly sympathised
> In true plain words by thy true-telling friend;
> And their gross painting might be better used
> Where cheeks need blood; in thee it is abused.

This may be true enough, but it is not without its own vein of ingenious flattery. William Shakespeare was a clever man, not without his own weapons of defence: we see that he can hold his own.

The next Sonnet continues the theme of his simple affection against the other's rhetoric:

> I never saw that you did painting need
> And therefore to your fair no painting set. . . .
> There lives more life in one of your fair eyes
> Than both your poets can in praise devise.

Nevertheless it is discouraging to have Southampton's praise 'richly compiled', celebrated 'with golden quill',

> And precious phrase by all the Muses filed

Certainly Marlowe's phrases were more eloquent, more rhetorical and polished; like an 'unlettered' parish clerk, the country-poet can only say Amen

> To every hymn that able spirit affords
> In polished form of well-refinèd pen.

Such is the situation, poised in expectancy – we may well wonder how it would develop – when suddenly, drastically, it comes to an end. Something has happened to the Rival Poet; he disappears; he is never mentioned again: the rivalry has had a sudden end. The sonnets that have been describing it are all in the present tense; Sonnet 86, which brings it to an end, is in the past. The whole character of it is valedictory, and it is a very remarkable – and recognisable – personality that it describes.

> Was it the proud full sail of his great verse

that daunted Shakespeare? Everyone would recognise the description: 'Marlowe's mighty line' as Ben Jonson wrote of him. His prime achievement had been to marry great poetry to the drama – the patentee of splendid dramatic blank verse. Shakespeare then asks,

> Was it his spirit, by spirits taught to write
> Above a mortal pitch, that struck me dead?

That Marlowe knew the formulas, Latin and English, for summoning up the spirits we know from *Dr Faustus*. Nothing surprising in his trafficking with the spirits – many Elizabethans did. What is more interesting is that Shakespeare agreed with Drayton in recognising Marlowe's poetry as surpassing mortal power.

What would have happened, if he had lived, we cannot tell: we can only say here, shortly, that his premature death at twenty-nine was the greatest loss our literature ever suffered.

William Shakespeare knew, like everybody else, what had happened to him: it was a matter of public scandal, like so much about Marlowe, at the time. He was always in trouble and would have come to a sticky end at some time or other. His exquisite poem, *Hero and Leander*, only half-finished – even so, a more finished work of art than *Venus and Adonis* – was not published till five years later, in 1598. William Shakespeare was then writing *As You Like It*: reading the poem brought it all back to mind; three times his mind recurs to the dead poet. There is an extended reference, turned to comic effect, to Leander swimming the Helles pont. Again, someone pointedly says, that 'strikes a man more dea than a great reckoning in a little room'. That was how Marlow had died, in a quarrel over 'le reckoning', according to the inquest in the little tavern room at Deptford. Then there comes Shake speare's touching reference to him, the only time he quoted a lin from any contemporary:

> Dead shepherd, now I find thy saw of might:
> 'Who ever loved that loved not at first sight?'

That was one of Marlowe's many famous lines. Shakespeare' phrase brings back something of what those felt who loved an understood him. It rings like a knell in the phrases with whic Edward Blount dedicated the poem to Sir Thomas Walsingham who had befriended him. Marlowe had needed all the friends h could muster in those last troubled, hysterical months: no wonde he was looking for another patron. Now Edward Blount wrote o him:

> Sir, we think not ourselves discharged of the duty we owe to our frien when we have brought the breathless body to the earth. For, albeit th eye there taketh his ever farewell of that beloved object, yet the im pression of the man that hath been dear unto us, living an after-life i our memory, there putteth us in mind of farther obsequies due unto th deceased . . . and to the effecting of his determinations prevented by th stroke of death.

Nevertheless, the experience, though over, placed a strain upon th relations of the poet and his patron: they were never quite the same The very next Sonnet finds Shakespeare ready to take his leave:

> Farewell! thou art too dear for my possessing. . . .
> Thyself thou gav'st, thy own worth then not knowing,
> Or me, to whom thou gav'st it, else mistaking. . . .

Next:

Upon thy part I can set down a story
Of faults concealed, wherein I am attainted,
That thou in losing me shall win much glory. . . .

In the following, ingenious as ever, he returns upon the theme, embroiders it:

Thou canst not, love, disgrace me half so ill,
To set a form upon desirèd change,
As I'll myself disgrace. . . .

Still more seriously in the next:

Then hate me when thou wilt; if ever, now;
Now, while the world is bent my deeds to cross,
Join with the spite of fortune, make me bow,
And do not drop in for an after-loss.

This is pretty plain speaking: this is 1593, when things both publicly and privately – as we shall see – were at their worst. And in the midst of them he no longer could feel sure of Southampton's support, though it was now more than ever necessary:

But do thy worst to steal thyself away,
For term of life thou art assurèd mine,
And life no longer than thy love will stay,
For it depends upon that love of thine.

The need is urgent, the accent that of intense sincerity: Shakespeare says what he means, other poets were dying in this time of stress, and he had heavier obligations than any of them. He repeats the reproach:

Then need I not to fear the worst of wrongs,
When in the least of them my life hath end.
I see a better state to me belongs
Than that which on thy humour doth depend. . . .

There is the essential independence of spirit of the man at this crisis: he does not fear to charge the young man with 'inconstant mind', when Shakespeare specifically says that his life depended on his patron's change of mind. In either case, he would be

> Happy to have thy love, happy to die!

In the event, the patron did not let him down; but, after this, the relationship had lost its innocence:

> So shall I live, supposing thou art true,
> Like a deceivèd husband; so love's face
> May still seem love to me, though altered new;
> Thy looks with me, thy heart in other place.

This is followed by a famous sonnet which, devastating as it is, reveals a man of the people charging this young aristocrat with the typically aristocratic failing: coldness, or at least coolness, of heart. Perhaps unfair, it was understandable in the circumstances:

> They that have power to hurt and will do none,
> That do not do the thing they most do show,
> Who, moving others, are themselves as stone,
> Unmovèd, cold, and to temptation slow. . . .

they remain in control of themselves, and therefore of others:

> They are the lords and owners of their faces,
> Others but stewards of their excellence.

We shall see that in the great affair of Shakespeare's heart – his infatuation for the Dark Lady – in which he was now involved, he was far more deeply affected than ever Southampton was. The poet, with his sensitive nature, his extreme susceptibility to women, was abnormally vulnerable. Southampton was able to expose himself to temptation, without committing himself: he could flirt with the fascinating loose woman without losing control, since he was not really responsive. Nevertheless, his faithful poet gives him a tutorial warning:

> But if that flower with base infection meet –

the flower of chaste virtue, being Southampton –

> The basest weed outbraves his dignity.

In fact, by involving himself with this woman – even though the original responsibility was Shakespeare's, as it was – the young Earl was exposing himself to ill-fame, with which his poet was already besmirched:

> How sweet and lovely dost thou make the shame
> Which, like the canker in the fragrant rose,
> Doth spot the beauty of thy budding name!

All through these Sonnets there is a quasi-parental element, an anxious sense of responsibility for the fatherless youth, so apt to be misguided, almost as if Shakespeare was *in loco parentis* – to use a university term. Besides, William Shakespeare was a parent himself. The warning that he gives the youth is courteously phrased, and with characteristic ingenuity – for he could not exist without his patron's support – he turns everything, even reproaches into poetry; but the warning is unmistakable:

> That tongue that tells the story of thy days,
> Making lascivious comments on thy sport,
> Cannot dispraise but in a kind of praise;
> Naming thy name blesses an ill report.

We have no information about what the young peer was up to at this time – it was five years yet before he got Elizabeth Vernon with child and Essex made him marry her; even then he was found equally responsive to the masculine charms of the soldierly Captain Piers Edmonds.

The faithful poet gave his advice:

> Take heed, dear heart, of this large privilege;
> The hardest knife ill-used doth lose his edge.
>
> Some say thy fault is youth, some wantonness;
> Some say thy grace is youth and gentle sport. . . .

With his looks and advantages, 'the strength of all thy state',

> How many gazers mightst thou lead away. . . .
>   But do not so; I love thee in such sort
>   As, thou being mine, mine is thy good report.

Through good and ill the poet continues his faithful love, with a solicitude equal to his affection.

After this, there follows a period of absence – probably the spring of 1594 in the country – and with absence, as is often the case, a renewal of affection if with a decipherably different accent, with the experiences the relationship had undergone.

Such, alas, is inevitably the way in human affections.

CHAPTER 6

The Dark Lady

We must retrace our steps by some months. It would seem to have been towards the end of 1592 that a still more serious complication entered the relationship, to endanger it further. The snake had already entered Paradise, and destroyed its pristine innocence, with a woman. This was the woman with whom Shakespeare became infatuated – and who made him suffer correspondingly – and with whom he had involved his patron. Shakespeare recognised that the fault was his: he had got the young peer, in the contemporary manner, to write to the equivocal, and equivocating, lady on his behalf. This was customary enough in that age, but the young woman – since we now know at last, after centuries, who she was – being no better than she should be, naturally saw a better prospect in an unattached and rich Earl, three years younger and much more inexperienced than herself, than in an indigent player-poet, six years older, with a wife and family to boot.

Two sections of the Sonnets deal, with the utmost candour, with the affair. Since it was triangular, to use a convenient vulgarism, the first section, Sonnets 34 to 42, describe it from the point of view of Shakespeare's relationship with Southampton, are concerned primarily with him. But the later Sonnets – in numbering, not in time – from Sonnet 127 to the end describe the affair from Shakespeare's point of view. They are naturally even more revealing, with his 'honest, open and free' nature; they lay bare his soul with all its subtlety and sensitiveness, his rueful self-awareness in the midst of his humiliation, guilt and suffering. In the end, though deeply wounded, he is able to laugh at himself and place his imbroglio in a lighter context. Perhaps he achieved catharsis by writing, for again he turned everything he experienced, ill along with good, into poetry.

The first breach between the older man and the youth is announced in Sonnet 34, and that it concerns Shakespeare's mistress is made clear by the references to his loss, the youth robbing him, stealing all his poverty, reproaching him that he might at least refrain from his – his poet's – seat. The reproach was not without its effect upon Southampton's better nature: he repented with tears.

> Nor can thy shame give physic to my grief;
> Though thou repent, yet I have still the loss.

Upon this Shakespeare consoles the golden boy:

> Ah! but those tears are pearl which thy love sheds. . . .

The next Sonnet, 35, continues the consolation, turns it to good account in verse – needs must: one must live:

> No more be grieved at that which thou hast done. . . .
> All men make faults, and even I in this,
> Authorising thy trespass with compare. . .
> Excusing thy sins more than thy sins are. . . .

What those faults were is made clear by Shakespeare accusing himself as accessory

> To that sweet thief which sourly robs from me.

The next Sonnet, 36, gives us a fine statement of the situation between older and younger man, very characteristic of Shakespeare in its spirit of candour and acceptance. At this moment, early on in their delighted discovery of each other – charm of youth on one side, facetious grace on the other – they are emotionally close together. But Shakespeare accepts the fact that their different lives necessarily divide them: there is 'a separable spite' which keeps them apart. This is evidently Shakespeare's career as an actor, and his attachment to his dubious mistress is known and commented upon uncharitably. And so,

> I may not evermore acknowledge thee,
> Lest my bewailèd guilt should do thee shame,
> Nor thou with public kindness honour me,
> Unless thou take that honour from thy name.

The three Sonnets, 40, 41, 42, reveal that the young peer's flirtation with his poet's mistress has gone further: Southampton was learning the ways of women at last, but regrettably in an ill quarter. Moreover, it places Shakespeare in an humiliating position: his rich patron is taking his girl away, and the poor poet cannot afford to do anything about it, even if he would. All he can do is to turn it into verse.

> Take all my loves, my love, yea, take them all;
> What hast thou then more than thou hadst before?

Everything that Shakespeare has is the youth's already: he cannot blame the boy for being involved with the lady partly out of affection for the older man. Though subtle, anyone of psychological perception can see that that might happen. What Shakespeare blames him for, quite consistently from the very beginning of the Sonnets, is his willingness to taste forbidden fruits, while refusing marriage:

> But yet be blamed, if thou this self deceivest
> By wilful taste of what thyself refusest.

Shakespeare forgives the youth the injury he does to his friend and poet – needs must anyway:

> I do forgive thy robbery, gentle thief,
> Although thou steal thee all my poverty.

No one understood better than Shakespeare that it was only

natural to err with women; there were the temptations of youth, his extreme attractiveness laid him more open than usual.

> Ay me! but yet thou mightst my seat forbear. . . .

for in this instance there was a double breach of trust:

> Hers, by thy beauty tempting her to thee,
> Thine, by thy beauty being false to me.

Shakespeare minds the loss of Southampton's heart more – we shall see more clearly why this would be so in a moment. To anticipate, the lady was not in love with the older man anyway.

> That she hath thee is of my wailing chief,
> A loss in love that touches me more nearly.

Shakespeare would excuse these young people on the grounds that they loved each other for his sake, who had introduced them. But this was mere poetry: they needed no such excuse.

The second section of the Sonnets, 127 to the end, deals with the affair between Shakespeare and his Dark Lady from the point of view of their relationship and records his hopes and expectations, his reactions, torment and utter disillusionment. These Sonnets, though placed later in numbering, naturally begin earlier than Southampton's involvement. We learn about its initiation two facts, the first of which has never – so far as I know – been noticed. *Shakespeare first fell in love with the girl out of pity for the situation she was in:*

> If thy unworthiness raised love in me,
> More worthy I to be beloved of thee.

The second fact is well known: Southampton became acquainted with her through writing on Shakespeare's behalf.

What does he tell us about her?

The first thing is that she was extremely dark: raven black eyes, black hair, eye-brows and eye-lashes. This was unfashionable in a time that rated fairness, and especially red-gold hair, so highly, and it called the more attention to the lady, for she was already well known. Some people would not allow that she was beautiful:

> some say that thee behold
> Thy face hath not the power to make love groan.

It gives the susceptible poet, however,

> A thousand groans but thinking on thy face . . .
> Thy black is fairest in my judgment's place.

He continues:

> In nothing art thou black save in thy deeds,
> And thence this slander, as I think, proceeds.

From the beginning then, she is a bad lot; Shakespeare fell for her, young as she was, out of pity and then became infatuated: it was simply sex that held him in thrall.

The second thing we learn about her is that she was musical: the very next sonnet has a description of the poet standing beside her while she plays upon the virginals, envying the wooden keys – 'those jacks that nimble leap'

> To kiss the tender inward of thy hand . . .

while Shakespeare longs to kiss her lips. He does not have to wait long before he is permitted to do so, and more besides. The next Sonnet, 129, is the famous virtuoso-piece about fornication:

> The expense of spirit in a waste of shame
> Is lust in action. . . .

The literary inspiration for the poem came, as so often, from Philip

Sidney, but again characteristically, it expressed, with power and urgency, personal experience:

> Enjoyed no sooner but despisèd straight. . . .
> Before, a joy proposed; behind, a dream.

We may note that this very language is shortly carried over into *The Rape of Lucrece*, which has a comparably sombre atmosphere of guilt, repentance, remorse to the Sonnets describing his experience with this woman; just as her darkness, black hair and eyes are celebrated in the character of Rosaline in *Love's Labour's Lost*, written privately for this circle in this year 1593.

In spite of this woman's ill conditions and qualities Shakespeare falls more and more under her spell – once more there recurs the humiliating position of an older in relation to a younger, as we shall see. Highly sexed and heterosexual as Shakespeare was, he could not resist, though totally without illusions as to her character:

> Yet none knows well
> To shun the heaven that leads men to this hell.

(In Elizabethan English 'hell' meant women's sexual organs.) The young lady behaved haughtily to her middle-aging lover – verging on thirty the actor was no lamb, especially then when people aged more rapidly; and, in fact, his life was well more than half over. There is nothing surprising in his being still more conscious of the disparity of age between him and Southampton, which was nine and a half years. Now that we know the facts her attitude becomes more understandable too:

> Thou art as tyrannous, so as thou art,

and in the next he admits to

> Knowing thy heart torments me with disdain. . . .

Perhaps now, for the first time, we may sympathise with the

young woman's point of view; it must have been a bore to be so obsessively pursued by an impecunious player, when one would have preferred him out of the way for the more obvious attractions of a rich and unattached peer younger than oneself. That this was the situation the very next sonnet tells us:

> Beshrew that heart that makes my heart to groan
> For that deep wound it gives my friend and me!
> Is't not enough to torture me alone
> But slave to slavery my sweet'st friend must be!

In the next Shakespeare admits that she has got hold of the youth, while he himself is still 'mortgaged to thy will' – remember always the double meaning of 'will' in Elizabethan English, not only desire but the sexual organs. The poet would willingly forfeit himself to free him, but she is not going to let go her hold:

> He learned but surety-like to write for me
> Under that bond that him as fast doth bind.

So now she has a hold on both of them.

The two notorious sonnets playing on the word 'will' that follow see her sitting pretty. They never have hitherto been explained fully, though we shall see that the tentative guess at the second Will referred to, as referring to a husband, is borne out by the newly discovered facts:

> Whoever hath her wish, thou hast thy will,
> And Will to boot, and Will in overplus;

i.e. she has her sex, her husband, and William Shakespeare, too, to bother her. That this is his situation is immediately made clear;

> More than enough am I that vex thee still,
> To thy sweet will making addition thus.

The meaning is perfectly plain and blissfully bawdy:

Wilt thou, whose will is large and spacious,
Not once vouchsafe to hide my will in thine?

He goes on to say that she has accommodated others, so why not him?

The second 'Will' sonnet carries on the joke that has so baffled the professors:

If thy soul check thee that I come so near,
Swear to thy blind soul that I was thy Will;
And Will, thy soul knows, is admitted there. . . .

This very cleverly – but, we shall see, perfectly plainly – plays upon the fact that there are two Wills: her husband and Will Shakespeare. The first, *thy soul knows*, i.e. is quite conscientiously admitted there; very well, 'swear to thy blind soul', i.e. turn a blind eye, and say that I am your Will too. How clever, and how naughty – what fun it must have given the poet and the patron! So long as the young woman will take him, he doesn't mind others, provided he may be one:

Ay, fill it full with wills, and my will one.

After this, it is perhaps a piece of masculine vanity to reproach the poor lady with being a 'bay where all men ride', and again 'the wide world's common place'. The relationship had become disingenuous on both sides:

When my love swears that she is made of truth
I do believe her, though I know she lies,
That she might think me some untutored youth,
Unlearnèd in the world's false subtleties.

Shakespeare likes the illusion that she thinks him young,

Although she knows my days are past the best. . . .

Keeping up pretences with each other – how recognisable the situation! –

Therefore I lie with her and she with me

– in both senses of the word 'lie', of course.

And so the older partner is reduced, humiliatingly, to ask her that, though she loves elsewhere,

in my sight,
Dear heart, forbear to glance thine eye aside.

Even though she does not love him, he would rather hear her say that she did – 'if I might teach thee wit', indeed: a man older even than her precocious experience could certainly instruct her to be more intelligent. (Wit, in Elizabethan English, meant intelligence.) He, therefore, asks her to

Bear thine eyes straight, though thy proud heart go wide.

Notice the epithet, her *proud* heart: a haughty woman, with pretensions.

The next sonnet, quite logically, reproves her pride: she cannot reproach Shakespeare with adultery in loving her; or if she does

not from those lips of thine
That have profaned their scarlet ornaments
And sealed false bonds of love as oft as mine,
Robbed others' beds' revenues of their rents.

Shakespeare's candour, as usual, shines through the falseness of the situation: he is no better than she is, he has been just as free with professions of love. Now he is reduced to the humiliation of asking her to take pity on him, if she wants others whom she is chasing to take pity on her. This serious sonnet is followed, in Shakespeare's manner, by a light-hearted one, 143, in which he depicts himself ludicrously like a child crying after its mother, while she is chasing after a cock in the farmyard:

So runn'st thou after that which flies from thee. . . .

This is followed by a sombre sonnet summing up the triangular affair:

> Two loves I have, of comfort and despair . . .
> The better angel is a man right fair,
> The worser spirit a woman coloured ill.

A new turn is given by the suggestion that the lady is tempting Southampton away, partly to ensure Shakespeare's subjugation,

> Wooing his purity with her foul pride.

The older man is in an agony of uncertainty as to how far relations between the young people have gone – his charge, as he feels, so much more innocent and inexperienced than the woman:

> And whether that my angel be turned fiend
> Suspect I may, yet not directly tell. . . .

At this moment Shakespeare is away from them both and kept out of their confidence:

> But being both from me, both to each friend,
> I guess one angel in another's hell.

We now know the meaning of the word, and his suspicion of what was up between them:

> Yet this shall I ne'er know, but live in doubt,
> Till my bad angel fire my good one out.

The suggestion here, as others have seen, is of venereal disease; and anyone who knows the facts of Elizabethan society knows that there is nothing improbable in that, nor that this loose young woman might be affected by it. Here was yet another reason for Shakespeare to fear for his young friend; himself he could not help.

No wonder all this is followed by the philosophic repentance of

'Poor soul, the centre of my sinful earth' – so much admired by Santayana – and the psychological torment of the next:

> My love is as a fever, longing still
> For that which longer nurseth the disease. . . .

A middle-ageing man has an absolute fixation on a bad lot of a young woman: it is a familiar enough situation, from the newspapers and murder-cases. The only difference is that the man in this case was utterly self-aware about all that was happening to him, every facet of the emotional entanglement, as in a drama, and in addition – so like an obsessed writer – was driven to writing it all down, expressing everything, turning it all to account in the realm that, after all, mattered more than anything: that of Art.

He understands everything that is happening to him: in spite of his loss of control, he can see himself and the whole mad affair from the outside *at the same time as he is going through it*: this is what it is to have genius. Reason, which is the physician to the emotions, has left him:

> Past cure I am, now reason is past care,
> And frantic-mad with evermore unrest.

This is what sex can do for highly sexed heterosexuals. A whole sonnet, 150, is devoted to describing it:

> O, from what power has thou this powerful might . . .
> To make me give the lie to my true sight . . .
> Whence hast thou this becoming of things ill,
> That in the very refuse of thy deeds
> There is such strength and warrantise of skill. . . . ?

Though young, she had the skill and experience to handle him, in addition to the spell of sex upon him.

> Who taught thee how to make me love thee more
> The more I hear and see just cause of hate?

Life had taught her in a hard school, we shall see. Other people knew her circumstances and her story, and detested her character:

> O, though I love what others do abhor,
> With others thou shouldst not abhor my state.

Evidently with other people she was being malicious about him, laughing at him – one sees the whole situation, and the openness of his nature which had first fallen for her out of pity:

> If thy unworthiness raised love in me,
> More worthy I to be beloved of thee.

This is followed, in the usual way, by a light-hearted bawdy sonnet, which would indicate that the Dark Lady Sonnets follow an intelligible order just as much as the Southampton sequence. Her sonnets are often coupled in pairs like his, and we have a comic one following a serious one in a kind of antiphony. Shakespeare now uses the theme of betrayal – after all, he is in a ludicrous position – for a joke. Just as she betrays him, so his body betrays his nobler part, his reason:

> flesh stays no farther reason;
> But, rising at thy name, doth point out thee
> As his triumphant prize. Proud of this pride

– we all know what 'proud flesh' means, swelling or stiff –

> He is contented thy poor drudge to be,
> To stand in thy affairs, fall by thy side.

This must have given the young man, at least, a laugh for his money:

> No want of conscience hold it that I call
> Her 'love', for whose dear love I rise and fall.

'Hold it', indeed – the ingeniousness of it all, perfectly spontaneous and natural, passes belief. It is a well-known psychological phenomenon that homosexuals do not go in for this kind of bawdiness.

At the very end Shakespeare returns to the falseness and treachery, the horror of his situation in all his helplessness:

> In loving thee thou know'st I am forsworn. . . .

'Forsworn' means perjured, faith broken; of course Shakespeare is an adulterer, and not for the first time, as he has just told us. But she is doubly forsworn, for now she has broken the promise she made to him, when in bed with him, swearing new love to him after a breach. This is what these two lines mean:

> In act thy bed-vow broke and new faith torn
> In vowing new hate after new love bearing.

Some previous commentators have thought that the broken bed-vow revealed that she was a married woman; actually the vow she made and broke was to Shakespeare, though we shall see that she too was married – perhaps another touch of the poet's linguistic duplicity. In the end, he sums up decisively and simply: he has known all along that she was a bad lot, a false dissembling bitch – other people knew it, he knew it himself but had been blinded by 'love', or – as we should say – sex. He had stood up for her against those who abused her:

> Who hateth thee that I do call my friend?
> On whom frown'st thou that I do fawn upon?

He had been loyal to her, against the evidence of his own eyes – we all know why; now the affair has come to an end,

> And all my honest faith in thee is lost. . . .

But notice – what the imperceptive generations have missed – that it is the young woman who has sent him packing. It is she who has ended it, 'by vowing new hate' after promising to renew relations.

It was evidently a distracting affair: no wonder so susceptible a man was distracted. But no one has seen the young woman's point of view, or at least expressed it with any sympathy. She was evidently temperamental and promiscuous, as well as proud and inconstant, changing her mind and driving Shakespeare frantic. But it must have been tiresome to have him hanging on to her skirts – as he described himself in the farmyard scene – mad about her, always pressing her, when she was after Southampton.

To such humiliating straits are highly sexed men reduced. Fortunately Shakespeare retained his sense of humour, in the midst of his straits; and he rounds off his account of the affair with a couple of ruefully comic sonnets about Cupid and the heats of love, which form a kind of coda, and are perfectly in place where they are. The affair broken off, he hies himself to the bath for cure of his disease:

> I, sick withal, the help of bath desired
> And thither hied, a sad distempered guest.

He found there no cure: physical satisfaction was the only cure for sexual desire.

It is thought that this refers to a visit to the waters of Bath, a regular resort for Elizabethans suffering from sexual distempers. There is, indeed, nothing improbable in this, and indeed Shakespeare in the plays expresses the quite usual Elizabethan attitude towards having caught the pox – a matter again for a bawdy joke, for laughing at oneself, if somewhat ruefully.

Something of this experience is reflected, and indeed the whole circle, in Shakespeare's very personal play of this year, 1593, *Love's Labour's Lost*. Everyone can see that this is a private play in essence, written for a restricted circle, with its own private jokes and personal parodies. All the same, a play is a public performance – one does not expose all one's personal griefs and humiliations in it – and anyway it relates to the earlier, happier stage of the affair. For everyone knows that the character of Rosaline in the play is drawn from the personality, at least the looks of the Dark Lady, described in very nearly the language of the Sonnets. Rosaline is extremely dark; the King of Navarre in the play describes her as 'black as ebony'. To this her lover, Berowne, replies:

> Is ebony like her? O wood divine! . . .
> No face is fair that is not full so black.

And again,

> O, if in black my lady's brows be decked,
> It mourns that painting and usurping hair
> Should ravish doters with a false aspect;
> And therefore is she born to make black fair.

One might be reading the Sonnets – and indeed several passages of the play are written, by the fluent author – in sonnet-form.

Again, it has always been recognised that her lover, Berowne, expresses Shakespeare's point of view. The theme of the comedy is that Navarre and his friends are abjuring the society of women for a year to devote themselves to their studies. Berowne-Shakespeare thinks this academic notion nonsense – it was, of course, the idea that prevailed at the universities then and for long afterwards. Berowne says that it is love, as it is learned in women's eyes, that

> Courses as swift as thought in every power,
> And gives to every power a double power,
> Above their functions and their offices. . . .
> Love's feeling is more soft and sensible
> Than are the tender horns of cockled snails.

The horns of these snails appear also in *Venus and Adonis*, just now appearing – Shakespeare had no objection to repeating himself. His irresistible *yen* for women makes him conclude:

From women's eyes this doctrine I derive;
They sparkle still the right Promethean fire;
They are the books, the arts, the academes,
That show, contain and nourish all the world.

This polite tribute may well be expressed partly in inverted commas, but people who hold to it too absolutely are apt to have to pay for their illusions.

A more original point than this: when Rosaline turns to describing Berowne, it is Shakespeare describing himself, a skit on himself, with jokes at his own expense:

but a merrier man,
Within the limit of becoming mirth,
I never spent an hour's talk withal.
His eye begets occasion for his wit;
For every object that the one doth catch
The other turns to a mirth-moving jest,
Which his fair tongue, conceit's expositor,
Delivers in such apt and gracious words
That agèd ears play truant at his tales,
And younger hearings are quite ravishèd.
So sweet and voluble is his discourse.

Underneath this descant we may recognise the truth about himself, witnessed to by Aubrey: 'he was a handsome, well-shaped man: very good company, and of a very ready and pleasant smooth wit'. And Shakespeare goes on to embroider upon other recognised points of his euphoric personality – his liking for good food and plenty of sleep, his *tendresse* for women and amorous propensities.

The play takes for its point of departure the earlier Southampton theme, with which the Sonnets began and which inspired *Venus and Adonis* – that of the young man who is not yet responsive to women. Already becoming a joke it was a very suitable, indeed obvious, theme for a skit on Southampton, his friends and acquaintance, by the poet of the circle. Here was the Dark Lady known to it: I have all along said that, if she were ever to be discovered, it would be someone known to just these people. This turns out to be true – a complete vindication of fact and argument uncovered by rigorous dating and proper chronological method, instead of absurd conjectures and guesses *in vacuo*, devoid of any historical knowledge.

The other themes of the play, that of the breaking of oaths and the skit upon academic and literary disputes, were much to the fore at the moment. Navarre, now Henri IV, was considering whether to abjure Protestantism for the sake of winning Paris; he was under instruction and English leaders were much exercised whether he would go back on his undertakings. We have seen that Shakespeare could have been *au fait* with at least the names that appear in Richard Field's tracts, as in the play. Navarre, Berowne (Biron), Longaville, Dumain (Mayenne). The other theme, the verbal warfare with its quibbles and puns, tags and riddles, personal jokes to which we have lost the key, relates to the Harvey–Nashe row going on at the time. This pamphlet war would have been much enjoyed in that circle. We need not expect fantastic characters like Don Armado and Holofernes to be straight caricatures: they appear to contain recognisable elements from inflated and pedantic Gabriel Harvey and John Florio, Southampton's Italian tutor, an *habitué* of the household; while 'tender Juvenal' was the nickname for young Nashe, who so much enjoyed flea-biting the leathery Harvey.

A respectable editor of the play, no genius, tells us, 'of all Shakespeare's plays this is the most personal. A solution of the puzzle he has set here (and I had better say at once that I cannot provide it) would not only satisfy the most rabid detective ardour but illuminate Shakespeare's own early life and the conditions that shaped his career and his first plays – an essential background of which at present absolutely nothing is known.'

We perceive how silly it is to say that 'absolutely nothing is known' about it, and even sillier to say that Shakespeare 'set a puzzle' in writing the play. Shakespeare no more wrote the play to set a puzzle than he wrote the Sonnets to set a puzzle. He wrote them straightforwardly, in his open and free way; it simply happens that the key was lost.

Now that we know the story, the cogency of it is brought home by the fact that, when Southampton entertained King James at Southampton House in 1605, the play he chose to entertain the royal party with was an old one, *Love's Labour's Lost*: it had a particularly personal reference, and belonged to him. It was a private play, not for the public theatres, though in between it had been presented at Court before the Queen.

The end of the affair with the Dark Lady – with its self-questioning, its remorse of conscience, and conflict between reason and lust – has its reflection in *The Rape of Lucrece*, published in 1594. Not, to be sure, in the character of that chaste matron, who is anyway fair with skin as white as her virtue, but in the dark, sombre atmosphere, heavy with guilt and reproach. Here, too, we find the complete writer making use of every bit of experience, ill as well as good, dark as well as fair.

We have already intimated the parallel between Sonnet 129, about lust being

> Enjoyed no sooner but despisèd straight,
> Past reason hunted, and no sooner had
> Past reason hated. . . .
> Before, a joy proposed; behind, a dream.

Before the rape of Lucrece Tarquin argues with himself:

> What win I, if I gain the thing I seek?
> A dream, a breath, a froth of fleeting joy.
> Who buys a minute's mirth to wail a week?
> Or sells eternity to get a toy?

Shakespeare must have argued with himself thus:

> Shameful it is; ay, if the fact be known:
> Hateful it is; there is no hate in loving:
> I'll beg her love; but she is not her own

– and this was true of the dark woman: she was already married. Tarquin presents Shakespeare's dilemma between reason and will:

My will is strong, past reason's weak removing.

Nor could William Shakespeare resist any more than Tarquin:

What could he see but mightily he noted?
What did he note but strongly he desired?
What he beheld, on that he firmly doted . . .

and there follows a description of the female charms Shakespeare found so overwhelming. Then lustful desires charge home,

Nor children's tears, nor mothers' groans respecting,
Swell in their pride, the onset still expecting.
  Anon his beating heart, alarum striking,
  Gives the hot charge and bids them do their liking.

All, so like him, true to nature and to life.

He has, in fact, told us everything about himself and his dark mistress, except her name.

We should never have known that, if it had not been for Simon Forman's habit of noting down everything relevant about his clients; and we should not have known it now, if the historian had not been led to it by the exact coincidence of dating, the corroboration of fact in circumstance and every detail so that there can be no mistake about it: as made clear in the manuscripts, for nothing whatever has appeared about her in print. Hence the key was lost: here it is.

Three years later, on 13 May 1597, there came to consult Forman, medical practitioner and astrologer, a young man called William Lanier, of the well-known family of Court-musicians.* He lived in Longditch, Westminster, near the bridge that led to Canon Row, practically a part of Whitehall, where peers and grandees lived. He was twenty-four and had a suit in hand; he was about to go on Essex's Islands Voyage, the expedition upon which

* MS. Ashmole 226.

Southampton served with success, at last, in command of the *Garland.*

Four days later, Lanier's wife came concerning the suit. She was a daughter of one of the well-known Italian musicians of the Queen, Baptist Bassano and Margaret Johnson, with whom he lived as man and wife. Emilia, for such was her name – Emilia Bassana, Forman calls her, now Lanier – was twenty-seven, three years older than her husband. Forman tells us, 'she hath had hard fortune in her youth. Her father died when she was young; the wealth of her father failed before he died and he began to be miserable in his estate. She was paramour to my old Lord Hunsdon that was Lord Chamberlain and was maintained in great pride. Being with child, she was for colour married to a minstrel', i.e. Lanier.

On 3 June she comes again, about her husband's suit and for herself. 'She seems to be with child of twelve days or weeks – much pain in her left side – but it will hardly stay with her: she hath many false conceptions. . . . She was brought up in the country [i.e. county] of Kent, and hath been married four years.' Forman had to be precise with dates and figures, for astrological forecasts; so this takes us back to 1593. 'The old Lord Chamberlain kept her longer' – so that takes us back to before 1589. She would have been born about 1570. 'She was maintained in great pomp. She is high-minded – she hath something in her mind she would have done for her. She hath £40 a year [a good dowry for those days] and was wealthy to him that married her, in money and jewels. She can hardly keep secret. She was very brown in youth.'

Forman never notes this of anyone else: evidently she was exceptionally dark, to a degree that struck people.

'She hath a son, Henry' – named after the father, Henry Carey, first Lord Hunsdon, Lord Chamberlain, first cousin to the Queen. The Italian girl had been the old man's mistress from the age of nineteen or before – probably from 1588, Armada year, when he came south from the Scotch Border – where he was Lord Warden of the East Marches – to command the Queen's body-guard in the hour of danger.

Her very existence has hitherto been unknown.

On 16 June she comes again to inquire whether her husband shall come to any preferment, i.e. be knighted, before he comes home. Remember, she is 'high-minded', according to the perceptive Forman, as well up in the ways of women as William Shakespeare. On 2 September she wants the figure cast to know whether she shall be a Lady, and how she shall speed. The expedition had not yet returned. Forman tells us more of what he had learned from her. 'She hath been favoured much of her Majesty [that may be as it may be] and of many noblemen, hath had great gifts and been made much of – a nobleman that is dead hath loved her well and kept her. But her husband hath dealt hardly with her, hath spent and consumed her goods. She is now very needy, in debt and it seems for lucre's sake [very oddly, Forman wrote 'Lucrece sake' – but he was undoubtedly psychic] will be a good fellow, for necessity doth compel. She hath a wart or mole in the pit of the throat or near it.'*

There follows Forman's astrological forecast, which is of less interest to us: we are interested only in the facts. The figure seemed to indicate that she would become a Lady or 'attain to some greater dignity' (she has certainly achieved that); her husband would be 'knighted hardly', i.e. doubtfully, and 'get little substance. . . . It seems he will not live two years after he come home.' In fact, he disappears from view: nothing more is known of him. Elsewhere Forman has a caustic comment: Will Lanier had 'gone to sea with the Earl of Essex in hope to be knighted – though there was little cause why he should'. He added later, 'he was not knighted, nor yet worthy thereof'.

Always alert where women were concerned, Forman was ready to take the opportunity afforded by Will's absence: his experiences followed a pattern we shall recognise. An unattached note, difficult to interpret, seems to relate to her. The figure 'shows the woman hath a mind to the quent, but seems she is or will be a harlot. And because . . . she useth sodomy.' This Italianate sophistication was what the figure indicated, we must remember; but Forman sounds disapproving, in his old English way. However, on 10 September,

* MS. Ashmole 354.

he puts the question, 'if I go to Lanier [note the disrespectful omission of Mrs] this night or tomorrow, whether she will receive me, and whether I shall be welcome et halek' – that is his regular term for intercourse.

Next day, 'a certain gentleman longed to see a gentlewoman whom he loved [i.e. wanted] and desired to halek with'. He set the figure to know whether it were best send her a message or whether she would bid him come. He sent his man, by whom she returned word he would be welcome. 'He went and supped with her and stayed all night. She was familiar and friendly to him in all things, but only she would not halek. Yet he felt all parts of her body willingly and kissed her often, but she would not do in any wise. Whereupon he took some displeasure, and so departed friends, but not intending to come at her again in haste.' To this he added, 'but yet ready were friends again afterward but he never obtained his purpose' (he meant then). Later, keeping his notes up to date, 'she was a whore, and dealt evil with him after'.

It may be more precise, as well as more polite, to describe her as a *cocotte*.

Six days later, on 17 September, she simply sent for Forman, in her high-handed way.* He cast the figure whether best to go or not; the indication was that she seemed to be afraid, but in fact wasn't. He did not obey her command. A week later, 'she sent her maid to me, and I went with her to her'.†

October 29 was a full day for Forman. In the morning he went to see the Queen, in robes of state, open Parliament. At the show he stood beside a gentlewoman, Joan Harington, who made a date with him, and at 4 p.m. came to him 'and did halek etc very friendly'.‡ We see how free and easy Elizabethans were apt to be, like medievals. He had just before put the question whether 'to go to Lanier's this night or no'. She sent both her man-servant and her maid – so she still lived like a gentlewoman – to fetch him. 'I went with them and stayed all night.'

The astrologer's relations with Emilia Lanier were not purely

* MS. Ashmole 226. † MS. Ashmole 354. ‡ MS. Ashmole 226.

physical. At the end of 1597 he reminds himself, in the obscurity of Latin – appropriate to the subject, and also in case anyone was prying into his note-books – to put the question concerning her tales as to the invocation of spirits, and whether or not an incuba (meaning her), 'and whether I shall end it or no'. Two years later he was still in touch with this deleterious woman, for on 7 January 1600 he sets the question 'to know why Mrs Lanier sent for me: what will follow, and whether she intendeth any more villainy'.*

Did she perhaps deal in spells and the invocation of spirits? There would be nothing surprising in that in the Elizabethan age. Forman himself did, and we have already noticed it as probable that Marlowe did. There is not the slightest likelihood that Shakespeare did – though we are reminded of one of his last sonnets to her:

> O, from what power hast thou this powerful might
> With insufficiency my heart to sway?

In William Shakespeare's case sex (female) exerted quite enough of a compulsive spell. But Proust – whose extraordinary searching mind understood everything – regarded loving as 'like an evil spell in a fairy-story against which one is powerless until the enchantment has passed'.

This is all that Forman tells us; after that she sinks back into the darkness out of which, poor woman, she came. But we have great reason to be grateful to him; without him she never would have been identified, for there is nothing about her that has survived in print. What he tells us completely corroborates what Shakespeare tells us in the Sonnets. The young discarded mistress of the old Lord Chamberlain, exceptionally dark, half-Italian and musical, she was married off to another musician, Will Lanier, in 1593. She was then twenty-three, her husband twenty; Southampton was not twenty till October that year, Will Shakespeare was twenty-nine.

These dates and respective ages tell us whole volumes, and confirm the story – where vague conjectures, for generations, have told us nothing, merely created confusion.

* MS. Ashmole 236.

The 'Will' sonnets become perfectly clear, as they were originally – not written to create a puzzle:

> Whoever hath her wish, thou hast thy will,
> And Will to boot, and Will in overplus.

Again in the next:

> Swear to thy blind soul that I was thy Will;
> And Will, thy soul knows, is admitted there. . . .

Her husband Will is properly admitted there; very well, turn a blind eye to conscience and Will Shakespeare is willing to take the other Will's place.

The external documents that remain corroborate the account of Emilia in the Sonnets and what Forman tells us about her in every detail. She came from the Bassano family of musicians at Court, who were recruited to the King's service from Venice at the end of Henry VIII's reign. They were a numerous clan, but there is no difficulty in tracing Emilia. She was the daughter of Baptist Bassano and Margaret Johnson, who is sometimes referred to as Bassano, for they lived as man and wife. Both were buried in the parish of St Botolph, Bishopsgate, just outside the walls of the City, on the way to Shoreditch where the early theatres were and many of the theatre-folk lived.

Forman's account is confirmed by the parish register and Baptist Bassano's will. Bassano, 'the Queen's musician', was buried on 11 May 1576, leaving Emilia a little girl of six. Her mother, Margaret Bassano, as she is named, was buried on 7 July 1587, leaving the girl alone to take the chances of life at seventeen. The provision her father had been able to make for her was scanty, indeed – as Forman said; there was another daughter, Angela, safely married to a gentleman, Joseph Holland. So, Baptista Bassany, as the English called him, left to Emilia Bassany, 'daughter of the body of Margaret Bassany alias Margaret Johnson, my reputed wife, the sum of £100 . . . to be paid at her full age of 21 years or day of marriage'. The two daughters were left the rents of the three houses of which he had the lease in the parish. The keeping of Emilia and her bestowal in marriage was left to her mother; but she died in 1587, leaving the girl to her own resources. She really had only her own dark beauty, and no doubt had been taught to play on the virginals.

It cannot have been long after that the elderly Lord Chamberlain took her as his mistress. Forman tells us that she had been brought up in Kent, perhaps in the vicinity of the Court at Greenwich; Lord Hunsdon had a grant of the manor of Sevenoaks there. Henry Carey, first Lord Hunsdon, was some ten years older than his first cousin, the Queen. He was the son of Mary Boleyn, who had been a mistress of Henry VIII some years before he fell passionately in love with her sister Anne, who made him make her Queen. Mary Boleyn, discarded, had been married off to William Carey, a gentleman conveniently in waiting, who died. Their only son was born about 1524 and named loyally after the King.

When Anne Boleyn's daughter came to the throne, Henry Carey's fortune was made and he proved worthy of it. All the Careys were, of course, in clover but he turned out a good servant of the state, naturally loyal and to be depended upon. A stout soldierly fellow, forthright and honest, he was straightforward in speech, a great swearer. The Queen kept him mostly up on the Scottish Borders, in garrison at Berwick; in addition to his numerous family, he had there a natural son, Valentine Carey, who became a respected ecclesiastic, Bishop of Exeter.

From the year of Shakespeare's birth, 1564, Lord Hunsdon – no Puritan – had his own company of players. James Burbage was one of them, and, as we have seen, builder of the first theatres out in Shoreditch. His son, Richard, became the star of the Lord Chamberlain's Company, Shakespeare's fellow and friend of many years. In 1585 Hunsdon was made Lord Chamberlain: this was a great blessing to the players – hitherto a not very respectable profession – for the Chamberlain gave them support at Court, against the City authorities always itching to suppress them.

Though Hunsdon had his residence in Somerset House, he also had a lease at this time of the buildings within Blackfriars, which Burbage and his fellows – Shakespeare among them – later turned into an indoors theatre. Hunsdon's son, who succeeded him, after an interval, as Lord Chamberlain lived in Blackfriars – as did Richard Field, who printed Shakespeare's poems. Blackfriars was familiar ground to him.

In the crisis of Armada year, 1588, the Lord Chamberlain came south to take command of the Queen's body-guard, in case of invasion. The invigorating excitement of that year (like 1940 or 1944 to us) would have made a propitious time to pick up a pretty dark girl for consolation; this can hardly have taken place much later, for Forman tells us that she had been kept by the old Lord Chamberlain for longer than the four years she had been so far married to Will Lanier – the musician to whom she was married off 'for colour' when with child. The child was called Henry, as the Lord Chamberlain had been called after his mother's lover, the King.

We have seen that Shakespeare's love for the discarded dark girl had its origin in pity for her condition:

> If thy unworthiness raised love in me,
> More worthy I to be beloved of thee.

If she turned out as badly as she did, poor girl, who can blame her after such a life?

Will Lanier, to whom she was married – a youth of Southampton's age, three years younger than herself – evidently cared nothing for her and married her for what she had got off the Lord Chamberlain. The Laniers were another prolific family of Court musicians, who had come in from France, from Rouen, a generation later than the Bassanos. But Will Lanier made no career as others of them did; he simply disappears. Emilia's boy by the Lord Chamberlain, Henry Lanier, got a place at Court in 1629 as one of Charles I's musicians; only four years later he died, leaving a son called William, after Emilia's husband, the putative grandfather.

And this is all we know of them.

The old Lord Chamberlain died in 1596, two years after the formation of the famous company under his patronage. It would be fairly certain that the Chamberlain's Men, the leading members of the company, would be presented to him. It is a piquant thought that William Shakespeare should have succeeded him for a time with his mistress, in the seat of her favours.

It is now all quite clear. When one comes to think of it, who else, who more convincingly, would the Dark Lady have been?

CHAPTER 7

The Turning-point: the Lord Chamberlain's Company

In May 1594 Shakespeare fulfilled the promise he had made, in presenting *Venus and Adonis*, of offering his patron some 'graver labour' by publishing *The Rape of Lucrece*. Once more it was printed by Richard Field with the formal dedication by his full title 'To the Right Honourable Henry Wriothesley, Earl of Southampton and Baron of Titchfield'. Titchfield was the transformed abbey where he lived in the country and in the parish church of which one sees him upon the magnificent family tomb, a little boy kneeling in armour at a prayer-desk. Everyone can perceive the warmer, affectionate tone, the greater assurance, with which the poet addresses his young patron, after all that had passed between them: 'The love I dedicate to your lordship is without end. . . . What I have done is yours, what I have to do is yours, being part of all I have, devoted yours. . . . Your lordship's in all duty, William Shakespeare.'

It is the language of the Sonnets, with the similar emphasis on duty – how people have failed to see that the Sonnets, like the poems, are offerings of duty passes comprehension. A more subtle point, which people may be pardoned for not grasping, is the tone: it is both deferential and familiar, and at the same time has the independent spirit of the gentleman he was set on being. I know no dedication in the literature of the time that strikes quite that note or has quite that subtlety. But we are now appreciating what a clever, subtle writer he had become.

We have now to trace the last phase in the relationship between the poet and his patron. We saw that the strains imposed upon it by Southampton's readiness to receive a rival poet and by his trespassing upon Shakespeare's preserves with his mistress had well nigh ended good relations. The sonnets following 87 have a valedictory note; on one side, the poet's reproaches, on the other his fear

> that thou mayst take
> All this away and me most wretched make.

There followed after this periods of absence in the winter and spring of 1593–4, when Shakespeare is touring in the country again.

Absence renewed inspiration, not the less moving – as is the way with poets – for being nostalgic, looking back on the more innocent past. One of the finest sonnets, 104, not only expresses this but gives us an intelligible chronology consistent with all our findings.

> To me, fair friend, you never can be old,
> For as you were when first your eye I eyed,
> Such seems your beauty still.

Then,

> Three winters cold
> Have from the forests shook three summers' pride

– that is, the winters of 1591–2, 1592–3, 1593–4 –

> Three beauteous springs to yellow autumn turned. . . .
> Three April perfumes in three hot Junes burned,
> Since first I saw you fresh. . . .

Precisely, the springs and summers of 1592, 1593, 1594. For want of precise dating, or even perceiving its indispensable necessity, commentators with no historical sense have totally lost themselves and the whole coherence of the Sonnets.

Now, with the famous Sonnet 107, it is the summer of 1594, as two contemporary topical references make certain, for these two events coincide in time:

> The mortal moon hath her eclipse endured. . . .

In Elizabethan English 'endured' means 'come through'; 'the mortal moon' always refers to the Queen: she had come through the shadow upon her life of the Lopez conspiracy. The Queen's personal physician, Dr Rodrigo Lopez, was charged with agreeing with Spanish agents to poison the Queen. Though he had no intention of doing so, he was in touch with Spanish agents who presented him with a costly jewel. He could never clear himself, and Essex – Lopez had unwisely spread the word that he had a venereal infection, probable enough – hounded the doctor to his death. Lopez was tried and condemned – by Essex! – at the end of February. In March Paris at last surrendered to Henri IV; this ended the civil wars in France and gave hope of general peace:

> Incertainties now crown themselves assured,
> And peace proclaims olives of endless age.

It is unintelligent not to see the logical as well as the chronological necessity of *two* events coming at the same time: these give us certainty. We are in the summer of 1594.

In this year, with the plague over, Shakespeare returns to playing and is concentrating once more on his true dramatic vocation. He is more and more absent from Southampton; several of the sonnets apologise for neglecting him. Southampton makes a serious reproach of this, as we see from Sonnet 117:

> Accuse me thus: that I have scanted all
> Wherein I should your great deserts repay. . . .

Shakespeare gratefully recognises what he owes to his patron's support and affection:

> Whereto all bonds do tie me day by day. . . .

His time has been much taken up by people outside their relationship:

> That I have frequent been with unknown minds,
> And given to time your own dear-purchased right. . . .

But Shakespeare has his own reaction against the profession by which he must earn his living – all the more strongly at this moment when he was coming to a decision about the future. It is psychologically convincing that it is in just three sonnets, 110, 111, 112, that he expressed most strongly his resentment at his luck in life:

> Alas, 'tis true I have gone here and there,
> And made myself a motley to the view –

i.e. he has been touring about the country as a player –

> Gored mine own thoughts, sold cheap what is most dear,
> Made old offences of affections new. . . .

The next sonnet breaks out with unwonted bitterness:

> O, for my sake do you with Fortune chide,
> The guilty goddess of my harmful deeds,
> That did not better for my life provide
> Than public means which public manners breeds.

If only he had been born in independent circumstances! No one has ever spoken out more openly what he really felt about his luck in life and his wish that his birth and fortune had been better.

> Thence comes it that my name receives a brand

– he is branded with the name of a common player, which he is. And he gives a deeper reason for resenting it:

> And almost thence my nature is subdued
> To what it works in, like the dyer's hand.

That is, he is afraid that acting will affect his own inner nature cheapen it, make him false – the thing he hated more than anything All through his writing we find that he is exceedingly conscious o the thin line between 'seeming' and 'being', appearance and reality falseness and truth. He was the most honest of men.

Several times over in these sonnets, returning to his trade, pre paring to give himself up wholly to it, he asks for sympathy:

> Your love and pity doth the impression fill
> Which vulgar scandal stamped upon my brow.

He is recalling the vulgar attack on him as an upstart player darin to take upon him to write, with which Greene had branded him His only consolation had been Southampton's countenance:

> So you *o'er-green* my bad, my good allow.

No doubt he had been one of the 'divers of worship' who, accord ing to Chettle, had vouched for the common player's honesty.

But observe how this picture of himself conforms with Greene' (Roberto's) description of the provincial player with gentlemanl pretensions.

One way and another, William Shakespeare had been through great deal in these years. He tells us so, as he tells us everything:

> What potions have I drunk of Siren tears
> Distilled from limbecks [alembics] foul as hell within,
> Applying fears to hopes and hopes to fears,
> Still losing when I saw myself to win!

This refers mainly, but not only, to the unhappiness his affair with the Dark Lady had brought him.

> What wretched errors hath my heart committed,
> Whilst it hath thought itself so blessèd never!

There is a winning simplicity about that confession; many of u have made similar mistakes, and been deeply hurt – but he has expressed it as few ever could. The misery of that affair had gravely prejudiced his relation with his young friend, a better source of happiness, and well nigh overthrown it. A thought follows that was important to him, for it occurs again and again in the plays:

> O benefit of ill! now I find true
> That better is by evil still made better. . . .

He consoles himself with

> And ruined love, when it is built anew,
> Grows fairer than at first, more strong, far greater.

We may well wonder. The relationship, so innocent at first, opening up what vistas of discovery for both the older and the younger man, had been gravely shaken:

> That you were once unkind befriends me now

– for now the younger is reproaching the older in turn with unkindness:

> For if you were by my unkindness shaken
> As I by yours, you've passed a hell of time. . . .

This is followed by Shakespeare's most forthright statement of how he regarded himself, a confession of transparent candour, with no illusions about himself – and therefore none about others. He has no moral self-esteem, and no use for moral pretences: there is no humbug in Shakespeare. (We may interpolate – what a prime condition for a dramatist, as also for the understanding of politics! Everyone recognises the essential truth of his rendering of human nature. This is the reason why.)

> 'Tis better to be vile than vile esteemed,
> When not to be receives reproach of being

It is worse to be thought bad when one doesn't deserve it, if one forfeits one's pleasure simply on account of other people's opinion. For other people's opinion is not worthy of respect – that is what William Shakespeare really thought:

> For why should others' false adulterate eyes
> Give salutation to my sportive blood?

He was free with the women – why should that attract people's disapproval when they themselves were no better?

> Or on my frailties why are frailer spies,
> Which in their wills count bad what I think good?

William Shakespeare thought sex was good, and comes clean with resounding candour:

> No, I am that I am, and they that level
> At my abuses reckon up their own.

What more could a man tell us about himself? The fascinating thing is that it is the world's great writer who is doing so. It is this transparent sincerity that helped to make him so. This is what emerged more and more in time, and in the end enabled him to triumph over time.

In these last sonnets, 124 and 125, the poet is taking leave of his patron. With the formation of the Lord Chamberlain's Company that summer Shakespeare was provided for, his future assured. These last sonnets are not only valedictory but sum up what in his eyes this rare relationship had been – almost unique, when one considers whom it concerned, and the consequences for literature. Looking back over it now, he says:

> If my dear love were but the child of state . . .

that means, if his affection had merely been a matter of policy and self-interest, it would be subject to time and circumstance. The topical reference to the executions of Jesuits and seminary priests, which were a marked feature of the winter of 1594–5, shows us when these last sonnets were written and when the period of patronage came to its term. Summing it up, Shakespeare asks,

> Were't it aught to me I bore the canopy,
> With my extern the outward honouring. . . ?

Did it mean anything that he had borne the canopy over his young patron, externally honouring him as the peer he was?

> No, let me be obsequious in thy heart,
> And take thou my oblation, poor but free,
> Which is not mixed with seconds, knows no art
> But mutual render, only me for thee.

It is a wonderful ending to the Sonnets, the historic friendship of poet and patron to which our literature owes so much and could not more appropriately, more consistently or more convincingly, be expressed. William Shakespeare is saying that he will follow the young man in heart, not with the external formality that went with his rank; that his offering, 'poor but free', is of affection, 'only me for thee'.

It is most moving that at the end he states the whole relation in terms of human equality, man for man. This, too, shows how he ranked himself: as an equal.

From the literary point of view we can now see that the Sonnets are a rounded and complete work of art: a full record of duty, affection, friendship for Southampton; infatuation for the woman, torment, utter disenchantment with her; the friendship tarnished and threatened, then recovered – a kind of *redintegratio amoris*. The next sonnet in numbering, 126, a light-hearted piece about Cupid and love, simply serves as a buffer, then the sonnets about the Dark Lady begin. They too are, as we have seen, in intelligible order, though, in point of time, they come within the Southampton sequence, 1 to 125. There is no real problem; when the publisher Thorpe got the manuscript, years later, it was intelligently handled and intelligibly ordered – even if the poet, though we do not know, did not see it through the press, as he had done at the time with *Venus and Adonis* and *The Rape of Lucrece*.

As a player-playwright he could turn his hand, like a Johannes Factotum, to other services for his patron than presenting poems and sonnets. He had written *Love's Labour's Lost* specially for Southampton and his circle. Sonnets 98 and 106 show that he was thinking of telling 'a summer's story', and reading Chaucer for the purpose. This took shape, along with Ovid and folklore from the English countryside, in *A Midsummer Night's Dream*. This lovely work was shaped to celebrate a grand wedding, it is not difficult to see whose. The grandees whose wedding provides the framework for the real business of the play are an elderly courtly couple, a Duke and his bride. When they proceed to their wedding it suddenly transpires that, instead of its being Midsummer, the young people are returning from celebrating Mayday.

Southampton's mother, the widowed Countess, married Sir Thomas Heneage on 2 May 1594. Heneage was an important Court official, Vice-Chamberlain of the Household, of which Hunsdon was Lord Chamberlain. Heneage was a reliable Protestant, who had the confidence of the Queen; she in turn was friendly to the Countess, who, though a Catholic, was not a political Catholic like her first husband. Since the young Earl was showing no disposition to marriage, but remained averse to it, it was sensible of the Countess to do what she could to reinsure the family. She was a thoroughly good woman, grieved at the course her son was taking – doing nothing to continue the family or win the Queen's good opinion.

The wedding of the elderly couple was private, and the Queen did not attend it. That the wedding was one at which the Queen was *not* present should be obvious to persons of social sensibility, for the very first scene has lines in disapprobation of the virgin state:

To live a barren sister all your life,
Chanting faint hymns to the cold fruitless moon. . . .

The Queen was always praised in terms of the chaste moon, the terrene moon, the mortal moon, the virginal Cynthia.

But earthlier happy is the rose distilled
Than that which, withering on the virgin thorn,
Grows, lives and dies in single blessedness.

This is, of course, the Southampton theme, in which the Sonnets originated. The play ends with a masque of fairies winding their way through the chambers of a great house, to consecrate them for the occasion; most editors of the play have seen this: the house would almost certainly be Southampton House.

It is usually held that the play was revised for public performance by the Lord Chamberlain's Company. Among the lines written into the play were those describing at some length the exceptionally wet summer of 1594.

The Countess's marriage did not last long, for Heneage was an elderly man; but they were happy while it lasted, Heneage paying affectionate tribute to her kind care of him, obviously devoted to her. In accordance with Elizabethan usage she retained her title, Countess of Southampton; she refers to him in her letters, also according to regular usage, as 'Master Heneage'. It was quite common to refer to a knight as Master, or Mr in its modern form – Sir Francis Bacon is often referred to as Master Bacon, and so on; it was impossible to address any Lord as Mr. When the Sonnets were dedicated by Thorpe to Mr W. H., who had simply got the manuscript in his possession, this could never refer to a Lord; but it could, and almost certainly did, refer to Sir William Harvey, the Countess's third husband, to whom she bequeathed all her household goods and chattels.

That autumn the adolescent Earl did nothing to improve his image in the Queen's eyes – she must have known about his goings-on and never regarded him with approval, let alone favour – by the part he played in helping his friends, Sir Charles and Sir Henry

Danvers, to escape after the killing of Henry Long, heir to his family. Down in Wiltshire there was an embittered feud between two of the leading families, the Danverses of Dauntsey and the Longs of South Wraxall. There had already been a killing among the retainers, mutual insults and confrontations, when the feud culminated in a terrible affair in a house at Corsham on Justices' Day, 4 October 1594. These two aristocratic swordsmen, the Danvers brothers, burst into the house at the head of their followers; the Long faction were at dinner with Anthony Mildmay and others. There was a violent altercation, and the younger Danvers killed the heir of the Longs.

They then fled to the shelter of Titchfield, where Southampton secreted them in a lodge in the park, provided food for the party, spent a night with them, and helped to arrange their getaway to France. In the inquiry after their escape one of the Earl's stablemen recognised Sir Henry Danvers's maidenhair-coloured saddle all bloody – this was the younger brother who had killed Long. Southampton was emotionally attached to him; he never married. When the Sheriff came over Itchen Ferry to inquire into the escape, a couple of the Earl's servants – one of them 'Signor Florio, an Italian' – threatened to throw the officer overboard.

The Queen did not pardon the brothers for some years; they entered the service of Navarre, now Henri IV. When they were allowed back they dedicated their swords to Essex: the elder perished on the scaffold for him in 1601, when Southampton was let off the death-sentence. Henry Danvers survived the catastrophe but, not marrying, became a very rich man, a benefactor to Oxford and his native county. (To Oxford he gave the beautiful Botanical Garden we enjoy today, with gateway designed by Nicholas Stone.)

Such, at any rate, were some of Southampton's young friends – all of them devoted to Essex, increasingly at cross-purposes with old Lord Burghley and the respectables at Court. When the poet-playwright of the circle – though now a free man – came to write his next play that winter he chose an Italian love-story placed in the framework of a family feud. There is the theme of friendship to the fore in Mercutio's emotional relationship to Romeo, the aristocratic young swordsmen too free with their weapons. And Shakespeare, now a Chamberlain's man, wrote *Romeo and Juliet* for his fellows.

Two days after the Long murder, on 6 October 1594, Southampton came of full age. There were complicated affairs to settle, the inheritance of his estates, obligations to clear and debts to pay. He had earned the disfavour of the Lord Treasurer: no help in that quarter. Southampton now had to face the music. The Jesuit Superior, Garnet, who was likely to know the private affairs of a Catholic peer, reported that he was made to pay £5000 for his breach of promise – and Burghley found a better match for his granddaughter. The young man was made to face the financial facts (at least) of life, and for several years ahead found himself in considerable difficulties. It was a good thing that his poet was now safely established; but it was the golden youth, always generous, who enabled him to be so.

The information came down through Sir William Davenant, who was likely to know, that Southampton gave Shakespeare a goodly sum to go through with a purchase he had a mind to. It is generally taken that this was a purchase of a share in the Lord Chamberlain's Company on its formation earlier this year. They were on tour later in the summer – and in Wiltshire, we may observe, that autumn. It is easy to see how the last sonnets refer again and again to his absence, being aware of neglecting his patron – the Earl's awareness of it, too – while

> I have frequent been with unknown minds,
> And given to time your own dear-purchased right.

Among the unknown minds would be the fellowship of the Chamberlain's men, some of whom he would have known before in the profession and have acted with: the greater part of them are those with whom he would spend the remainder of his working days. For the turning-point had been reached, the decision made, by circumstances, by his nature and gifts: however much he might wish for a better lot in life, the theatre was his vocation. He was a good actor, he had been acting for a number of years; he had now made the grade as a dramatist; he had staked his claim as a poet; he had had the experience of serving a patron, and seen what that involved:

> Being your slave, what should I do but tend
> Upon the hours and times of your desire?
> I have no precious time at all to spend,
> Nor services to do, till you require.

There is a shade of irony in that, and of reproach in what follows:

> Nor dare I chide the world-without-end hour
> Whilst I, my sovereign, watch the clock for you,
> Nor think the bitterness of absence sour
> When you have bid your servant once adieu.

William Shakespeare was a busy, hard-working man: he cannot have liked hanging about, watching the clock for however lordly a young man, thinking

> . . . where you are, how happy you make those.

And in the next,

> That God forbid that made me first your slave,
> I should in thought control your times of pleasure,
> Or at your hand the account of hours to crave,
> Being your vassal, bound to stay your leisure!

It can hardly be doubted that, when the time came, he would opt for independence. Indeed, he had opted for independence before his service to his patron came to an end – hence the complaints from Southampton referred to in the last Sonnets. It would be like his prudence – learned in a hard school – not to end his service until the Chamberlain's Company was securely established with fair promise for the future. He was now a man of thirty, several years over the half-way mark in his life; it was high time for the decision to be made, the more so because belated, owing to earlier adverse circumstances, the long apprenticeship, the insecurity of the plague years, from which the patron had saved him.

Many men of mark come to a threshold like this in life, when they have to make up their minds, for good and all, to step over it. As he himself said, only a few years later, when he was in a position to see how favourably things had worked out:

> There is a tide in the affairs of men,
> Which, taken at the flood, leads on to fortune. . . .

By the time that was written his fortune was being made; the decision had turned out right, but which

> Omitted, all the voyage of their life
> Is bound in shallows and in miseries.

He had had plenty of experience of that.

We need not repeat all that he owed to the relationship with Southampton, between emergence from obscurity with the *Henry VI* plays to the firm establishment of the Chamberlain's Company. It was, however, these decisive years that matured and equipped him – the increased sophistication with the introduction to cultivated society, the refinement of the senses observable in his imagery; the artistic development with cultural contacts with other arts, in addition to literature, the deep and lasting love of music, if only a superficial acquaintance with painting. Then there was the exploration of other emotional areas of friendship, love and sex than those offered by a provincial country town.

We have gone into all this in detail, mostly in his own words, for it is rarely that one of the world's writers takes us into the innermost crevices of his own heart and experience. But William Shakespeare was without any disguise, singularly honest and open. We shall have no such opportunity again. Henceforth, he will be utterly and completely a man of the theatre, more so than any other dramatist, so absorbed in his work that there will be no time for any more sonnets or poems – with the exception of 'The Phoenix and the Turtle', an occasional poem on the theme of a happy marriage. Even when he buys a large property at Stratford he is so busy that his brother has to take possession of it for him.

As Bentley says, Shakespeare became a dedicated professional, 'more completely and more continuously involved with theatres and acting companies than any other Elizabethan dramatist'.* He is 'the only one known who not only wrote plays for his company, acted in the plays, and shared the profits, but who was also one of the housekeepers who owned the building. For seventeen years he was one of the owners of the Globe Theatre, and for eight years he was one of the housekeepers of the company's second theatre, the Blackfriars, as well.' He had no time for bumbling about the town getting into trouble, like Ben Jonson – so there is no mystery about our hardly hearing about him in any other capacity than the theatre. There is obviously a good deal in what Aubrey heard about him; 'the more to be admired because he was not a company keeper: lived in Shoreditch, wouldn't be debauched and, if invited to, writ he was in pain'. We can tell from the plays that he had a dislike for drunkenness. All this is consistent with Chettle's experience, who had never met him till he received a call protesting at being insulted by a literary journalist. No time to publish any more works – not even his own plays: everything he had went henceforth into the theatre. No time for any more sonneteering: there is not the slightest likelihood that he wrote any more after this time.

This has the fundamental consequence for his biography that, henceforth, almost everything about him is external information – except for hints we are given in the plays. The brief period of continuous inner illumination is over.

During the plague years at least three companies disappeared, not only Sussex's and Pembroke's – with which Shakespeare had had an earlier connection, for they possessed his *Henry VI* plays and

* G. E. Bentley, *Shakespeare and His Theatre*, pp. 49, 66.

Titus Andronicus – but also the Queen's, which had set a new model in 1583 and taken the lead with the best actors. Out of the quicksands – with the plague over and normal conditions returning – the first company to give a new lead was the Lord Admiral's, with the finest of tragic actors as its star, Edward Alleyn, and his wife's stepfather to manage it, Philip Henslowe. They had most of Marlowe's plays, which continued to hold the stage through the 1590s. Henslowe's account-books, which survive, show the leaders of the Company calling on the old Lord Chamberlain at Somerset House in connection with the business, and payments 'for drinking with the gentlemen'.

The Burbages took the lead in the organisation of a new company under the Lord Chamberlain's own aegis, for James Burbage was, as we have seen, Hunsdon's man. William Shakespeare was only less important than the Burbages themselves, the creators of the enterprise; in the documents his name appears first; he must have taken a leading part in the new venture. He could bring to it his skill as an actor, the plays he had written – and those he was going to write, henceforth exclusively for the Company – perhaps his social contacts and graces, which James Burbage was without. Burbage, more than thirty years older, had begun life as a joiner, then turned to playing; when he built the first Theatre and the Curtain out in the Liberty of Holywell in Shoreditch his carpentry must have come in handy. He had begun life poor; he was a tough customer, as he needed to be, rude and not overly honest in earlier days. He had two sons, Cuthbert and Richard, who became the star of the Company. All three Burbages were entirely theatre-men: no other business; where their rival Henslowe had varied interests, and was not primarily a theatre-man at all. Then Edward Alleyn gave up acting to attend to his affairs; Marlowe's plays continued popular, but he was dead. The combination that appeared to have the lead fell behind in the race; no one could have foretold that the combination of the Burbages with Shakespeare would achieve first place, let alone attain such continuous success.

Things were still rather tentative in June 1594 when the Admiral's and Chamberlain's men played together at Newington Butts – it may be owing to fear of the renewal of plague that they went out there, along Southwark High Street, into the country. After mid-June the Admiral's men went to their own theatre, the Rose, on Bankside, the Chamberlain's to theirs, the Theatre, on the other side of the river outside Bishopsgate. They never played together again; henceforward each had its independent existence. The leading companies came to be these two only, in rivalry with each other, which occasioned some disputes – in which the prudent, gentlemanly playwright did not involve himself.

Of the men who came together that June to form the fellowship in time to become so famous Richard Burbage and William Shakespeare were the indispensable key-men; in fact these were the two associated together in popular fame and gossip. Burbage created the part of Richard III, the success of which play surpassed that of the *Henry VI* plays before the plague years. It is likely that *Richard III* was the most popular of all Shakespeare's plays with the Elizabethan public; it provided a superlative part for Burbage, the success of it must have given the new combination confidence and an initial impetus. Even when the play was printed three years later, in 1597 – the shortened version of it, adapted for stage production with a number of minor parts that could be doubled for a reduced number of actors – it went into five more editions before the full text was published in the Folio.

Even today, people who know nothing else of Shakespeare will say,

> A horse! a horse! my kingdom for a horse!

– Richard's last despairing cry. In his own day Burbage was so celebrated for this rôle that stories were told of him in it. The guide who took people over Bosworth Field in the next generation was apt to confuse Richard with Burbage:

> For when he would have said, King Richard died,
> And called 'A horse! A horse!' – he 'Burbage' cried.

The tale went round London – reported by one of the young lawyers addicted to the theatre – that a woman fell for Burbage in this rôle and at the theatre gave him an assignation to come to her that night under the name of Richard III. But the playwright overheard it and got free from the theatre beforehand, gained admittance and was 'at his game ere Burbage came. Then, message being brought that Richard III was at the door, Shakespeare caused return to be made that William the Conqueror was before Richard III.'

Ben trovato – but it is just like the things that happened at the theatre, as we know from Forman's notebooks.

When the Company made their first performances at Court that Christmas, on 26 and 27 December 1594, payments for the two plays were made to Burbage, Shakespeare and Will Kemp, their leading comic actor. Burbage may not have had any musical gift, as Alleyn had, but he had a gift for painting. The portrait we have of him is a self-portrait; it gives us an impression of a strong personality with its large nose, wide-awake, intelligent eyes with well-formed arched eye-brows, sensuous lips, and powerful oval-shaped head: it gives one a sense of power and punch. At the end of Shakespeare's career, in 1613, we find him still co-operating with Burbage over an *impresa* for the Earl of Rutland. This was a painted shield, with emblems and mottoes, for use in tournament or pageant; Shakespeare wrote the words. (Rutland and his brothers were friends of Southampton, and had been involved like him in the Essex conspiracy.) In the accounts we find the payments: 'To Master Shakespeare' – note that he becomes generally referred to henceforth by the respectful title – 'in gold about my Lord's impresa, 44*s*. To Richard Burbage [note: he is only an actor] for painting and making it, in gold 44*s*.' When Shakespeare died three years later, the three fellows of the Company whom he singled out, with bequests to buy mourning-rings to remember him by, were Burbage, Heming and Condell. We may take it that these were closest to him.

Burbage in the end graduated to the style of 'gentleman', though neither he nor Shakespeare achieved that of 'esquire'. When he died, three years after Shakespeare, his death so much grieved the Earl of Pembroke, then Lord Chamberlain, that he could not bear to attend a grand supper and play for the French Ambassador: 'which I, being tenderhearted, could not endure to see so soon after the loss of my old acquaintance, Burbage'. If this is what one earl felt about an elderly actor, we should be able to understand how much more there was between Shakespeare and his younger, more impressionable, peer. But we have no evidence of any further closeness: Shakespeare had far too much to do, writing, acting, producing, helping to direct the affairs of the Company. There was no time to lose if he were ever to make himself independent.

Several tributes were paid to Burbage, though nothing like so many as his friend received. Here is one that brings them together, the actor and the parts his fellow wrote for him:

> He's gone, and with him what a world are dead,
> Which he revived, to be revivèd so.
> No more young Hamlet, old Hieronimo,
> Kind Lear, the grievèd Moor, and more beside
> That lived in him, have now for ever died.
> Oft have I seen him leap into the grave,
> Suiting the person which he seemed to have,
> Of a sad lover, with so true an eye,
> That there I would have sworn he meant to die.
> Oft have I seen him play this part, in jest [gesture]
> So lively that spectators and the rest
> Of his sad crew, whilst he but seemed to bleed,
> Amazèd thought even then he died indeed.

Evidently this is Burbage in the part of Romeo; Hieronimo is, of course, the leading part in Kyd's earlier *Spanish Tragedy*.

Without going into the play that brought the new combination its early great success, we should say that *Richard III* is Shakespeare's grand tribute to Marlowe – a Marlovian villain dominating sole everybody else in the play. Though it does not plumb the spiritual depths of the last act of *Dr Faustus* and the poetry is less majestic, *Richard III* is more varied and complete, with more humour and a subtler rendering of character. For material Shakespeare read up Holinshed, Hall's Chronicle, and More's account; with his marvellous understanding of human beings and their motives, he got very near the truth about Richard. Again there is a good deal of play-acting within the play, the farce put up by Richard and Buckingham over the 'offer' of the crown, with touches from the profession:

> Tut, I can counterfeit the deep tragedian;
> Speak and look back, and pry on every side,
> Tremble and start at wagging of a straw,
> Intending deep suspicion; ghastly looks
> Are at my service, like enforcèd smiles. . . .

Elizabethan acting was declamatory and gestural; there was a code of gestures, well recognised by the public, to express thoughts and motives as well as actions. We should find it primitive and elementary; as against that, there was its soaring poetry and a range of imagination we can not reach. Then, too, the audience was almost part of the play, it felt itself so much part of the action, so excitable, mercurial and responsive – we have difficulty in imagining how different Elizabethan theatre, like Elizabethan society, was.

But we have evidences; we are told how the audience would 'generally take up a wonderful laughter and shout altogether with one voice, when they see some notable cosenage practised, or some sly conveyance of bawdry brought out of Italy'. This was from a disapprover; but even this sourpuss could not resist a comedy: 'comedies make our delight exceed, for at them many times we exceed so extremely that, striving to bridle ourselves, we cannot – delight being moved with variety of shows, of events, of music, the longer we gaze, the more we crave'. Remembering this delight, we go again and again: 'yet will not my countrymen leave their plays, because plays are nourishers of delight'. At a scene of love, 'the beholders rose up, every man stood on tip-toe and seemed to hover over the prey; when they sware, the company sware; when they departed to bed, the company presently [i.e. immediately] was set on fire'.

Stimulated, they went home to bed with their wives; those that hadn't any could easily make a date, and for the rest the theatres on Bankside were conveniently close to the brothels.

For the specific response to Shakespeare, we have Nashe's word how patriotism thrilled at *Henry VI*, seeing brave Talbot, 'the terror of the French', brought on the boards. Or there is Leonard Digges to witness:

> So have I seen when Caesar would appear,
> And on the stage at half-sword parley were
> Brutus and Cassius – O, how the audience
> Were ravished! With what wonder they went thence!
> When some new day they would not brook a line
> Of tedious, though well-laboured, *Catiline*.
> *Sejanus* too was irksome, they prizèd more
> 'Honest' Iago, or the jealous Moor.

This introduces us to the difference that developed between Shakespeare and his junior, of the next generation: Ben Jonson. Shakespeare was always popular, against the text-book rules; this irritated the pedant in Ben, but got him approved by the intellectuals. Both *Catiline* and *Sejanus* were dead from the first.

For the present, it is enough to register the extraordinary *rapport* between stage and theatre, players and audience, almost a kind of unity with ripples and bursts not merely of applause or derision but in antiphony – like provincial Italian opera, or an English football-match today.

In the uncertainties as to the future, the disturbed conditions before Shakespeare reached firm ground with the formation of the Chamberlain's Company, he needed to be able to turn his hand to anything. He was called in to revise a couple of scenes in a play on *Sir Thomas More*, which had been sketched out by Anthony Munday, with help from Dekker and Chettle. In writing *Richard III* Shakespeare read More's account of Richard and followed him closely. But to write a play on More was a ticklish business under the Tudors; moreover the 'Evil Mayday' riots of 1517, which More had dealt with, were paralleled in 1593 by an agitation against immigrants. It is a tribute to Shakespeare's expertness that he should have been called in to handle this awkward subject; one can see from his treatment of it that he would never be one to give trouble to the authorities.

Indeed, he agreed with them in his view of the mob and how it should be handled. What is remarkable is the consistency of this scene with the Jack Cade scenes in *1 Henry VI*, and the treatment of the crowd in *Julius Caesar* and *Coriolanus* later. From the literary angle, the scene is immensely superior to the rest of the play, in the writing, the humour as well as the serious argument, the neatness dramatically. There is the further interest that the balance of informed opinion holds that this addition to the manuscript is in Shakespeare's hand. It is written with ease, conviction and speed, the author pausing occasionally for a second thought as he went along. But the play was not proceeded with – too awkward ground; and shortly he had better things to do.

The 'fellowship' within the Company – which meant its leading actors – was very close. They acted day in and day out together, in the theatre during the season, at Court during the Christmas twelve-day holiday or at Shrovetide; they rehearsed most days in the week. When not acting in London they toured together; they must have eaten together, even when they had families and homes of their own. How close they were we can see from their wills, always remembering their Fellows, bequests of money, mourning-rings, apparel, musical instruments. Sometimes a player lodged in the house of another and was looked after by the family. Then there were the hired men, who sometimes acted as servants, and the boy-actors of the Company who were in the position of apprentices to a craft.

Shakespeare did not have a house or home in London: there he was a lodger, in different places at different times. This had its advantages, which it does not require much imagination to appreciate. There had been the affair with the Dark Lady. We shall see that he was concerned in the intimate affairs of another none-too-respectable household later. To lodge alone is more stimulating to the imagination and to work, and obviously leaves more time for writing: we may say that this was indispensable to him. Family-wise, his sights were fixed on Stratford – and his investments were to be directed there: an independent country-gentleman at the end of the long hard road.

Aubrey had heard that 'Mr William Shakespeare was wont to go into Warwickshire once a year, and did commonly in his journey lie at this house [the Crown tavern in] Oxford: where he was exceedingly respected. I have heard parson Robert Davenant say that Mr W. Shakespeare here gave him a hundred kisses.' The tavern-keeper was John Davenant, 'a vintner there, a very grave and discreet citizen'; his wife 'a very beautiful woman, and of a very good wit and of conversation very agreeable'. Her other son, named William, became the famous poet and dramatist, Sir William Davenant. 'Now Sir William would sometimes, when he was pleasant over a glass of wine with his most intimate friends, say that it seemed to him that he writ with the very spirit that Shakespeare, and seemed contented enough to be thought his son.'

There is no reason why this should not be so – there is usually something in what John Aubrey says. What is striking is that Sir William Davenant not only took after Shakespeare in genius, as poet and dramatist, but in the nature of his genius; he was equally good-natured, affable and euphoric. He was equally bent on the pursuit of women, a cause in which this poet-laureate lost his nose – a subject of mirth to Elizabethans, Shakespeare among them.

The organisation was as follows: James Burbage and his son Cuthbert, theatre-owners and managers of the property, with Richard as part-owner. The nucleus of the fellowship was formed by the leading ten or so actors, who shared in the profits, as Fellows of a college shared in its revenues. Then came the hired men, who were paid weekly wages, acted as supernumeraries, musicians, and performed useful menial functions as stage-keepers, door-keepers, what not. Lastly came the few boys, aged from six to eighteen, who acted the women's parts – usually three or four – or those of children, sometimes of very old men. The boys often lived as apprentices with the leading actors, giving rise to the suspicions sometimes voiced – by Marston, for instance – and probably justified well enough by Marlowe, though not himself an actor.

We now understand – as the Victorians did not – how the personnel of the Company determined the shape and casting of the play. This is in marked contrast with today. The leading actors were a continuous body, though there were changes by deaths or some leaving; so there had to be rôles for the chief actors, and no part written for which there was not a suitable actor. It must have been a remarkable boy who could take the part of Cleopatra; yet, on second thoughts, there is something tomboyish about the character, and conventional folk are apt to overlook the emotional and intuitive eroticism of youths anyway. Usually there were a dozen or so parts, the rest small ones which easily could be doubled.

It has been noticed that in the first years of the Company there were two gifted boys, one short, the other tall, to take the parts of Helena and Hermia in *A Midsummer Night's Dream*, Portia and Nerissa in *The Merchant of Venice*, Beatrice and Hero in *Much Ado about Nothing*, Rosalind and Celia in *As You Like It*, and Olivia and Viola in *Twelfth Night*, with which the sequence comes to an end. Those boys had outgrown their parts. On the other hand, the frequent disguisings of sex the comedies resort to, the girls dressed as boys, turn the disadvantage of boys playing women's parts to good use. When an English traveller went to the theatre in Venice he was surprised to find that women could act as well as the boys at home.

Will Kemp must have been next in importance in the early years of the Company, for he had a streak of genius as a comic actor and was independently famous for his jigs – dancing and miming, with words: some of them were published. He probably began as one of Leicester's Men, was one of his troupe in the Netherlands and went on – as a considerable number of English actors and musicians did – to Denmark. We know that he played the part of Peter in *Romeo and Juliet* and Dogberry in *Much Ado*. Would he not then have played the part of Falstaff, which early became famous? By 1599 he was seeking a change – evidently an independent spirit; for he sold his share in the Globe, to which they had moved, to the other four Fellows holding a moiety, Shakespeare, Heming, Phillips and Pope. So that they now had one-eighth each of the Globe profits; apart from anything else: they were 'sharers'; this was how the money was made, not just by acting or writing plays. Next year Kemp performed his celebrated morris-dance, with pipe and tabor, all the way from London to Norwich, and hung his buskins in the Guildhall there. This was trumpeted all over the country, and was written up in a pamphlet, *Kemp's Nine Days' Wonder* – evidently the more individual and spectacular publicity he preferred. 'I have danced myself out of the World,' he wrote, meaning the Globe. After a visit abroad he came back to it briefly. One of the *Parnassus* skits at Cambridge names him as a third with Burbage and Shakespeare. But shortly he was dead, his place taken by Robert Armin, a very different spirit, more subtle and intellectual with a vein of melancholy, for whom Shakespeare wrote his later clown-parts, like Feste and the Fool in *Lear*.

With John Heming and Henry Condell we come to a couple of reliable fellows who stayed with the Company. Heming came to the Chamberlain's Men at the beginning, from the troupe of Ferdinando, Lord Strange, as several others did. He had business ability, acted regularly as receiver for performances at Court, and was regarded with confidence by his fellows. He appears in several of their wills, as executor or legatee; he was 'master' to one actor, hired man or servant, and a trustee for Shakespeare's Blackfriars property. In time he acquired a larger interest in both the Globe and Blackfriars, along with house-property and parish offices in St Mary Aldermanbury. A good citizen, he was one of those actors, going up in the world, to take out a coat-of-arms – though not until 1629; 'John Heming of London, gent., of long time servant to Queen Elizabeth of happy memory, also to King James her royal successor and to King Charles his son'. A Worcestershire man, of Droitwich.

Henry Condell was not an original sharer in the Globe, but he came to be so; a regular Fellow in the Company he appears as trustee, executor or legatee in several of their wills. He, too, became prominent in the affairs of St Mary Aldermanbury, and was buried there. The profession by then had become not only respectable, but reputable – largely the work of such people as Ned Alleyn, Burbage and Shakespeare. With the money Alleyn made he bought the manor of Dulwich, built the almshouses and the school; as an elderly man he married a daughter of John Donne, Dean of St Paul's. At his death Alleyn was expecting a knighthood for his good works. (Many men have been knighted for less.) Other actors staked their claim to a coat-of-arms – none so soon as William Shakespeare; scoffed at by the serious-minded or merely envious, it was a sure sign of the profession's upgrading.

Augustine Phillips was one of those who took out a coat-of-arms. Austin Phillips they called him, as we know from Forman's casebooks, for Phillips came to him from time to time about his ailments. He was one of the original combination of 1594, and remained continuously till 1605, when he died, not old. By then he had a country-house and land out at Mortlake, by the Thames, and made a characteristically generous will, like all these Fellows. Five pounds to 'the hired men of the Company which I am of' – sometimes a sum like this was specified for a supper together; pieces of 30*s* to his Fellows, Shakespeare and Condell, and his 'servant', the actor Beeston; pieces of 20*s* to his colleagues, Robert Armin, Richard Cowley, Laurence Fletcher, Nicholas Tooley, Alexander Cook; silver bowls to Burbage, Heming and Sly; as much as £20 to Timothy Whithorne, overseer of the will. Samuel Gilburn, his late apprentice, is left 40*s* and my 'mouse-coloured velvet hose, a white taffeta doublet, a black taffeta suit, my purple cloak, sword and dagger, and my bass viol'. James Sands, his present apprentice, is left 40*s*, 'a cithern, a bandora and a lute'. Actors often bequeathed musical instruments; they were sometimes singers. We know what frequent opportunities Shakespeare provided for music in his plays.

Thomas Pope was another of the Fellows in at the beginning from Lord Strange's troupe. He, too, had visited Denmark – to the players there was nothing remote about the Court of Denmark or the Castle at Elsinore; he, too, gained interests in both Globe and Curtain, and took out a coat-of-arms. There was a fuss about this, as there had been about Phillips's. A Herald complained that 'Pope the player would have no other arms but the arms of Sir Thomas Pope, Chancellor of the Augmentations' – and founder of Trinity College, Oxford, we may add. (He came of no very grand family: perhaps the actor *was* related.)

William Sly was one of Shakespeare's original Fellows, coming from Strange's men, and was henceforth with the Chamberlain's men to his end. Not one of the original shareholders of the Globe, he was admitted one before his death in 1608. A base-born son was baptised in St Giles's, Cripplegate, in 1606, as was another next year of Edmund Shakespeare, the youngest brother, another player. Sly left bequests to Cuthbert Burbage and James Sands, the rest of his property to the Brownes, the family in which he lived and who had looked after him. Robert Browne's young family had been wiped out by plague in 1593: this must have been a second. Browne spent a number of years acting in Germany; George Bryan was another of those who had been there and in Denmark. He was one of the fellowship for a few years only, but was payee for Court performances in December 1596. Richard Cowley, (pronounced Cooley), was one of the original combination; he was payee for the Company in 1601, and remained with it, dying two years after Shakespeare. His will was witnessed by three of his colleagues and Ravenscroft, the musician.

Such were the men with whom Shakespeare spent most of his days, working professionally with them, for the next two decades. In that time he made a modest independent fortune, such as he had had in view all along, concentrating his holdings at Stratford, with which he remained constantly in touch and to which he retired. It should be obvious what a tremendous incentive sharing the theatre-profits gave to the Fellows, the inner corps of leading actors who dominated the Company. From this time on Shakespeare put the whole of his creative energy, his dramatic gifts as well as business ability into it, while Burbage went on to take Alleyn's place as the great actor of the time. No wonder the Chamberlain's Men won the race; their primacy was acknowledged, when James I succeeded to the throne, by his taking over their patronage and their becoming the King's Men, their leaders Grooms of the Chamber. Of the other Companies, only three or four lasted as long as twenty years; 'only Shakespeare's Company continued for nearly half a century', right up till the disastrous Civil War put an end to it.

To complete the picture, there was the Lord Chamberlain at the apex. It is a thousand pities that the Burbages' papers have not survived as Henslowe's have done. If only they had we should have known much more about the performances and dates of Shakespeare's plays, their takings and receipts. Since the Lord Admiral's Men had to go to Somerset House about their reorganisation, we must suppose that the Chamberlain's men also must have settled their affairs with old Lord Hunsdon. James Burbage was his man and well known to him; it would be interesting to know if he also met the player who had, for a time, succeeded him in the favours of his mistress.

She had been married off in 1593. Three years later Hunsdon was on his death-bed: on 21 July he called his son and heir to him and asked that 'he would not leave him that night'.* The old Lord was on good terms with his son, who was 'to possess all and whatsoever I shall leave behind me. So I do think you worthy of it, and much more, for I have always found you a kind and loving son.' He did not wish his wife to be 'troubled with so broken and hard estate as I shall leave . . . being able to leave her nothing in respect of that which so good a wife to me hath deserved'. In the event the Queen was kind and provided for her by passing the keepership of Somerset House to her; the second Lord Hunsdon went to live in Blackfriars.

'Her Majesty hath sent me sundry gracious promises that, on the word of a prince, she would fully relieve my estate. . . . And therefore doubt not but she will bestow mine offices upon you – which, if she do, you may be the better to my poor servants, which I am not able to recompense.' Emilia had been generously recompensed three years before, £40 a year with money and jewels, and

* Prerog. Court Cant., Prob. 11/88, f. 54.

a husband found. For the present the Queen gave the office of Lord Chamberlain to Lord Cobham, a favourite with her, Robert Cecil's father-in-law. The Cobham family were descended from the wife of Sir John Oldcastle, the Lollard knight who had been Prince Hal's companion-at-arms, and they objected to his name being used for the old buffoon of *1* and *2 Henry IV*. Hence the substitution of the name Falstaff (suggested by Sir John Fastolf in the chronicles), and the excuse hastily stuck on at the end: 'Oldcastle died a martyr, and this is not the man.'

The Queen gave Hunsdon's widow an outright gift of £400, and to the daughters £800 for his funeral. This enormous sum enabled them to put up to his memory the largest tomb in Westminster Abbey.*

However, Lord Cobham died in March next year, 1597; the second Lord Hunsdon succeeded as Chamberlain, and to the patronage of the Company. He was installed as Knight of the Garter at Windsor on St George's Day, 23 April 1597; it has been suggested that *The Merry Wives* was presented on the occasion – certainly it was written for a Garter feast at Windsor, probably later. Naturally the plays of the Chamberlain's dramatist were in request and favour with the family circle. Sir Edward Hoby invited Sir Robert Cecil to his house in Canon Row on 9 December 1595, 'where, as late as shall please you, a gate for your supper shall be open, and King Richard present himself to your view'. Lady Hoby was daughter to the old Lord Chamberlain, sister to the new. Later we find Cecil joking to Essex about Richard II – a subject about which the Queen was queasy – and Southampton's wife (he was caught at last) jesting about Falstaff.

The new Lord Chamberlain's sisters, Lady Hoby and Lady Scrope were fearful for his health – we find them consulting Forman about the degeneration of his condition. A well-informed Court lampoon tells us what that was:

> Chamberlain, Chamberlain,
> He's of her Grace's kin:

* *Cal. S. P. Dom. 1595–7*, 309.

Fool hath he ever been
With his Joan Silverpin.
She makes his cockscomb thin
And quake in every limb:
Quicksilver is in his head,
But his wit's dull as lead
– Lord for thy pity.

Fourteen years younger than the Queen, his first cousin once removed, he died in the same year, 1603.

CHAPTER 8

Success

THE whole emphasis of this book is biographical not critical, but there are points upon which the two approaches converge. The fact that Shakespeare's dramatic poetry generated far greater power than his non-dramatic, that the tensions of drama reached immeasurably wider ranges, depths and summits of imagination, in itself shows that his real vocation was for the stage. He had made the right, probably the inevitable, choice. One cannot imagine him dedicating his life to writing a *Faerie Queene*, still less a *Polyolbion*, like his fellow Warwickshireman, Drayton. Shakespeare's genius was all for action and its expression in drama. 'Shakespeare the poet has . . . the special feeling for the theatre, for the actor's art and for that most objective of all literary forms, the drama. . . . Phrases and images throughout his work show how naturally he thought of life as itself a kind of play in which men and women shape their rôles and their way of addressing their world and their fellows.'*

This is a more challenging and difficult *genre* than writing a narrative poem, a novel, or even an epic – for all these proceed 'sur le papier, qui souffre tout'. Whereas a play is three-dimensional, it has the dimensions of life; it operates with human beings in the flesh, and there are all the difficulties and limitations of personnel and casting. The dramatist has to think three-dimensionally how best to achieve his effects with the means at his disposal. The means are a *donné*: they are the conditioning blank or rhymed verse or prose, according to the persons of the drama, and songs for the singers. Blank verse was not such a problem to the Elizabethans: anyone

* Helen Gardner, *Religion and Literature* (1971), pp. 68–9.

who lives in the documents of the time knows that formal speech was already practically blank verse. All the same, what poetry Shakespeare made out of it!

A really illuminating critic, who approaches the subject from the point of view of the stage, tells us that Shakespeare's 'primal starting-point was how to tell a story upon the stage. He ransacked history and fiction for stories that could be made significant and told, or retold, upon a stage. He was a supreme stage story-teller and perceived that the basic source of all meaning that can be presented through his medium was the image of a human action.'* It is the action that supplies the matter, with appropriate language, though sometimes the action is enough without speech: there is the language of gesture, even more important then and expressed according to a code well understood by the audience. Shakespeare himself tells us so:

> for in such business
> Action is eloquence, and the eyes of the ignorant
> More learnèd than the ears. . . .

His gift for creating a scene must have been innate. Again we see that there was probably something in the rumour Aubrey reported, of Shakespeare as a boy helping his father, 'when he killed a calf, he would do it in a high style and make a speech'. The development of the gift must have been partly intuitive, partly deliberate and consciously worked out. 'It is easy to show that Shakespeare saw the scene 'in the mind's eye' (a phrase he invented) with peculiar sharpness. . . . It was a gift he had from the start, to tell his story three-dimensionally, as well as in lines. . . . Action with him is always paramount; theme, character, discourse and imagery (to take them in the order of their dramatic importance) all issue from the intrinsic shape and quality of the story. . . . The narrative is the *donné* and the succession of scenes is determined by Shakespeare's basic skill as a story-teller.'

* Nevill Coghill, *Shakespeare's Professional Skills* (1964), p. 3.

Cognate with this is the very different nature of the Elizabethan theatre, which has only come to be comprehended fully again in our own time; this has put out of court a vast amount of comment on the plays, for even the Restoration picture-stage was closer to ours than it was to the Elizabethan. Shakespeare's stage was a large area of board jutting out into the middle of the pit, open to the air, with the audience crowding round three sides of it, in immediate *rapport*: no changes of scenery to impede the action or interrupt the response of the audience. They must have been carried along more powerfully by the continuous flow, pauses and change of *locale* marked only by an occasional rhymed couplet; while the contrasting action between 'scene' and 'scene', the shifts of mood between one episode and another, were more exciting, no emotion dissipated.

Productions were 'basically *placeless*, and Shakespeare composed all his plays with far less attention to the place of the action than modern readers assume'.* Modern changes of scenery, pauses, intervals, all disperse and suspend the impact. In the Elizabethan theatre the actor was paramount – we must never forget that Shakespeare was one of them. Hence, too, 'the dramatic impact of a particular scene is greatly enhanced by the sharply contrasted tone or content of the scene which preceded it. Such effects depend upon continuous performance; any break or interruption between such paired scenes spoils, or greatly reduces, the effect.' Then there is the effectiveness of asides and soliloquies, when the actor was in collusion with the audience – largely lost for us. No wonder Elizabethans, one way or another, were stunned – as I have been at the uninterrupted impact of a Greek tragedy.

As for the actors, 'they brought out new plays as often as they could get them and the rest of the time repeated old favourites. So that, in any given month, as many as ten or fifteen different plays might be acted, allowing for a number of repetitions. . . Under this system Shakespeare, or any other hired man, might well act in as many as fifty or sixty different plays in the course of a year. Such

* Bentley, *Shakespeare and His Theatre*, pp. 53, 62.

training was very strenuous, but it helped young actors to learn their profession more thoroughly than most modern ones can. Through some training of this sort the young man from Stratford must have been going during at least part of the lost years.'*

All Elizabethan education was based on training the memory, to an extent that is hardly conceivable with our option for soft options. To this Shakespeare added the further training of the actor's memory. No wonder he was a perfect magpie for phrases, collocations of words, images, picked up here, there and everywhere; often his subconscious reshaped them and turned them out anew, more apt and striking than ever.

The phrases and images that stuck in his mind were those of Spenser, Sidney and – most of all – Marlowe; this was natural: genius speaks to genius. Shakespeare himself had begun as a dramatist by practically patenting the English history-play, with the *Henry VI* trilogy. Here Marlowe had followed the example of his junior in his last play, *Edward II* – better constructed, more mature and effective than Shakespeare's three. Now, with the book of English history open before him in Holinshed's *Chronicles*, and with his rival dead, with enriched experience and maturing powers, he was ready to go beyond him with *Richard II*.

Though *Edward II* was its starting-point and inspiration – the story of a weak and ineffectual king upon the throne, his deposition and final tragedy – how different a play! Marlowe's main interest is in the homosexual side of Edward II and his relations with Gaveston, his lack of sympathy for women is evident in the deplorable portrait he gives of Queen Isabella, 'the she-wolf of France' – there is no chord of sympathy with her plight, as there would have been with Shakespeare. Marlowe's play is swift and savage, and – now that one can see it again on the stage – more effective than one had realised. Shakespeare's play is full of human understanding and compassion, suffused with charm and pity, a gentler, more lyrical poetry. The two men stand revealed in their work: the ruthlessness

* G. E. Bentley, *Shakespeare: a Biographical Handbook*, p. 93.

of Marlowe's imagination, the extremism of his temper; the normal and equable humanity of the other.

Richard II was written in 1595, following upon *Romeo and Juliet* with which it has some affinities; and was followed by *King John*, with which it has much more. Shakespeare read up, with more than usual care, not only Holinshed and Hall but Berners' Froissart and apparently a French source. To this he added Samuel Daniel's *The Civil Wars*, out in 1595. Daniel was, in some ways, close to him in spirit: a man of modest beginnings, yet independent-minded, of transparent sincerity and sympathy of soul. Daniel had found a patron, encouragement and support in Sidney's sister, Countess of Pembroke, at Wilton, as Shakespeare had in Southampton. Closest to Shakespeare's Sonnets are those of Daniel, and there are other mutual influences. They would certainly have known each other, for Daniel's brother-in-law was John Florio.

We must resist the temptation to go into this appealing play – no less dramatically effective than the contrasting *Richard III* – and confine ourselves to flecks of the biographical and touches of the time, the real not the critical. Marlowe's is an altogether grimmer world, like that of his shady, questionable life. Richard and his Queen love each other, unlike Marlowe's couple. Then, too, Marlowe had no special respect for royalty: there was no sacredness about it to that rational mind, to whom nothing was sacred, except poetry itself. It is likely that Marlowe did not care enough about human beings to attach much importance to social order. Shakespeare, the family man, a responsible member of society, did. With his wiser sense of the collective folly of human beings, he saw the necessity of upholding society, in spite of intrinsic failings: undermine the social order and worse ensues with its breakdown.

This is the lesson of every one of his historical plays, whether English or Roman. He well knew how thin is the crust of civilisation and how easily a society plunges into the dark waters beneath. His own life fell in the blissful interval of the Elizabethan age – immediately before, all the turmoil and destruction of the Reformation, the scars were visible everywhere he toured about the country:

he comments on them in the Sonnets. A generation before that there had been the ferocity of the Wars of the Roses; a generation after his death the worse destructiveness of the Civil War. In his own house at Stratford, in July 1643, his daughter gave hospitality to Charles I's Queen in the distractions of that time – the sympathies of the town were with Parliament, evidently those of Shakespeare's family with the monarchy, as one would expect.

This does not mean that he had any illusions about inadequate monarchs or royal failings. The play shows that Richard II was no good at the job, Bolingbroke much better at it. Nevertheless, the usurpation of Henry IV was the seed of the Wars of the Roses; in historic fact Henry seems to have repented it in his later years: it had all been a question of self-preservation. Shakespeare's sympathy was engaged by the personal tragedy of Richard; that of Henry is naturally developed in the two plays that depict him worn down by the burdens of rule, with the strains and successive crises which prematurely aged him.

In *Richard II* Henry's character is reserved, not yet developed: evidently Shakespeare had the whole cycle in mind, was planning forward, as we saw with the Sonnets. There are distinct touches of the contemporary Essex in Henry's courtship of the people as Bolingbroke. The latter's popularity was a strong weapon in his hand against Richard; Queen Elizabeth was well aware of the threat Essex's cult of popularity (Bacon warned him against it) implied for her. Shakespeare's friend and saviour was becoming Essex's foremost follower; this may have posed a problem in loyalties for the dramatist. Giving himself wholly to the theatre, he was well out of the pressure of events, on the sideline. His intellectual sympathies were all with order and authority; he must have seen what Essex was up to and

> Observed his courtship to the common people;
> How he did seem to dive into their hearts
> With humble and familiar courtesy,
> What reverence he did throw away on slaves,
> Wooing poor craftsmen with the craft of smiles. . .

Of revealing personal touches we need only mention the favourable notice taken of bowls – as again shortly after in *King John* – and the extended reference to the exit of a well-graced actor. One of Bolingbroke's complaints against Richard's low-born minions was that they had torn down his coat-of-arms and razed out his *imprese*,

> leaving me no sign,
> Save men's opinions and my living blood,
> To show the world I am a gentleman.

We have seen the importance William Shakespeare attached to that for himself; the Sonnets betray his sensitiveness about his reputation. 'As I am a gentleman' is a phrase very frequent in the plays: he would shortly take steps to place his gentility beyond question.

During these five years before the building of the Globe, from 1594 to 1599, the Chamberlain's Men played mostly at the Theatre, but occasionally also at the Curtain, the Cross Keys inn in Gracechurch Street, and – it may be inferred – at the newly built Swan on Bankside, besides their regular performances at Court, wherever it might be, Whitehall, Greenwich, or Richmond. There was quite a lot of moving about, apart from touring, as yet again in 1597. All this added to the work of the actors, learning their parts and rehearsing in different places, still more for the actor-dramatist having to write and produce the plays too. We do not hear of him as receiver for Court-performances again: he can have had little time for anything except his work.

Shakespeare was residing conveniently for it in the parish of St Helen, Bishopsgate, where he was rated for tax. Bishopsgate Street led through the gate in the City Wall, across the Ditch out to the fields of Shoreditch where the Theatre and Curtain stood. Immediately to the left one passed the church of St Botolph, where Emilia Lanier's parents were buried. Behind it was a quadrangle Petty France, into which foreigners had crowded and built up their tenements. Others of the Bassano clan lived further along in the parish of St Leonard, Shoreditch, where their names appear in the registers. Within the gate, turning round and going down Bishopsgate into the City was Crosby Place, familiar to everyone as Richard III's residence whence he executed his *coup d'état* in 1483 – Shakespeare needed no reminder, passing it frequently, and of course it appears in the play. Below Crosby Place Bishopsgate Street became Gracechurch Street, with the Cross Keys inn for occasional playing. His parish church was the fine former priory church of St Helen, crowded with the monuments that always attracted his attention.

In this parish there lived at this time the brilliant and attractive composer, Thomas Morley.* He and Shakespeare may have known each other, for Morley is almost the only composer of the time whom we know to have set one of the songs – 'It was a lover and his lass', and perhaps 'O mistress mine'. Incidentally, we should observe that a number of musical compositions were dedicated to Lord Chamberlain Hunsdon, so that Emilia Bassano's accomplishment on the virginals may have offered an additional attraction to him, as evidently to Shakespeare.

In 1596 Shakespeare was assessed for tax at the formal valuation of £5 – this was a common rating for middle-class people with no substantial holding in the parish. It was the same rating that Simon Forman, astrologer and doctor, enjoyed lower down near the river in St Botolph's, Billingsgate. Shakespeare was assessed to pay 5*s*, and next year 13*s* 4*d* – the same assessment as Forman's. Shakespeare did not pay, and his name was entered on the list of defaulters. He had moved away across the river to Southwark, whence he ultimately paid up from the Liberty of the Clink. This is where Francis Langley had built his new theatre of the Swan, of which we have a drawing of the interior, whence much of our visual picture of Elizabethan staging comes.

The Chamberlain's men may have acted here for a time, for a legal document shows one William Wayte asking surety of the peace against Francis Langley, William Shakespeare and a couple of unknown women. This kind of document is very common,

* cf. my *The Elizabethan Renaissance: the Cultural Achievement*, p. 102.

and rather a matter of form – Langley and Wayte, a disagreeable customer, had previously quarrelled: it had no sequel and no importance. All that it shows is that Shakespeare knew Langley, a respectable citizen who was a member of the Drapers' Company, had purchased the manor of Paris Garden in Southwark and built the Swan. Thither Shakespeare had moved, and that is all. A volume of conjecture has been built upon it: without value.

Shakespeare had family matters to occupy him in this year 1596. His only son Hamnet died in August, and was buried at Stratford on the eleventh of the month, a sad Wednesday for the family. With the boy of eleven perished Shakespeare's hope of perpetuating the family in his name. Going home to Warwickshire each summer, he would surely be at Stratford during his child's illness. Knowing the way of writers as we do, it is not possible that he was not thinking of his boy in the grieving lines in the play he was writing at the time, *King John*:

> Grief fills the room up of my absent child,
> Lies in his bed, walks up and down with me,
> Puts on his pretty looks, repeats his words,
> Remembers me of all his gracious parts,
> Stuffs out his vacant garments with his form. . . .

And then,

> I have heard you say
> That we shall see and know our friends in heaven:
> If that be true, I shall see my boy again. . . .

This check to his hopes of founding a family – he can hardly have expected his wife to breed again, eleven years since the twins, and now over forty – did not prevent him from carrying out the long-cherished wish of obtaining a coat-of-arms. It was sued out in John Shakespeare's name – his son would have the satisfaction of having been born a gentleman; no doubt he presented the case and paid the cash. The grant from Garter King of Arms, William Dethick, recited – what is otherwise unknown – that John Shakespeare's 'late grandfather for his faithful and valiant service' was advanced and rewarded by Henry VII. Was some imaginative person drawing the long bow? It is not impossible that Shakespeare's great-grandfather served at Bosworth Field; but we do not know. Then 'the said John hath married the daughter and one of the heirs of Robert Arden of Wilmcote in the said county, esquire'. But Robert Arden had never been an esquire; someone here is telling a tall tale – even if it remains likely enough that he went back to the Ardens of Park Hall. It was William Shakespeare who, by his own efforts, became the 'gentleman'.

There follow the familiar coat-of-arms, the silver spear across a field of gold, the crest of a falcon spreading its wings, and the proud claim: 'Non sanz droict.' But William Shakespeare was still not satisfied: three years later there was a request to impale the arms of Arden with those of Shakespeare. Evidently it was the Arden descent and name that he valued. Later on Dethick was criticised by a rival for granting the Shakespeare coat – without reason, as it turned out: just heralds' little ways. And so we come to see the arms proudly displayed on the monument at Stratford.

King John has affinities with *Richard II*, and E. K. Chambers also adduces 'close phrasal echoes' with *The Merchant of Venice:* we shall not be wrong in placing it between those two. The reference to the Armada 'scattered and disjoined' by tempest relates to the second Armada, which was dispersed by storms in the Bay of Biscay in the autumn of 1596.

What reveals Shakespeare significantly is the way in which he departs from Protestant propaganda about King John, as depicted in the rant of Bale and in the earlier play, *The Troublesome Reign*. In these King John was a Protestant hero in combat with the Papacy. Shakespeare is above all that; indeed, to him John was no hero at all: the real hero is his creation, the Bastard Faulconbridge, who has the spirit of Richard Coeur-de-Lion. In place of religion, which divided people, we have patriotism, which united them – as it did at that time, when there was every reason to be proud of the achievements of the country. It is obvious that people cannot understand or appreciate that today, for the worst of reasons. The last time that love of one's country could and did inspire to heroic efforts was during the unforgettable years 1940 to 1945, when the England that came down to us from the Elizabethan age, with all her achievements, came to an end.

The references to contemporary events relate the play to 1596; the blow of Henri IV's conversion, the question whether his word could be relied on, whether the alliance with France against Spain would hold. (It did not: France made peace in 1598, leaving the English and the Dutch to fight on.) Shakespeare's insight into the world of politics and the considerations that prevail there – quite beyond any other dramatists – is expressed in the Bastard's classic speech on Commodity, i.e. Expediency. This alone is of a maturity to make the suggestion that *King John* is an early play absurd. The expedition to Cadiz that autumn, of which Essex reaped all the glory, is referred to in

> a braver choice of dauntless spirits
> Than now the English bottoms have waft o'er
> Did never float upon the swelling tide,
> To do offence and scath in Christendom.

Though not an inspired play like *Richard II*, *King John* had a fine, bravura part for Burbage in the Bastard; a contrasting part in his legitimate brother, lean and thin-faced – a caricature-part that appears again and again, with Justice Silence, Slender, Aguecheek. It is thought that these were taken by the skinny Sinkler (or Sinclair). There were parts for four boys; with his bent for kingly parts, and his leading position in the Company, perhaps Shakespeare himself played King John. Once more, as so often, the theatre itself supplies an image: the men of Angers 'stand securely on their battlements, as in a theatre'.

Early in the year 1596 Calais had been besieged by the brilliant Parma, making a dash from the Netherlands. A powerful fleet was formed at Dover to go to the rescue, and among the young courtiers who hoped to see service was Southampton. He went down, to be received by Lord Admiral Howard on board his flagship, as befitting his rank. Then came the Queen's command that he, and two other young peers, Derby and Mountjoy, should not go – the reason being that they had as yet no heirs: she would not have their peerages extinguished. Then Calais fell. The objective of the expedition was changed to Cadiz, where it achieved the most brilliant exploit of the war with the capture of the city. Essex, with his unfailing appeal, won all the popularity – even, chivalrously, in Spain. Southampton had had to chafe at home.

Two Spanish flagships were captured at Cadiz, one of them the galleon *St Andrew*. There is a reflection of this in *The Merchant of Venice* this winter:

> I should think of shallows and of flats,
> And see my wealthy *Andrew* docked in sand,
> Vailing her high-top lower than her ribs. . . .

The play is a last dramatic tribute to the influence of Marlowe, for the character of Shylock was suggested by Barabas and the core of the play by *The Jew of Malta*. The Lopez affair in 1594 had led to a revival of Marlowe's play: it was performed no less than fifteen times between the trial and the end of the year. Since it belonged to the Admiral's Men and brought in good takings, it was natural that the Chamberlain's Men should expect to take advantage too. One sees what a motive it was with Shakespeare to pit himself against a pacemaker, as Ben Jonson said, outshining first Lyly, then Kyd, then Marlowe. Perhaps Greene had sensed this powerful competitiveness?

Everyone appreciated that the heart of the play was the character and situation of Shylock: it was frequently referred to as *The Jew of Venice*. And that the point of departure was the Lopez affair is obvious from the passage about the Wolf that was hanged – the audience would recognise the reference (Wolf = *Lupus*, Lopez). When Shakespeare took up the character, he began with the common Elizabethan conception of the Jew; but shortly his dramatic intuition flowered into human understanding – or his humanity deepened the drama – and one gets the note of human sympathy so different from the unripened Marlowe: 'Hath not a Jew eyes? hath not a Jew hands, organs, dimensions, senses, affections, passions?' We may take this as Shakespeare's comment on the condemnation of Lopez – for which Essex had been responsible. This lets us into the ambivalence of the dramatist's situation, the tensions the politics of the time aroused, the closeness of observation that contributed so much to his understanding of politics – and also the inestimable advantage, for a prudent man, of being independent.

Shakespeare is not interested in the intellectual issues which engaged Marlowe's formally educated mind and exposed him, unwise and young, to danger. Shakespeare, wiser about people and more sceptical, saw that

In religion,
What damnèd error, but some sober brow
Will bless it, and approve it with a text . . .?

We see a glimpse of his own experience, too, in the rueful observation:

All things that are
Are with more spirit chasèd than enjoyed.

Here, as everywhere, there is his passionate love of music – another contrast with Marlowe – in the famous lines condemning

The man that hath no music in himself,
Nor is not moved with concord of sweet sounds. . . .

We know that Emilia's playing on the virginals was one of the arts by which he had been ensnared.

With these plays Shakespeare was achieving regular and continuous success in London. More than that, the Lord Chamberlain's Company in which he had invested everything, to which he had mortgaged his future, was establishing its ascendancy. This gave him the security he had long looked for, and never before enjoyed; his response was the wonderful creative flow which his earlier work had intimated and promised but was only fully released from 1594 onwards.

Taking out a coat-of-arms – he was the first of his profession to do so – was an outward and visible sign of success and confidence. It would not be lost on Elizabethans – far more important in their eyes than ours! It was immediately followed up by a suitable residence for an armigerous gentleman, the finest house in his native town: New Place. This was in the best part of Stratford, where the well-to-do lived, just across from the Chapel and School he had attended as a boy. The house had been built by Hugh Clopton, the leading townsman who had made money in London in the previous century. It stood well back from Chapel Street, with a little forecourt; in front a gallery and servants' accommodation, behind a three-storey house of five gables. Really rather grand – a marked translation from Henley Street!

Shakespeare bought it from William Underhill, in trouble for his Catholic recusancy, for only £60; so there may have been a mortgage on it, or Underhill owed him money. It was in need of repair, for Shakespeare sold the town a load of stone next year. Two barns, and two orchards and gardens went with the property. A few years later, in 1602, he bought a cottage and garden on the other side of Chapel Lane. The family must have settled in in 1597, for early next year a town-survey shows him as holding ten quarters of malt – a supply for a large household. 'Mrs Shakespeare no doubt looked after the brewing at New Place, and her daughters were soon old enough to help.'* Leading townsmen traded in malt, and in early 1604 some twenty bushels were sold to a neighbour, who also borrowed a small sum. Since he did not pay up, the increasingly well-to-do dramatist – more careful about money than his father – put his neighbour, Rogers the apothecary, through the court of record and collected it.

He was already thinking of making a permanent investment in land in Stratford, the proper equipment for his new status and the

* Mark Eccles, *Shakespeare in Warwickshire*, p. 91.

regular foundation of economic independence. For Lawyer Sturley, agent of the Lucys out at Charlecote, wrote to Richard Quiney in the New Year, then in London, what he had gathered from Quiney's father: 'it seemeth by him that our countryman [i.e. fellow Warwickshireman], Master Shakespeare, is willing to disburse some money upon some odd yard-land or other at Shottery or near about us. He [Quiney's father] thinketh it a very fit pattern to move him [Shakespeare] to deal in the matter of our tithes. By the instructions you can give him thereof and by the friends he can make therefore, we think it a fair mark for him to shoot at and not impossible to hit. It obtained would advance him indeed and would do us much good.'* Sturley followed this up with several sentences in Latin asking him to urge Shakespeare in the matter, for it was of importance to the town and would bring him honour and praise.

It is a most revealing letter – apart from the fact that it shows these two products of Stratford Grammar School conversing easily in Latin. Richard Quiney was in London on the town's business that Christmas and had had a meeting with Shakespeare, very busy, for this was the season for performance at Court: the Company were playing there on 26 December 1597, 1 and 6 January 1598, and again on 26 February. His fellow-townsmen – regarding him respectfully as Master Shakespeare, and knowing his grand London associations – were anxious to advance his interests at home as a landed gentleman, and do the town a good turn by getting a local man to make a purchase in the tithes.

But John Shakespeare's son was a prudent man where money was concerned; he 'did not draw his bow at a venture'. It was not until 1602 that he made his purchase of land, 107 acres of the best in Old Stratford, and in 1605 a moiety of the tithes in the villages round about. And that made him independent – even of the theatre.

Meanwhile, in the autumn of 1598, Richard Quiney was again in London on the town's business, stopping as usual at the Bell in Carter Lane, near St Paul's. Finding himself short of cash, he addressed himself to Shakespeare: 'Loving Countryman. I am bold

* E. I. Fripp, *Master Richard Quyny*, pp 124, 137–8.

of you as of a friend, craving your help with £30 upon Master Bushell's and my security, or Master Mytton's with me. . . .You shall friend me much in helping me out of all the debts I owe in London. You shall neither lose credit nor money by me, the Lord willing. And now but persuade yourself so, as I hope, and you shall not need to fear; but with all hearty thankfulness I will hold my time and content your friend [i.e. in case Shakespeare needed to raise the cash from another], and if we bargain farther, you shall be the paymaster yourself. My time bids me hasten to an end, and so I commit this to your case and hope of your help.'

I detect a note of dubiety on Quiney's part whether he was going to succeed in raising any cash from his loving countryman. He may not even have dispatched the letter, for all the urgency of its tone, since it fetched up among his own papers later. My suspicion is strengthened by what Sturley replied to Quiney about the proposition 'that our countryman, Master William Shakespeare, would procure us money: which I will like of as I shall hear when, where, and how. And I pray let not go that occasion, if it may sort to any indifferent conditions' (i.e. agree with impartial terms).

The consequences of his father's improvidence had indeed been brought home again at this very time. In 1597 John Shakespeare was able to offer the Lamberts – Mary Arden's sister and son – the £40 for which he had mortgaged part of his wife's inheritance at Wilmcote. No doubt the money was William Shakespeare's. But the Lamberts were not giving up: John Shakespeare had not tendered the money when due, and now the land was worth more. The inheritance was permanently lost to Mary Arden's son: in 1602 it was sold. So William Shakespeare had to look elsewhere than the old family property: it was in this year that he made his considerable purchase in Old Stratford.

In London this year he reached the peak of his achievement in the *genre* of English history-play with the two plays on *Henry IV*. What we must notice is that they form the keystone of a grand overarching design: they follow upon *Richard II*, while *Henry V* followed upon them and linked up with the three plays on *Henry VI*.

Which oft our stage hath shown; and, for their sake,
In your fair minds let this acceptance take.

He himself spoke as Chorus what he had penned at the end of *Henry V*. There is again this evidence of a forward-reaching ambitious mind, planning ahead in his work – as we have seen with regard to his establishment at Stratford.

One more evidence of this forward planning is the character of Prince Hal and his transition to kingship as Henry V – the way the transformation is prepared beforehand, his wildness accounted for and dignity saved, in spite of the bad company he keeps and the pranks he engaged in. This has bothered generations of literary critics, Victorian and later, who have not understood the dramatic logic any more than the historical necessity of it. Their trouble is anachronistic: they do not understand the medieval conception of kingship, the exigencies imposed and expectations to be fulfilled. Nor do they appear to know that to the Elizabethans Henry V was a hero: hence, in part, the different character and tone of the play.

I have said what I have to say about these historical plays, in some detail, in *William Shakespeare*; here I have something new to add. It has only recently been made clear that Shakespeare was far closer to the truth about Henry V than any of us realised. K. B. McFarlane probably knew more about fifteenth-century England than any historian has ever done, the leading authority on it in our time. He tells us now that, after Henry's early death, 'memories of his wild youth came to replace the full story of his devotion to duty and hard work. It was on these memories that Shakespeare built. They were up to a point accurate memories. Disbelieved by Victorian scholars, they have been proved to have contemporary support. In contrast to his self-discipline and single-mindedness as king, his youth had had its disorders as well as its achievements. That with some wild friends he had lain in wait and robbed his own receivers, that he attracted to himself low and riotous company, that if not dissolute himself he was far from chaste, and that William Gascoigne, the Chief Justice, had then so far offended him as to be dismissed at the beginning of his reign, can now hardly be doubted

The interest lies in the suddenness and completeness of the reformation at his father's death.'*

In fact, the night of his father's death and of his accession to the throne, when he spent the whole night in confession and consultation alone with the anchorite in Westminster Abbey, Henry underwent a conversion. He was a medieval man, not a modern. He *had* to send Falstaff and his crew packing: generations of unhistorical sentimentalists about Falstaff have not grasped the point. McFarlane, the least sentimental of historians, says simply of Henry V as king, 'take him all round and he was, I think, the greatest man that ever ruled England'.

As an historical scholar McFarlane was a technical medievalist. But he thought that the medieval chroniclers were not to be compared with Shakespeare as historians, for historians are capable of interpreting what they find. 'That is what we mean by calling them historians rather than chroniclers. *Shakespeare was by far the greatest of them*. He accepted much from Hall and Holinshed, but he brought to his work a power which they lacked and one essential to a great historian: whereas Hall's kings and statesmen are scarcely even two-dimensional, some at least of Shakespeare's are *alive*.'†

The wholeheartedness and complete conviction of this tribute to Shakespeare as an historian from such an academic source is impressive – and it goes as much for Shakespeare's understanding of Richard III as of Henry V. It puts the proper appreciation of this sequence of plays in historical perspective; the least that must be said is – what I have urged all along – that they cannot be properly grasped without historical understanding.

It remains only to elicit the personal points that reveal him and the topical references that recall the circumstances of the time. The part of Falstaff would have been taken by Will Kemp, and that was the popular hit of these plays, the character that has made their fame ever since. We have mentioned that the name had been changed from Oldcastle because the Cobhams objected to their

* K. B. McFarlane, *Lancastrian Kings and Lollard Knights*, pp. 123, 133.
† Ibid, p. 6.

(collateral) ancestor appearing as a buffoon on the stage. But there was more to it than that: the Cobhams were politically allied to Robert Cecil and Ralegh, to whom Essex and Southampton were bitterly opposed. So that this uproarious portrayal, which would carry overtones to an Elizabethan audience, came out of the enemy's camp. Falstaff may have meant something special in the Essex circle; for next year, when Essex wrote that some maid-of-honour was marrying 'Sir John Falstaff', it was apparently a joke on Cobham, who *was* a buffoon. A year later, when Southampton had at length been caught by his maid-of-honour and was made by Essex to marry her (she was his cousin), she wrote to Southampton in Ireland: 'all the news I can send you that I think will make you merry is that I read in a letter from London that Sir John Falstaff is by his mistress, Dame Pintpot, made father of a goodly miller's thumb, a boy that's all head and very little body; but this is a secret'. Evidently their dramatist's creation of Falstaff was a favourite, and meant something special to them.

There are few country images in these plays: they are dominated by the life of the Court – of which Shakespeare was a close observer from many performances there – and of the City, where he resided and had more familiar acquaintances. The renderings of London life, the scenes at the Boar's Head in East Cheapside, characters like Hostess Quickly and Doll Tearsheet, the talk of the carriers – 'I have a gammon of bacon and two razes of ginger to be delivered as far as Charing Cross': it is all quite Dickensian. Evidently London life had grown on him in the years there, and he had a sharp eye for the humours and characters of the town. The endearments of Falstaff and Doll Tearsheet are convincing and even moving: the author was well acquainted with the ways of such. 'Come, I'll be friends with thee, Jack: thou art going to the wars; and whether I shall ever see thee again or no, there is nobody cares.' But to Ensign Pistol: 'You, a captain, you slave! For what? for tearing a poor whore's ruff in a bawdy-house?' And then Falstaff, the old rogue: 'Come: it grows late; we'll to bed. Thou'lt forget me when I am gone.'

All the same, his home neighbourhood is given a good show, as in

Henry VI. There are the nostalgic scenes at Justice Shallow's house in the Cotswolds, with his senile reminiscences of life as a gay lad at Clement's Inn. 'There was I, and little John Doit of Staffordshire . . . and Will Squeal, a Cotswold man.' We have 'the red-nosed innkeeper of Daventry', and Hinkley Fair; and old Puff of Barson, i.e. Barcheston, where the Sheldon tapestries were made. A great deal of Warwickshire is there. And perhaps Stratford, too. We have seen that Shakespeare was building, or making repairs, at New Place this year. Very well, everything was grist to his mill; there are two extended passages about building:

> When we mean to build,
> We first survey the plot, then draw the model;
> And when we see the figure of the house,
> Then must we rate the cost of the erection;
> Which if we find outweighs ability,
> What do we then but draw anew the model
> In fewer offices, or at last desist
> To build at all?

Again, repetitively, we

> Question surveyors, know our own estate,
> How able such a work to undergo . . . .
> We fortify in paper and in figures. . . .

It betrays no very intimate knowledge of the operations – just such an acquaintance as a newly become householder might have who is much away from home.

At the end of the second *Henry IV* play there is an Epilogue, with a very personal note. It was evidently spoken by Shakespeare, and has his characteristic propitiation of the audience – so unlike Ben Jonson. 'First my fear, then my curtsy, last my speech. My fear is your displeasure; my curtsy, my duty; and my speech, to beg your pardons. If you look for a good speech now, you undo me; for what I have to say is of mine own making.' He had no need to fear, with the prodigious success of Falstaff, and would have had none really – all that was polite obsequiousness. But there was something behind it: 'I was lately here in the end of a displeasing play, to pray your patience for it and to promise you a better.' Could that have been one which he had sponsored, and was now apologising for? 'I meant, indeed, to pay you with this. . . . Here I promised you I would be, and here I commit my body to your mercies. . . . Then he knelt down to pray for the Queen.

'One more word, I beseech you. If you be not too much cloyed with fat meat, our humble author will continue the story, with Sir John in it, and make you merry with fair Katherine of France. Where, for anything I know, Falstaff shall die of a sweat – unless already a' be killed with your hard opinions. For Oldcastle died a martyr, and this is not the man.'

Then a final, irresistible plea for sympathy – had he played the part of Henry, or Prince Hal? 'My tongue is weary; when my legs are too [for the play was followed by dancing a jig] I will bid you good night.'

What a man! how hard he must have lived and worked! It is riveting: here we have him in the flesh.

His established position with the public is now beginning to be reflected in the demand for versions of the plays in print – any version that could be got hold of rather than none at all. Hence the crude texts of the plays put together – without with your leave or by your leave – from what odd actors or auditors remembered: hence the long succession of Bad Quartos, which have provided employment for so many textual scholars. These were sometimes, not always, replaced by a better text – the Good Quartos – issued from within the Company, for the plays were the Company's property, and occasionally a text which came close to the author's manuscript. It is further evidence of how hard-driven a man he was that he seems to have had little time to bother with printed texts of his plays. In any case, the play itself on the stage was the thing: everything went into that and writing and producing it.

The position with regard to copyright was different in those days:

if a publisher got hold of a manuscript and published it, the author had no remedy – except to publish a better version. This was done with *Romeo and Juliet*, of which Cuthbert Burby produced a poor version assembled from memory in 1597; this was followed by a good one, 'newly corrected, augmented and amended', evidently from within the Company. This same year Andrew Wise printed a good text of the ever-popular *Richard III*. Wise also issued a good text of *1 Henry IV*, close on the heels of its performance; since the naughty Burby had got hold of a bad text of *Love's Labour's Lost*, it was offset by a good one also 'newly corrected, augmented and amended'. These issues gave opportunity for revision and improvements; the important point here is that there was a reading public avid for the plays, though the dramatist had little or no time to attend to it.

In this year 1598 there appears upon our stage a striking and formidable personality henceforth to be important in Shakespeare's story: Ben Jonson. Born in 1572, he was eight years younger. Of Border stock and of Border fighting qualities – for a time he was a soldier – he transmitted his aggressiveness to literature and the theatre, which resounded with his affrays. In complete contrast with the courtly suavity of the 'gentle' (i.e. gentlemanly) Shakespeare, who was all intuition and imagination – and a cleverer man into the bargain – Ben had the intellectualist and dogmatic bent of his Scotch ancestry. Fortunately, he had genius to mitigate it.

Ben had come up the hard way too, his father having died before he was born; but he went to Westminster School and, though he could not go on to the university, he emerged with a scholarly, bookish bent. His stepfather apprenticed him to his own trade of bricklaying, which Ben hated. Upon his return from soldiering he drifted into acting, as Shakespeare had; never a good actor, he was better at instructing. A literary opponent, Dekker, depicted him in his early impoverished days: 'I have seen thy shoulders lapped in a player's old cast cloak. . . . Thou hast forgot how thou ambledst in a leather pilch [rug] by a play-wagon in the highway, and tookst mad Jeronimo's part, to get service among the mimics.' The appearance with the 'terrible mouth' and the face 'like a rotten russet apple when it is bruised' would be appropriate in such a part; his enemy did not mention the fine, luminous eyes which bespoke his intelligence.

Ben was first employed as a writer by Henslowe's rival company, but he remained independent to write for whom he chose. Shakespeare gave him his first big opportunity by accepting his first masterpiece, *Every Man in His Humour* and himself performing in it in this year 1598. We have the list of 'the principal comedians', valuable as the first extant list of the Chamberlain's Men. We have met them all, except Christopher Beeston and John Duke who left the Company together in 1602; they both lived in Shoreditch, where their children were baptised in St Leonard's.

Shakespeare took Ben's work under his wing, protected and advanced his interests – to be rewarded in time to come by an exceptional service after his death, from so rugged a type not much given to be beholden to anyone. He certainly needed it, for within a few days of the opening of his comedy, he killed the actor Gabriel Spencer in a duel and was lucky to escape the gallows; pleading benefit of clergy, i.e. as a literate person, he was branded on the offending thumb. In prison, to add further to his troubles, he became for a time a Catholic. When he came out, he wrote plays and satires for the boys' company, the Children of the Chapel, but he followed up with another masterpiece for the Chamberlain's Men, *Every Man out of His Humour*, in which Shakespeare did not act. Though Ben's quarrelsome temper made difficulties and for a time there was a breach with the Company, his two greatest comedies, *Volpone* and *The Alchemist*, were written for it, as also his marmoreal monuments of classicism, *Sejanus* and *Catiline*, to which the public did not take. However, Shakespeare did his best for his *protégé* and acted at least in *Sejanus*.

Evidently it was not possible to quarrel with William Shakespeare for long – a clever man in this too! All the more remarkable because Jonson did not really see eye to eye with him in professional matters, and made no bones about expressing it. There was a fundamental romanticism in Shakespeare's nature and imagination, which responded to and had been shaped by Sidney and

Spenser. These meant little to the new-comer, with the slant of a younger generation. Nor did he care for the earlier drama with its lack of classic rules – he positively detested *The Spanish Tragedy* he had had to act in and was paid to bring up to date. He had no respect for the public's judgment or taste, and was constantly flinging the fact in its face. Though he loved the man, William Shakespeare, and admired his genius 'this side idolatry', he was bothered by his unfailing instinct for what would go on the stage, contrary to his (Ben's) rules. A very positive and unsceptical intellect, he does not seem to have grasped that Shakespeare's plays had their own imaginative logic, their own aesthetic and intuitive decorum, even a successful classicism of their own kind – witness *Julius Caesar* and *Coriolanus* – which never failed, where Ben's never took wings. This bothered him, as their success irritated him.

His own genius was for satire, ridiculing the follies, manners and types of the age; he had a formidably critical intellect – which made him a favourite with the younger generation of intellectuals, which, wrong as usual, rated him above Shakespeare. In his heart of hearts, Jonson knew better, and in the end placed him with Aeschylus, Sophocles, Euripides – what more generous tribute could there be? But, then, Ben was a large-minded man, a genius himself, not without his own vein of romanticism and poetry. Besides, never forget, he loved the man.

This year 1598 brought back an earlier, and more touching, memory: the shadow of Marlowe. His *Hero and Leander* was at length published; Shakespeare's engaged, and engaging, mind was caught by it, as we can tell by no less than three references in the play he was writing at the time, *As You Like It*, and yet another in *Much Ado* which followed. We do not need to go into them again here, except to underline his knowledge of how Marlowe had come by his end in the little tavern at Deptford, and the moving tone of the reference to the 'dead shepherd' – the only time that a contemporary was mentioned in all his work.

There are unmistakable touches of the personal in *As You Like It*. The story came from Lodge's romance, *Rosalynde*, which he had dedicated to old Lord Hunsdon. But the magpie dramatist took a suggestion from Greene's *Orlando Furioso* in the scene of Orlando's hanging his love-poems on the trees in the forest. The forest is the Forest of Arden. But note that the theme wrought out in Arden was the gentility theme. Was this wholly unconscious? Orlando had been robbed of his proper inheritance, education as a gentleman, by his brother: 'my father charged you in his will to give me good education: you have trained me like a peasant, obscuring and hiding from me all gentlemanlike qualities.' When he takes to the Forest of Arden, he is followed by an old family-retainer, Adam; by an old tradition Shakespeare took that part.

We have a number of topical references to the voyages of the time, foreign travel and contemporary modes and manners. Jacques sums up the human condition in terms of the theatre – it must have been doubly effective glancing all round:

> All the world's a stage,
> And all the men and women merely players;
> They have their exits and their entrances;
> And one man in his time plays many parts. . . .

It is the Epilogue again that so bespeaks the author, with the easy confidence with which he plays with the audience: 'My way is to conjure you; and I'll begin with the women. I charge you, O women, for the love you bear to men, to like as much of this play as please you; and I charge you, O men, for the love you bear to women – as I perceive by your simpering, none of you hates them – that between you and the women the play may please.'

CHAPTER 9

At the Globe

BEFORE end the of 1598 the Chamberlain's Men were preparing a new move across the river to the more up-to-date and accessible theatre-area on Bankside – conveniently reached by London Bridge or the Thames wherries, which were the taxis of that day. Here the Admiral's Men had their permanent theatre, the Rose, while Shakespeare's temporary association with the Swan may have prepared the move. Land was leased near these two, but exceptional arrangements for ownership were made. One half was assigned to the Burbage brothers, to whom their father had left the old Theatre; the other half was shared among Shakespeare, Phillips, Pope, Heming and Kemp. When Kemp sold his share on leaving next year, Shakespeare came to own one-eighth of the new Globe. This unique arrangement gave added incentive to the leaders in the Company to pull together, for the greater part of the theatre-takings came to these actors themselves, who prospered by it. Thus the core of the Company held together; the Globe became the most famous of London theatres, the permanent public home where Shakespeare's plays were to be seen. To this there was added later the private Blackfriars theatre, while the favour of the Company at Court was maintained and increased with James's reign.

The Theatre in Shoreditch, which had served the Chamberlain's Men well, was demolished and the timbers taken across the Thames for use in building the new house of their maturity, with which their name would be for ever associated. Indeed, the Globe, with the proud challenge of its appropriate name – who thought of it? – marked the primacy the Chamberlain's Men had won. It was a large house, holding an audience of perhaps 2,000, packed in the pit open to the weather, while galleries in tiers all round sheltered those willing to pay more. A much larger stage than the average today jutted out into the pit, cellarage underneath for graves, ghosts, noises; stage entrances at the back, a curtained space for surprise or intimate scenes, a balcony above and a 'lords' room' for grandees – either could be used for musicians. In spite of the greater size, 'the bulk of the audience was nevertheless closer to the actors than in our present-day theatres'.* This 'made possible more intimate effects and more rapid transitions from mood to mood. . . . Since the Elizabethan public theatres used neither sets nor intermissions between scenes, cumulative effects from scene to scene were commonly attained to a degree that is impossible in our playhouses.'

These features gave Shakespeare 'three great assets unfamiliar in normal modern theatres: flexibility, speed, and intimacy of effect. Flexibility made possible the nineteen changes of scene in *Hamlet* with no greater degree or loss of concentration than if every scene had been written for the same background.' And think of the cumulative emotional effect, or – we should say – effects, for contrasts of mood were sharper, more dramatic. Elizabethan people were more demanding of excitement: they would never put up with the dissipation of effect we suffer from scene-shifting and intermissions, like the interrupted coitions that make American football so boring to an English spectator.

Until our time exact knowledge of Elizabethan theatre-conditions, production and staging had been largely lost; now that we have recovered it, it happily puts out of court a mass of Victorian (not only in a period-sense) commentary on Shakespeare's plays. We appreciate better today that 'he *thought* essentially in scenes. . . . Very early in his career – quite notably, in fact, in *Titus Andronicus* – Shakespeare obtained a brilliant command of the individual scene. Shakespeare works in "big" scenes (which, however, seldom tax the audience's attention for more than fifteen minutes) interspersed with scenes of relaxed tension.'† The gift was innate, but rendered

* Bentley, *Shakespeare: A Biographical Handbook*, pp. 132–4.

† J. I. M. Stewart, in *New Statesman*, 7 May 1972, reviewing E. Jones, *Scenic Form in Shakespeare*.

unfailing by professional practice: the complete man of the theatre always knew what would go.

The Globe was ready in time for *Henry V* in 1599. The Prologue refers to it, with the usual propitiation of the audience:

> But pardon, gentles all,
> The flat unraisèd spirits that hath dared
> On this unworthy scaffold to bring forth
> So great an object.

There is the characteristic self-depreciation, out of politeness, not to be taken literally: 'this unworthy scaffold' (he was probably proud of it), the 'flat unraisèd spirits' (that had written the play indeed!)

> Can this cockpit hold
> The vasty fields of France? or may we cram
> Within this wooden O the very casques
> That did affright the air at Agincourt?

– the wooden O being the Globe itself. He concludes:

> Admit me Chorus to this history;
> Who prologue-like your humble patience pray,
> Gently to hear, kindly to judge, our play.

It would seem that – Burbage playing Henry V – Shakespeare spoke the part of Chorus: an indispensable part in this play to link up the wide changes of location and time, which also sounds the personal note of the writer of the play:

> Vouchsafe to those that have not read the story,
> That I may prompt them; and of such as have,
> I humbly pray them to admit the excuse
> Of time, of numbers and due course of things,
> Which cannot in their huge and proper life
> Be here presented.

And here he speaks the Epilogue again, surely in his own person:

> Thus far, with rough and all-unable pen,
> Our bending author hath pursued the story,
> In little room confining mighty men,
> Mangling by starts the full course of their glory.

'Rough and all-unable pen'! – it is his signature-tune, reminding us of the Sonnets, himself 'a worthless boat' 'inferior far' to Marlowe, that 'able spirit', that 'worthier pen'. We must not assume that this is what he really thought: it was his gentlemanly way of putting it – in striking contrast to Ben Jonson. Nevertheless, he had always had underlying confidence, and by this time knew the score well enough.

The play particularly reflects the bellicose atmosphere and circumstances of the time. There was a real feeling of crisis about Ireland: Tyrone had organised in Ulster the most dangerous resistance the English had yet met with and inflicted a disaster upon the army at the Yellow Ford. The government was preparing the largest force ever sent there to retrieve the situation:

> The armourers, accomplishing the knights,
> With busy hammers closing rivets up,
> Give dreadful note of preparation. . . .

So too with the shipping: behold

> Upon the hempen tackle ship-boys climbing;
> Hear the shrill whistle . . .
> behold the threaden sails,
> Borne with the invisible and creeping wind,
> Draw the huge bottoms through the furrowed sea. . . .

Essex took command of the army; the populace, ever faithful to this *homme fatal*, poured forth out of the City to give him a grand send-off in March 1599.

> But now behold . . .
> How London doth pour out her citizens!
> The mayor and all his brethren in best sort,
> Like to the senators of the antique Rome,
> With the plebeians swarming at their heels,
> Go forth and fetch their conquering Caesar in. . . .

And so, with an immediate transition to Essex, who was accompanied by Southampton and many of his personal following –

> As by a lower but loving likelihood,
> Were now the General of our gracious Empress,
> As in good time he may, from Ireland coming,
> Bringing rebellion broachèd on his sword,
> How many would the peaceful city quit
> To welcome him!

Essex did nothing of the sort. He may have set out for Ireland like Henry V; he returned like Richard II, having accomplished nothing. Worse, having wasted the forces with which he had been equipped with much effort, in useless marches through the country, he ended with something like covert treason. Instead of coming to grips with Tyrone, he made a truce – and discussed with him the conditions of bringing in James of Scotland upon the Queen's demise.

With her, he wasted time and temper in a fruitless correspondence about Southampton. She had expressly vetoed him from being Lord General of Horse; when they arrived in Ireland, Essex used his authority as Lord Lieutenant to appoint him. The Queen: 'for the matter of Southampton, it is strange to us that this continuance or displacing should work so great an alteration in yourself, valuing our commandments as you ought. . . . We not only *not* allowed of your desire for him, but did expressly forbid it, being such a one whose counsel can be of little, and experience of less, use.' There was the Queen's opinion of Southampton; she added a tart reminder of his misdemeanour last year, in getting Elizabeth Vernon with child and marrying her at the last moment secretly for Essex's sake. 'Yea, such a one was, were he not lately fastened to yourself by an accident – wherein for our usage of ours we deserve thanks [she had sent him briefly to the Fleet, instead of to the Tower like Ralegh] – you would have used many of your old lively arguments against him for any such ability of commandment.'

That was that: Southampton was divested of his grand promotion as Essex's right-hand man, and served, gallantly enough, as a plain captain. The truth was that Essex was building up his own following in the hope of controlling the succession to the throne; and, when he held his quasi-treasonable discussion with the great rebel at a ford on the Ulster border, Southampton was with him. While the young Earl had been General, however, he promoted a tough fighting captain, Piers Edmonds, his Corporal-General. We learn of this officer, that 'he ate and drank at his table and lay in his tent. The Earl of Southampton would cull and hug him in his arms and play wantonly with him.' No doubt: war has its consolations no less than peace.

Meanwhile, from home his wife, very much in love with him, was writing him faithful love-letters, regretting that she had not produced a son, and relieved that he was not 'troubled for my not being as, I protest unto you, I infinitely desire to have been. . . . Though I be not now in that happy state, yet I doubt not that in good time God will bless me with bearing you as many boys as your own heart desires to have.' She made him a good wife, and in time to come their family-life was noted as exceptionally happy; but not until he had learned – spoiled as he had been by everybody – from adversity.

After Essex's hasty return from his humiliating fiasco in Ireland, he was placed under restraint at York House. Southampton and his wife went to keep open house at Essex House with the Earl's wife and sister, Penelope Rich (Sidney's Stella). When the ladies went into the country, Southampton, with young Rutland for company, passed their time 'merely in going to plays every day'. Among the plays to be seen this winter were *Henry V* and *Julius Caesar*, *As You Like It* and *Much Ado about Nothing*. Again in March 1600 we hear that 'all this week the Lords have been in London and passed away the time in feasting and plays'. Meanwhile, the Lord Chamberlain, the second Lord Hunsdon, was entertaining the Dutch envoy with his company's *Henry IV*.

Its dramatist, now at the peak of his production, was able to turn out plays with both hands: serious historical plays with one hand, comedies with the other. We have seen that, while writing *Henry V*, *Julius Caesar* was revolving in that forward-planning, crowding mind. With this play he 'turned to the great sequence of tragedies and virtually created our modern concept of what tragedy is'.*

We must resist the temptation to go into the play, but merely say that it reflects Shakespeare's increasing interest in political issues, the crucial issue of social order as against the (often unreal) plea for liberty – all displayed in the personal drama of Caesar as against Brutus. Shakespeare did his best to keep dramatic balance by writing Caesar down, emphasising his weaknesses, but there is no inner sympathy for a doctrinaire republican in the person of Brutus. The play was a success at the time and always has been since. Those are superficial critics who have not seen that the play has an essential unity, in spite of Caesar's death half-way through: his spirit dominates the rest of the play. As if Shakespeare didn't know far better how to write a play than any mere critics!

With the cycle of English history plays based on Holinshed virtually complete, Shakespeare now turned to Sir Thomas North's translation of Plutarch's Lives to open up new territory. North's prose was so good that Shakespeare could adapt whole passages easily into blank verse. He derived touches from elsewhere, Marlowe's translation of Lucan's *Pharsalia*, and Kyd's translation of Garnier's *Cornelia*. While writing Shakespeare was reading Daniel's *Musophilus*, a fine poem just out; for the dramatist adopts a thought from a stanza to become famous:

> And who, in time, knows whither we may vent
> The treasure of our tongue . . .
> To enrich unknowing nations with our stores?

* Gardner, *Religion and Literature*, p. 69

This becomes:

> How many ages hence
> Shall this our lofty scene be acted over
> In states unborn and accents yet unknown!

Everything transformable was grist to his mill – perhaps poor Greene had some inkling of that and what a formidable competitor the actor had it in him to become.

Certainly he did not cease to borrow the plumes of the intellectuals to set them off to better purpose. He was, of course, an intellectual himself, but with a better head. We notice what a reading man he was, in addition to everything else – this play has also an echo of Sir John Davies's philosophic poem, *Nosce Teipsum*, out that year. He was necessarily, though also by nature, a rapid reader, as he was a rapid writer – to Ben Jonson's disapproval, since Ben had to work hard at everything he accomplished.

This again irritated Ben, who jotted down in his note-book: 'Many times he fell into those things could not escape laughter – as when he said in the person of Caesar, one speaking to him, "Caesar, thou doest me wrong", he replied, "Caesar did never wrong but with just cause." And such-like: which were ridiculous.' In his play, *The Staple of News*, Ben ridiculed this little lapse; by the time the Folio came out someone had emended it. Some lines of Mark Antony are turned into fustian in *Every Man Out of His Humour*; and Caesar's too-famous last words, 'Et tu, Brute', are made nonsense of. A speech of Antony is further poked fun at in *Cynthia's Revels*. Ben could not leave *Julius Caesar* alone: its success, against *his* classic rules, irked him.

Once more we have Shakespeare's exposure of the mob, never more effectively than when their gullibility is made the subject of a whole scene in Mark Antony's trumping by mob-oratory of Brutus's absurd appeal to their (non-existent) reason. Shakespeare always writes of the people with friendly contempt – until he turns to unfriendly contempt in *Coriolanus*. The interesting thing psychologically is that the people themselves do not resent it, any more than Elizabethan audiences did; perhaps they recognise its truth: only intellectual liberals resent it on their behalf. We have a familiar image from his habitual environment: 'if the tag-rag people did not clap him and hiss him according as he pleased and displeased them, as they used to do players in the theatre, I am no true man'.

There are more affecting personal touches:

> When love begins to sicken and decay,
> It useth an enforcèd ceremony

– clearly goes back to the experience exposed in the Sonnets. As also the resigned note in:

> A friend should bear his friend's infirmities. . . .

Again, there is the note of absolute personal conviction in the famous lines:

> Men at some time are masters of their fates:
> The fault, dear Brutus, is not in our stars,
> But in ourselves, that we are underlings.

Just as *Julius Caesar* followed *Henry V*, so the double-minded dramatist followed *As You Like It* with *Much Ado about Nothing*, in 1599, before Will Kemp left the Company. In the Quarto of this play, based on Shakespeare's manuscript, the headborough and constable, Dogberry and Verges, are given the names of the actors Kemp and Cowley, who took the parts. Jack Wilson is given as the name of the singer who sang the lovely 'Sigh no more, ladies'. R. B. McKerrow comments, 'Dogberry and Verges were so life-like because they were not merely a constable and a watchman in the abstract, but actually Kemp and Cowley whose every accent and gesture Shakespeare must have known, *playing* a constable and a watchman.' Of course, and this goes for other parts in the plays, all of them related to the capabilities of the actors, and the resources of the company. For the dramatist never wrote in the abstract. Aubrey reports the rumour that 'Ben Jonson and he did gather humours of men daily wherever they came', and then 'the humour of the constable . . . he happened to take at Grendon [Long

Crendon] in Bucks, which is the road from London to Stratford, and there was living that constable about 1642, when I first came to Oxon'.

The situation of Essex at this time – cashiered, but maintaining his implicit challenge to the authority of the Queen – is glanced at in the reference to

> favourites,
> Made proud by princes, that advance their pride
> Against that power that bred it.

In that I think we see the dramatist's sympathy veering away from Essex, like that of most responsibly minded people. One senses there is personal feeling in this:

> my brother hath a daughter
> Almost the copy of my child that's dead. . .

and a thought so frequently repeated that we may call it Shakespearian:

> what we have we prize not to the worth
> Whiles we enjoy it, but being lacked and lost,
> Why, then we rack the value. . . .

It was in September of this year that a young Swiss doctor, Thomas Platter, saw a performance of *Julius Caesar* at the Globe, 'with a cast of some fifteen people. When the play was over, they danced very marvellously and gracefully together as is their wont, two dressed as men and two as women.'* He proceeds to give us our fullest contemporary description of the theatres. 'Thus daily at two in the afternoon, London has two, sometimes three plays running in different places, competing with each other, and those which play best obtain most spectators. The playhouses are so constructed that they play on a raised platform, so that everyone has a good view. There are different galleries and places where the seating is better and more comfortable. Whoever cares to stand below

* *Thomas Platter's Travels in England, 1599*, trans. C. Williams (1937), pp. 166–7.

pays one English penny, but if he wishes to sit he enters by another door and pays another penny; if he desires to sit in the most comfortable seats, which are cushioned, where he not only sees everything well but can also be seen, then he pays yet another English penny at another door.' This arrangement, with doors leading to different galleries, still operates at the seventeenth-century Sheldonian Theatre at Oxford. 'During the performance food and drink are carried round the audience. The actors are most expensively and elaborately costumed.' The theatres were becoming one of the attractions for foreign visitors to London.

Shakespeare's fame was now well established as the leading dramatist – there was no one to touch him. Quartos bad and good – memorial reconstructions put together or decent texts from the Company, close to the dramatist's manuscript – came out frequently to witness that he had a reading public for his plays. It may have given him more satisfaction to be recognised as a leading poet. Tributes from a younger generation appeared from such a charming poet as Richard Barnfield:

> And Shakespeare thou, whose honey-flowing vein,
> Pleasing the world, thy praises doth obtain.
> Whose *Venus* and whose *Lucrece*, sweet and chaste,
> Thy name in Fame's immortal book have placed.
> Live ever you, at least in fame live ever:
> Well may the body die, but fame dies never.

This comes as the *clou* of Barnfield's 'A Remembrance of Some English Poets', devoted appropriately to the four, Spenser, Daniel, Drayton, Shakespeare. Barnfield avowed himself a disciple of Shakespeare's poetry by numerous borrowings from his poems.

We have a number of contemporary tributes to these; perhaps one that Shakespeare would appreciate most came from an unexpected source, the admirable Jesuit poet, Robert Southwell, who had been executed in 1595:

> Still finest wits are stilling [distilling] Venus' rose.

Richard Carew, citing Shakespeare among the writers to be proud of in 'The Excellency of the English Tongue', compares him to Catullus. The Cambridge scholar, John Weever, has a tribute 'Ad Gulielmum Shakespeare' which virtually repeats Barnfield; but Weever's tutor, William Clovell, was in agreement with his pupil – as is not always the case: 'All praise-worthy Lucrecia. Sweet Shakespeare!' In fact, Shakespeare was markedly popular at Cambridge – not only among students but with dons – with the greater interest in what was topical and modern there than at Oxford.*

Since Francis Meres gave a list of Shakespeare's plays in his somewhat summary account of English writers to date, this passage has been discussed *ad nauseam*. What is more significant is that Shakespeare is the only writer to be mentioned in each section. Not only for the stage, though here he is described as the English Plautus and Seneca, 'the most excellent in both kinds', comedy and tragedy. He appears also among those who have greatly enriched and elaborated the language – true enough: the expansion of its vocabulary owed more to him than any other writer; it has been estimated that his is twice that of average English speech. Meres puts his works among the select company that will prove a perennial monument; he places him among the best lyric poets, and the most passionate love-poets.

This is always impressive, to go no further than 1599. In this year the publisher William Jaggard sought to recommend a miscellaneous volume he put out, *The Passionate Pilgrim*, as 'By W. Shakespeare'. He succeeded: two editions were at once called for, before somebody stopped it. Jaggard had got hold of a couple of Dark Lady sonnets, and added three more from *Love's Labour's Lost*, to help to make his book sell. In 1612 Jaggard, nothing daunted, brought out an expanded edition, using Shakespeare's name again and that of *Venus and Adonis*. Whatever the copyright position, there was no doubt of the appeal of the name.

All these tributes agree in regarding the poet as 'honey-tongued', 'sweet', and we hear of his 'sugared sonnets' circulating among his private friends. These epithets then had greater force – like the

* See my *The Elizabethan Renaissance: The Cultural Achievement*, pp. 11–12.

scent of musk and old damask-roses; after all, sugar was rather rare, and all the sweeter, even honey was stronger than the modern diluted variety out of a jar. These adjectives are consistent with the public conception of his personality as 'gentle', i.e. gentlemanly.

This was in some contrast with what they might expect, and got, from Ben Jonson, who did not hesitate to quip the master, when no one else did. The Chamberlain's men put on his next play, *Every Man Out of His Humour*, this year – a still more outrageous exposure of contemporary types and ways. It was bound to give offence – and in the event started the two-year theatre-war, between the public and private companies, which provided further spite to literary life, a favourite diet, and good sport to the wits about town. Shakespeare did not play in this piece. But it took notice of him – not ill-tempered, but it hit the mark. Ben has a scene making fun of taking out coats-of-arms and crests. And very good fun it is, at the expense of the Heralds' Office, and people putting down good money so that they can write themselves Gentleman, with a coat of a Boar's or possibly Bore's head, looking like 'Hog's Cheek and Puddings in a Pewter field'. For motto he suggests, 'Not without mustard', and for crest 'a frying pan had no fellow'. We remember that William Shakespeare's was, alliteratively, a falcon and his motto, somewhat boastfully, 'Not without right', in French.

The grandest tribute came from the Queen herself, evidently as much addicted to his plays as was Charles I. (His copy of Shakespeare's Plays still exists, with his appreciative markings.) Shakespeare had had to kill off Falstaff for the heroic *Henry V*, and the Queen – like readers of Dickens – wanted to see a favourite character again. She expressed her wish to see the fat knight in love, and the play written in a fortnight. No reason whatever to doubt the early tradition: the play was obviously fadged up in a hurry, mostly in prose, closing with a tribute to the Queen, and was written for a Garter Feast at Windsor on St George's Day, though we do not know in which year.

It incorporates some reminiscences of a visit a few years earlier by a German princeling, Count Mompelgart – 'Cousin Garmombles' of the play – who had not paid his bills and had been pestering the Queen ever since for the Order of the Garter. When he became Duke of Württemberg she gave it to him. There were several hits at Ralegh, not unkindly, for he was now restored to favour, passages taking off his obsession about gold in Guiana. There was another little jab at his friend Cobham – both were hostile to Essex and Southampton. To play the famous prank of shutting up Falstaff in the dirty-clothes' basket, Ford was disguised as Master Brooke – the Cobhams' family name. Nobody objected but the foolish Lord Cobham, and Shakespeare had to change the name to Broome.

There are any number of personal touches to fill out the play, some recognisable, others to which the key has been lost. The Cotswolds appear again: Slender asks, 'How does your fallow greyhound, sir? I heard he was outrun on Cotsall', evidently the old pronunciation of Cotswold. Bardolph is 'you Banbury cheese', which was made thin. Is there a reminiscence from Stratford days and youthful high spirits, in the attribution of the Lucys' coat of luces to Justice Shallow, and mispronounced 'louses' by the Welsh schoolmaster, Evans? (Shakespeare's schoolmaster had had a Welsh name.) There is a great deal of play about Ben Jonson's obsession with humours. Above all there is a lot of Windsor lore and familiarity with the places about: Datchet Mead and Frogmore, Herne's Oak in the Park, Eton and St George's Chapel.

Shakespeare knew it all well, from performances there. The play ends with the great bell of Windsor striking midnight, and

> Cricket, to Windsor chimneys shalt thou leap:
> Where fires thou find'st unraked and hearths unswept,
> There pinch the maids as blue as bilberry:
> Our radiant Queen hates sluts and sluttery. . . .
> Strew good luck, ouphes, on every sacred room;
> That it may stand till the perpetual doom,
> In state as wholesome as in state 'tis fit,
> Worthy the owner, and the owner it.

What could be closer?

. . .

Each play is a step in Shakespeare's career: in 1600 we come to one of the greatest with *Hamlet*. A perceptive critic has pointed out that we can discern three distinct stages in the development of the Elizabethan drama, each of them lasting roughly a decade.* In the 1580s there was the formal, rather rigid style, oratorical, with set speeches, set verse and simple, dominating themes – really rather primitive compared with what was to come. We may take Marlowe's *Tamburlaine* and Kyd's *Spanish Tragedy* as reaching the highest point in this line. In the 1590s the drama limbered up and became altogether more flexible and various, of more widely differing kinds, subtler characterisation, subtler verse. We may regard Shakespeare's comedies and histories as offering the best examples in these years when he had things – after Marlowe's death and until the rise of Jonson's star – much to himself.

The summit of Elizabethan drama is reached in the third decade, from about 1600. 'It was the time of nearly all the Elizabethan and Jacobean plays of the first rank – Shakespeare's major tragedies and dark comedies, Jonson's mature work, Chapman's and Tourneur's and Webster's tragedies – but it did not and could not last long.' In this it is like the crests of all artistic achievement, Attic tragedy or the marvellous peak of Haydn-Mozart-Beethoven, the French Impressionists or, in our day, the brief flowering of the silent film. On the threshold of this decade we meet one of its great masterpieces. Dramatically speaking, it is transitional, in itself spanning all three periods, harking back even to the first (to which its original belonged) as well as looking to the future: hence its extraordinary richness, its echoing fulness – and the feeling a lot of people have that all Shakespeare is in it.

We may safely disregard mountains of otiose commentary upon *Hamlet*, for the salutary reminder that it is but a play. And we must confine ourselves to revealing personal and topical touches. The Chamberlain's Men already possessed a *Hamlet*, a popular revenge-tragedy in the Kyd style. Thomas Lodge refers to it and 'the Ghost which cried so miserably at the Theatre, like an oyster-wife:

* Clifford Leech, *The John Fletcher Plays* (1962) pp. 26–29.

"Hamlet, revenge!"' Dekker refers to a *Hamlet's Revenge* at Paris Garden, which strengthens the likelihood that the Company had performed at the Swan at the time of the trouble between Wayte and Langley. Shakespeare took the old play and made something new and wonderful out of it – no wonder the predecessor did not survive. 'He transformed the "filthy, whining ghost" crying "Revenge" into the majestic, troubling, and questionable figure of Hamlet's father's ghost. No other dramatist has equalled him in presenting the awful visitation of madness, or in suggesting the degrading horror of witchcraft, or the destructiveness of malice.'*

When he embarked on *Hamlet*, *Julius Caesar* was still echoing in his mind – a whole passage refers back to it: it is clear that his mind was in continuous flow. And, just as there is the well-known salute to Essex in *Henry V*, so there are flecks of his personality in *Hamlet*:

> The courtier's, soldier's, scholar's, eye, tongue, sword;
> The expectancy and rose of the fair state. . . .
> The observed of all observers. . . .

We can see his situation reflected more specifically in

> His greatness weighed, his will is not his own;
> For he himself is subject to his birth;
> He may not, as unvalued persons do,
> Carve for himself; for on his choice depends
> The sanity and health of this whole state.

This was Essex's fortune and fate; his birth and the Queen's favour had raised him to a dangerous eminence and great expectations. He was locked in a political dilemma: he could neither go forward nor backward with safety; meanwhile the health of the state depended on him – and he was as psychotic as Hamlet.

* Gardner, *Religion and Literature*, p. 67.

Hamlet's uncle, the King, sums up:

> Madness in great ones must not unwatchèd go

and again:

> How dangerous is it that this man goes loose!
> Yet must not we put the strong law on him;
> He's loved of the distracted multitude,
> Who like not in their judgment but their eyes. . . .

This was precisely the Queen's dilemma with regard to Essex. He was dangerously popular; he had always courted the favour of the people, and was taking away that which she had earned by a lifetime of good government. He had had treasonable discussions as to what should take her place on her death – the sacred *arcana imperii* which could never be submitted to the people, so that her case against him went by default. On Essex's choice would depend the safety of the state: he was choosing wrongly and would try to overthrow it, with Southampton urging him on.

What is important for us is that the dramatist sees the whole situation – and is torn in two: hence the tension, the grandeur, the exceptional effort put into the play; as always, the most sensitive register of the time was responding to it. All along his sympathies had been with authority, the responsibility of government, maintaining social order. His mind and intellect were on this side. His personal associations were on the other. There is nothing more agonising for an intelligent man than to see his own friends, his own party, determined to run on the rocks. Francis Bacon saw it clearly too and, after warning Essex, prudently disengaged himself and passed over to the other side. Shakespeare, a mere player-playwright, on the side-lines of great events, wrote *Hamlet* and *Troilus and Cressida*.

The fact that the government was right did not mean that he liked the Cecils, Cobham or Ralegh; they were not his friends: Southampton was, up to the hilt with Essex in his staggering course. The late Lord Treasurer, prosy old Burghley – of whom Southampton had no kind memory – is clearly glanced at in the grave councillor, Polonius. Polonius had his wordly wise Precepts; those with which Burghley equipped his clever son Robert to succeed him are well known. Both are too long to cite here; but Burghley concludes with some words about popularity much to the point: 'Towards thy superiors, be humble, yet generous. With thine equals, familiar, yet respective. Towards thine inferiors show much humanity, and some familiarity: as to bow the body, stretch forth the hand, and to uncover the head, with such like popular compliments. . . . For right humanity takes such deep root in the minds of the multitude as they are easily gained by unprofitable courtesies than by churlish benefits. Yet I advise thee not to affect, or neglect, popularity too much. Seek not to be Essex; shun to be Ralegh.'

Whether Polonius was Burghley or no, Burghley was certainly a Polonius.

Meanwhile Jonson had set the town ringing with his invectives against his fellow-playwrights: Marston, actually an admirer at whom he had taken offence, and Dekker who had taken up the cudgels, or pen, on Marston's behalf. Ben, 'passionately angry, and passionately kind', pilloried them in a couple of satirical plays, performed by the boys' company at Blackfriars. Thus the theatre-warfare which raged during 1600–2 took on the character of a rivalry between the private theatre of the boys, and the public theatres of the men. The personal satire of the former appealed more to intellectuals and the fashionable; Jonson made the distinction between the new plays about 'humour', which appealed to the 'gentlemen', and 'the common sort, who cared not for't, but looked for good matter, they, and were not edified by such toys'. In *Cynthia's Revels* Jonson, who respected only an *élite*, if that, from the vantage-point of the private theatre, flouted at the 'common stages' and the 'common players'.

Shakespeare makes his comment on it in *Hamlet*: 'Faith, there has been much to-do on both sides. . . . There was for a while no money bid for argument, unless the poet and the player went to cuffs in the question. . . . O, there has been much throwing about of brains.' As for the boys, 'there is, sir, an eyrie of children, little eyases [note the bawdy pun], that cry out on the top of the question and are most tyrannically clapped for it. These are now the fashion, and so berattle the common stages – so they call them – that many wearing rapiers are afraid of goose quills and dare scarce come thither.' *The common stages – so they call them*: there is the old contempt in which the profession had been held and which he had done so much to correct – there is a trace of the old resentment too. He continues, 'what, are they children? Who maintains 'em? Will they pursue the quality no longer than they can sing? Will they not say afterwards – as it is most like, if their means are no better – their writers do them wrong to make them exclaim against their own succession?' *If their means are no better:* it recalls his own regret

> That did not better for my life provide
> Than public means which public manners breeds.

'Do the boys carry it away?' 'Ay, that they do . . . Hercules and his load too' – a comic gag for the Globe, with its sign of Hercules carrying it. It would survive; but the Chamberlain's Men would have to do something about the private theatre.

No play has more about the theatre and playing in it, including the best dramatic criticism of the age in Hamlet's instructions to the players. There is the use of a play, of the poisoning of Hamlet's father in the garden, to bring home Claudius's guilt, inset within the larger piece. There is Shakespeare's most impassioned declaration of the strangeness of the art, the psychological duplicity:

> Is it not monstrous that this player here,
> But in a fiction, in a dream of passion,
> Could force his soul so to his own conceit
> That from her working all his visage wanned,
> Tears in his eyes, distraction in's aspect,
> A broken voice, and his whole function suiting
> With forms to his conceit? and all for nothing!
> For Hecuba!
> What's Hecuba to him, or he to Hecuba,
> That he should weep for her? What would he do,

Had he the motive and the cue for passion
That I have?

But the extraordinary thing is that this, which has such sincerity and passionate conviction, is acting too, is just as much in inverted commas. Perhaps, after all, for Shakespeare – whose imagination was possessed by the sense of the thin line between being and seeming, appearance and reality – the theatre in the end was the real world.

By New Year 1601 Essex was reaching the end of his tether; there was no future for him now so long as the Queen lived, and if she died he was ready to raise insurrection. He was the leader to whom all the irresponsible and opposition elements looked – a motley crew of young peers, military men, and both Puritans and Papists: the extremes met in his unstable, neurotic personality. His followers were gathering round him in London for some move that was expected. James's envoys were on their way from Scotland: a threat to the state was implied by their collusion. On 3 February a final meeting was held at Southampton's lodgings at Drury House to decide on action: the Court at Whitehall was to be surprised, the two Earls to penetrate to the Queen and get her under restraint. When some drew back at this, Southampton demanded in passion, 'shall we resolve upon nothing then?' Next in rank, he was at Essex's right hand, egging him on.

The day before the outbreak into the City, a group of his closest followers dined together, Lord Monteagle, Sir Gelly Meyrick, Sir Joscelin and Sir Charles Percy and others, when Sir Charles proposed that they should cross the water to the Globe to see *Henry IV*. In order to put people in mind of the deposition of kings, they got the players to put *Richard II* on next day. After the outbreak Augustine Phillips was examined and said that his fellows had intended to play some other piece, 'holding that play of King Richard to be so old and so long out of use as that they should have small or no company at it'. So the conspirators offered an extra 40*s*, and the players performed it. It is remarkable that, if it were so out of use, they could perform it at such short notice – a tribute to the trained memory of the expert repertory company. Francis Bacon did not fail to make a point of this at the trial: 'neither was it casual, but a play bespoken by Meyrick'. The players were not held guilty in any way, and the matter was dismissed.

These bright sparks were addicts of the theatre, like Southampton, Rutland, Pembroke, Derby and so many others. The popularity of Shakespeare with them is attested by a letter from Sir Charles Percy from Dumbleton in Gloucestershire: 'if I stay here long in this fashion, at my return I think you will find me so dull that I shall be taken for Justice Silence or Justice Shallow'.

On the day of *Richard II*'s performance Essex, finding his way to Whitehall barred and the Court barricaded, broke out into the City hoping to cash in on his popularity with the mob. He was deceived, however, and retreated upon Essex House, shortly to surrender. At their subsequent trial in Westminster Hall, Southampton made a favourable impression, pleading his youth and being led away out of loyalty to his leader. He spoke eloquently and well, some people thought too plausibly. He was much pitied on account of his youth; he must have looked younger than he was, with his auburn hair flowing now over both shoulders and still only an incipient beard on his chin. In fact he was twenty-seven, but there was something of delayed adolescence about him. Both Earls were condemned to death.

Great interest was brought to bear to save the younger. We have the letters his mother wrote to Cecil, pleading that it was her son's despair of ever winning the Queen's favour that had brought him to such evil courses. Cecil took credit for saving the young Earl's life, though several were executed who were not more guilty than he, among them Sir Charles Danvers, brother of Southampton's boy-friend, Sir Henry. Southampton disappeared for the next two years into the Tower: we have the well-known portrait of him he had painted to celebrate his imprisonment. He looks older and thinner, a sadder and a wiser man; he is soberly but richly dressed, one arm resting on the window-sill of his comfortable apartment, a finely bound book with coronet and coat-of-arms at elbow. Inset is the Tower, with the somewhat arrogant inscription beneath, *In vinculis invictus* (i.e. in fetters unsubdued). Beside him – endearing feature – is his black-and-white cat: it is part of the Tower folklore that the cat found her way to him by coming down the chimney. If so, a further tribute to his charm and, perhaps, to his essential goodness of nature, that he was fond of cats.

As for the Queen, she had displayed a truly royal courage in the crisis, though it grieved her to the heart to have to execute the man who should have been a son to her. He admitted that she would never be safe if he lived. Later that year the Keeper of the Rolls at the Tower, the scholar William Lambarde, was presenting her with his account of them. She lighted on the reign of Richard II, and fired up, 'I am Richard II: know ye not that?' Lambarde deplored that such a wicked imagination had been attempted by 'the most adorned creature that ever your Majesty made'. Her Majesty: 'He that will forget God will also forget his benefactors. This tragedy was played forty times in open streets and houses.' This was a royal exaggeration, or perhaps what she had been told. But we have seen that Richard II meant something special in this circle; it is understandable that, so long as she lived and until James was safely on the throne, the deposition-scene had to be omitted from the play in print.

This was a time of sadness not only for the Queen but for her dramatist; it is in the air of all that he wrote, even in the comedy, *Twelfth Night*, or the queasy quasi-comedies, *All's Well That Ends Well* and *Measure for Measure*, let alone the bitterness and disillusionment of *Troilus and Cressida*. We must not make a simple transference from the circumstances of a writer's life to his work; all the same, these transpire.

In 1601 was published a garland of tributes to celebrate the long married happiness of Sir John Salusbury of Llewenny. (One of the family had been killed in the Essex affair, another was to perish for his part in Gunpowder Plot.) Sir John was an Esquire of the Body to the Queen, to whom he was kin; his wife was one of the Derby family. So it is not surprising that they were all dramatists who paid tribute – Shakespeare, Jonson, Chapman, Marston: someone rounded them up.

The subject was that of married happiness, a theme congenial to Shakespeare, and to the garland he contributed his exquisite poem, 'The Phoenix and the Turtle'. It is emblematic, rather than enigmatic, as has been often said; but, oddly, the whole tone is elegiac. It is a funeral poem: the birds have gathered together to sing the requiem of the chaste lovers united in death, the phoenix, a royal bird, and the humble dove, emblem of fidelity. When we read

> So they loved, as love in twain
> Had the essence but in one;
> Two distincts, division none:
> Number there in love was slain . . .

we remember, from the Sonnets:

> Let me confess that we two must be twain,
> Although our individed loves are one. . . .
> In our two loves there is but one respect,
> Though in our lives a separable spite. . . .

The subject of the poem was the death of love, nor need we doubt which love.

There is the same melancholy beauty and atmosphere of farewell in *Twelfth Night*, with its magical songs:

> Come away, come away, death,
>   And in sad cypress let me be laid . . .

and

> When that I was and a little tiny boy,
>   With hey, ho, the wind and the rain. . . .

It may very well have been produced at Court on Twelfth Night, 1601, for the Chamberlain's Men played there – but so did the Admiral's, Derby's and the Children of the Chapel. The Chamberlain's Men had established their lead with four out of the five previous appearances on Twelfth Night, culmination and end of the Christmas festivities. John Manningham recorded its performance at the Middle Temple, 2 February 1602 – so that its first production could have been on Twelfth Night, 1602. There can hardly have been time for the name Orsino to have been taken from the Duke of Bracciano in time to write the play for his visit in 1601 – anyway Orsino is a common enough Italian name. A volume of conjecture has been written about this. Dr Johnson says, 'whatever advantages Shakespeare might once derive from personal allusions ... have for many years been lost; and every topic of merriment, or motive of sorrow, which the modes of artificial life afforded him, now only obscure the scenes which they once illuminated'. But much has been recovered by fuller and more exact historical knowledge, not by conjecture.

A number of topical references relate the play to 1601, and show how alert the writer was to all that was going on and coming out: the Shirley brothers' account of their visit to the Sophy of Persia; Hakluyt's new map of the Indies, East and West, with rhumb-lines; the icicle on the Dutch navigator's beard in Nova Zembla; a snatch of song from Robert Jones's book of airs, out in 1600. From the first the main interest of the play was seen to lie in the character of Malvolio, though no amount of conjecture can satisfy us that he had a recognisable original:

> The cockpit, galleries, boxes are all full
> To hear Malvolio, that cross-gartered gull.

From this time on there are frequent references to the works of the dramatist: he has achieved fame with the *literati* as with the public. John Weever had another book out this year, inspired by Shakespeare: *The Mirror of Martyrs, or The Life and Death of Sir John Oldcastle*, with an epigram:

> The many-headed multitude were drawn
> By Brutus' speech that Caesar was ambitious:
> When eloquent Mark Antony had shown
> His virtues, who but Brutus then was vicious?

Abroad in exile the famous Jesuit, Father Parsons, who did so much harm by his writings – anything to damage the country that had rejected him – has a reference to Sir John Oldcastle, 'a ruffian knight as all England knoweth, and commonly brought in by comedians on their stages'. The Admiral's men had cashed in on Shakespeare's resounding success with Falstaff with a *Sir John Oldcastle*, put together for them by Anthony Munday and others.

The last of the *Parnassus* plays at Cambridge shows how well-known the Chamberlain's Men were there, and *Hamlet* was acted at both universities. The characters in the third *Parnassus* play are graduates looking for a job; Burbage and Kemp are brought on to try them out as candidates for the Company.

Burbage. A little teaching will mend these faults, and it may be besides they will be able to pen a part.

Kemp. Few of the university pen plays well: they smell too much of that writer, Ovid, and that writer, Metamorphoses. . . . Why here's our fellow Shakespeare puts them all down, aye and Ben Jonson too. O that Ben Jonson is a pestilent fellow: he brought up Horace giving the poets a pill; but our fellow Shakespeare hath given him a purge that made him bewray his credit.

When the candidates come on Kemp encourages them with the money to be made: 'they come north and south to bring it to our playhouse. And for honour, who of more report than Dick Burbage and Will Kemp? He's not counted a gentleman that knows not Dick Burbage and Will Kemp.' One of the students recites his passage from *The Spanish Tragedy*. Burbage then sees possibilities in another student, Philomusus.

Burbage. I like your face and the proportion of your body for Richard III. I pray, Master Philomusus, let me see you act a little of it.

Philomusus. 'Now is the winter of our discontent
Made glorious summer by the sun of York.'

Such was fame: henceforward the references to him and his work are too numerous to specify.

In his usual way Shakespeare had the story of Troilus and Cressida in mind for his next play before he had finished *Twelfth Night*. *Troilus and Cressida* was fairly certainly written in 1602. A unique play, it is arguable that it has more intellectual interest concentrated in it than any other of his works. Alas, that we cannot go into it here! It is a play for intellectuals, probably written for private performance, perhaps at an Inn of Court, where the scatological element would be appreciated by the young men no less than the legal word-play. Perhaps Shakespeare was responding to Ben Jonson's challenge with a satire of his own, and an element of mock-heroic; for the Prologue glances at Jonson's Prologue to the *Poetaster* of the year before. Jonson's Prologue had come in armed to express defiance to his detractors; Shakespeare's comes in,

> A prologue armed, but not in confidence
> Of author's pen, or actor's voice, but suited
> In like conditions as our argument

– for the argument was of war. It sounds mild and good-tempered enough; but some people have seen a glance at Ben's bull-headedness in the blockish character of Ajax.

Certainly the play is filled with political import and reflection on the late events, and it registers completely the edginess of this last year of the Queen's life, disillusionment with war and love, the faction-feuding, the jostling for position, the atmosphere of treachery and stupidity. The most sensitive register of the age could not but reflect it. The attitude is a *désabusé* 'plague on both your houses', the specific words of the play are 'fools on both sides'. The teeth are set on edge, there is the bitter withdrawal from commitment when one's own side commits the worst follies.

This is the least that must be said. We must add that there are recognisable touches of Essex, as in Hamlet.

> Things small as nothing, for request's sake only,
> He makes important.

This had been Essex's regular way with the Queen – it was one of the things she found insupportable: he had constantly turned the issue into one of confidence in himself.

> Possessed he is with greatness,
> And speaks not to himself but with a pride
> That quarrels at self-breath: imagined worth
> Holds in his blood such swoln and hot discourse. . . .

Shakespeare had completely seen through him, though it is true that there had been a deterioration in Essex's character in his last years:

> He is so plaguy-proud that the death-tokens of it
> Cry 'No recovery'.

There had been none; recovery, in fact, was impossible; he had forfeited sympathy.

And Southampton? Something of the relationship to Essex was glanced at in that of young Patroclus to the great Achilles. Essex and Southampton had sulked in their tent, like those two, contracting out of their duty and public life when they could not get their way. The consequences of the great man's fall are precisely described in a cutting passage: the rats deserting the vessel, the followers passing over to the other side – which was just the case, with Robert Cecil picking up Essex's former friends, as in the event he did Southampton. For the rest,

> when they fall, as being slippery standers,
> The love that leaned on them as slippery too,
> Doth one pluck down another and together
> Die in the fall.

One goes back to what he himself had said in taking leave of Southampton:

> Have I not seen dwellers on form and favour
> Lose all, and more, by paying too much rent,
> For compound sweet forgoing simple savour,
> Pitiful thrivers, in their gazing spent?

His own love, he had said, was not 'subject to time's love or to time's hate'; folded up and put away, it survives in the Sonnets.

Lastly, we must add that this play contains the most searching and incisive of all Shakespeare's comments on the problems of social order which we have always with us. No wonder that this brilliant, uncongenial play has never been popular: it is too stiff a medicine for people to take, like Swift, though in truth it gives them what they most need to be told – the evidence is in the break-up of society all round us: the absolute necessity of social order, authority and obedience, of people knowing their place and doing their duty. The crack-up when all this goes by the board is relentlessly exposed in *Troilus and Cressida*.

Somewhere along the line Ben Jonson received a reproof, and felt it; for he wrote later of the players,

> Only amongst them, I am sorry for
> Some better natures, by the rest so drawn
> To run in that vile line.

There he is, always in the right, and yet there is a rueful note in what is generally agreed to be a reference to Shakespeare – one more tribute to his good nature. The publication of this play offers problems no less than its performance. When it came to be printed, not until 1609, in the same year as the Sonnets, in a good text close to the author's manuscript, it carried a warm tribute to his comedies, 'that are so framed to the life that they serve for the most common commentaries of all the actions of our lives, showing such a dexterity and power of wit that the most displeased with plays are pleased with his comedies. . . . When he is gone and his comedies out of sale, you will scramble for them and set up a new English Inquisition.'

A publisher's blurb at once truthful and prophetic.

We know where he was living at this time, round about 1602, probably before: a lodger as usual, he was living in the French household of Christopher Mountjoy, a fashionable wig-maker, at the corner of Silver and Monkswell Streets in Cripplegate. Rather ironical when one thinks of Shakespeare's unkind comments on the profession in the Sonnets and in *The Merchant of Venice*:

> those crispèd, snaky, golden locks . . .
> Upon supposèd fairness, often known
> To be the dowry of a second head,
> The skull that bred them in the sepulchre.

This quiet little enclave was within the north-west angle of the City Wall; immediately without was St Giles's, Cripplegate, where Milton was to be buried later in the century. We can see, in Ralph Agas' map, the actual house with its twin gables and the pentice of the shop-front. Further down the street, was the little parish church of St Olave – the church, the whole area obliterated by the barbarian blitzes in the last war. There were in Shakespeare's time two or three City companies with their halls, Haberdashers and Surgeons – this is why the celebrated surgeon, John Banister, was a neighbour in Silver Street. (He died there in 1610.) Shakespeare would see the public-spirited almshouses on the right as he went up to Cripplegate; business would take him more frequently down Wood Street or Foster Lane to Cheapside or St Paul's churchyard, where the publishers had their bookstalls with frequent quartos of his plays on sale for sixpence. He had only to go one block east and he was in the parish of St Mary Aldermary, where Heming and Condell lived as substantial householders.

Shakespeare's householding was in Stratford; in London he was a lodger. But he must have been on confidential terms with the Mountjoys, perhaps particularly Mrs Mountjoy; for when it came to the marriage of their daughter to their apprentice, Stephen Bellot, 'Master' Shakespeare entered into the family discussions and actually performed the betrothal. Some ten years later, in 1612, there was a law suit about the dowry, and he was called upon to give evidence, being then 'of Stratford-upon-Avon, gentleman, of the age of forty-eight or thereabouts'. He said that it was Mrs Mountjoy who had solicited him to promote the marriage, though he could not now remember the amount of the dowry the daughter was to have, nor what goods. Others gave evidence that Mr Shakespeare had told them it was to be £50, whereupon the couple 'were made sure by Mr Shakespeare by giving their consent'.

A further set of interrogatories was prepared for him, but, alas, he did not appear to answer them. The case came to the notice of the French Huguenot church, who characterised both father and son-in-law as *débauchés*, and Mountjoy as living a licentious life. It was evidently a not very godly household, perhaps free and easy. More important to our purpose is that Shakespeare was certainly living there not long after writing the French scenes in *Henry V*, and perhaps before. If so, it would have been helpful to be on intimate terms with Mrs Mountjoy.

At Stratford his father died in September 1601, and was buried on the eighth; his widow, Mary Arden, seven years later, 9 September 1608. Someone in the next generation noted that he had once seen the old glover in his shop: 'a merry-cheeked old man, that said Will was a good honest fellow, but he durst have cracked a jest with him at any time'. This has often been quoted, without noticing that there is a certain awe, or at least respect, in the old man at his formidably successful son, who had more than retrieved the family's standing.

When Shakespeare at last made his first considerable investment in land – 107 acres in Old Stratford and Bishopton for the sum of £320 – he was not in Stratford on Mayday 1602 to take possession. His brother Gilbert did it for him in the presence, as witnesses, of neighbours Anthony and John Nash, Humphrey Mainwaring, Richard Mason and William Sheldon. Gilbert Shakespeare was a haberdasher and, as a bachelor, was free to move, like his brother, between Stratford and London, where he worked in St Bride's. He died at Stratford in 1612, at the age of forty-five; a third brother Richard died next year at thirty-nine. The youngest, Edmund, had followed the eldest into the theatre and become a player; he buried a base child at St Giles's, Cripplegate in 1607 and was himself buried on the last day of that year in St Saviour's, Southwark (now the cathedral). He was given a forenoon knell of the great bell, that icy winter's day when the Thames was frozen over. Who can have paid for that? None of the brothers lived to be old: the eldest, with greater stamina, lived longest.

On 24 March 1603, the eve of Lady Day, the Queen died – in her seventieth year, a great age for a monarch. Everyone realised that with her an epoch was passing; few could remember when she had not been there. A numbness fell upon the land, until her burial; when London, at the spectacle of her hearse – with the familiar figure, crowned and sceptred, upon it – fell into a passion of weeping. A ballad called upon the poets to lament her:

> You poets all, brave Shakespeare, Jonson, Green,
> Bestow your time to write for England's Queen. . . .
> Return your songs and sonnets and your says,
> To set forth sweet Elizabetha's praise.

But Henry Chettle observed that Shakespeare did not oblige:

> Nor doth the silver-tonguèd Melicert
> Drop from his honeyed muse one sable tear,
> To mourn her death that gracèd his desert
> And to his lays opened her royal ear.
> Shepherd, remember our Elizabeth,
> And sing her Rape, done by that Tarquin, Death.

For all her favour to the dramatist, she had executed Essex and condemned his friend Southampton to death: it was all too recent. Not for another decade was he to sum up, in his last play, the great age to which she gave her name and of which she and he were to go down to history together as the brightest jewels.

CHAPTER 10

The King's Men

JAMES I's smooth accession, skilfully managed by Robert Cecil – with Essex well out of the way – ended the insecurity, the period of queasy waiting that had got on people's nerves. As usual, there was a honeymoon period: James was anxious to be all things to all men – he was in a very euphoric mood himself, coming south into the promised land he had never before set foot in. All expectations, however, could not be satisfied: some were bound to be disappointed, first of all Ralegh.

But Essex's friends were now in favour. Southampton was immediately released from the Tower, and went out of town to meet the King, who graciously allowed him to bear the sword of state before him. More, he was given the privileged entry to the Privy Chamber – some thought he would become the favourite; but at twenty-nine he was a little old for the part, James was already equipped with James Hay, and Southampton was not his type. However, royal favour performed a miracle: he at last conformed, became a Protestant and, if he did not go to bed with the King, he at least went to church with him.

Grants flowed fast and free: Keeper of the Isle of Wight for life (Elizabeth's cousin, the second Lord Hunsdon had had that job); Keeper of the King's Game in Hampshire (James spent much of his time hunting in the forests); joint Lieutenant of the County with young Pembroke (to whom James was more inclined: a masculine type); Knight of the Garter. Best of all, Southampton got the lucrative monopoly of sweet wines (which Elizabeth had refused to renew for Essex); grants of manors and lands, some even to his retainers. Next year his mother, the Countess, received a sweetener of £600 (multiply by a hundred) out of the Exchequer, to console her for her troubles.

Mary Stuart's son, who had always been impecunious, had no idea of the value of money; to an impoverished Scottish king England was a land flowing with inexhaustible milk and honey. From the moment he arrived he began laying up financial trouble for himself, and for all the Stuarts in the future.

The Chamberlain's Men shared in the general euphoria. James immediately took them under his patronage; they became the King's Men, acknowledged as such to be the premier company – the Admiral's became Prince Henry's, Worcester's Queen Anne's. Fascinated by the English theatre after the dreary Calvinism of Scotland, neither James nor Anne could have enough of plays, masques, extravagant entertainments. They wanted to see all the plays they had not been able to see; performances at Court doubled in number, and soon the rate of pay was doubled – from £10 under the provident Queen to £20 under the improvident James. Money flowed in for Shakespeare and his Fellows.

More, as the King's Men, they had special licence to play in any town or university – no more nonsense from mayors and civic authorities. The leaders in the Company were sworn officers of the royal household, Grooms of the Chamber in ordinary. As such, Shakespeare and his Fellows received their livery of 4½ yards of scarlet cloth, to walk in the procession on the King's reception by the City. Again, next summer, they figured in the ceremonies attendant upon the Spanish plenipotentiaries in London to end the long war with a firm peace.

However, 1603 was a bad plague-year: the Court took to the country and in December was at Wilton, Pembroke's house, where the King's Men presented three plays. Southampton was there, too – it is fascinating to think what former patron and poet would have to say to each other, after all that had passed. On their return the Company played at Hampton Court on St Stephen's Day at night, and on Innocents' Day; in February they played at Whitehall on the nights of Candlemas and Shrove Tuesday. And they were paid considerable sums to compensate them for cancellations owing to plague. At the coronation in March 1604 the devices were written by the leading dramatists, Jonson included – all except Shakespeare, who was too busy. The King's Men walked in the procession, and Southampton made a graceful appearance at the tournament.

For the King's Men the Court was becoming a larger source of profit than the Globe, and correspondingly more demanding. 'In the ten years before they became the King's Company their known performances at Court average about three a year. In the ten years after they attained their new service their known performances at Court average about thirteen a year, more than those of all other London Companies combined. They were officially the premier Company of London; a good part of their time must have been devoted to the preparation of command performances.'*

By the time of the King of Denmark's visit to his sister, Queen Anne, in 1606, the royal family had seen most of the Company's repertory. A chamberlain of the Exchequer, Sir Walter Cope, reported to Cecil and Southampton, preparing to entertain them: 'I have sent and been all this morning hunting for players, jugglers and such kinds of creatures, but find them hard to find. Wherefore, leaving notes for them to seek me, Burbage is come and says there is no new play the Queen has not seen, but they have revived an old one called *Love's Labour's Lost*, which for wit and mirth, he says, will please her exceedingly. And this is appointed to be played tomorrow at my Lord of Southampton's. . . . Burbage is my messenger.'

This at least shows the familiar terms the King's Men were upon with Court officials; we hear the less of Shakespeare as the pressure of work became greater. It would be interesting if he were, as likely enough, among the performers at Southampton House, with which the play was intimately connected and where it was fairly certainly first performed. The increasing importance of the Court audience played a part in the new phase of his writing and the character of his dramaturgy – the great tragedies and the Roman plays, which

* G. E. Bentley, 'Shakespeare and the Blackfriars Theatre', *Shakespeare Survey 1*, p. 40.

were the peak of his achievement. His plays had to appeal to both audiences, the public theatre with its multifarious spectators, and a sophisticated Court: in their universal scope they succeeded in doing so.

The rewards were corresponding. In 1605 Shakespeare was able to make his largest investment at Stratford: £440 in one half of all the tithes on corn, grain and hay from Old Stratford, Welcombe and Bishopton (i.e. the rectorial tithes), and the vicarial, i.e. lesser, tithes, on wool, lambs etc. within the parish. It is a nice epitome of the Reformation, for these had belonged before it to the College of canons, whose house Shakespeare's friend, John Combe, occupied and in whose choir in the church he was to be buried: from the Catholic Church to the secular dramatist. The business-management of the tithes Shakespeare left to his friend, Anthony Nash, who was on the spot. It was some years since Abraham Sturley had suggested the investment in tithes as a good mark to shoot at; once more the prudent son of John Shakespeare had taken his time. The return on this investment alone, £60 a year clear, made the gentleman of New Place independent.

With the death of the Queen, with the passing of that figure that had for so long held her stage, we are entering a new world: an age was passing, in a sense more significant than is usually true of the hackneyed phrase. With our emphasis on the theatre and on Shakespeare as, above all, responding to its demands and opportunities, we should think of his next two plays as experimental. *All's Well That Ends Well* and *Measure for Measure* fit into no precise category; they are sometimes referred to as bitter comedies – but then we know what little regard Shakespeare paid to labelling plays. Categories are for the conventional: genius transcends them, and is very hard to fit in.

All's Well is an odd hybrid of folk-tale and morality, placed in an environment which permits a disenchanted comment on the values of the time – and that is something new in Shakespeare. An intelligent editor of the play has seen, as so rarely, that Shakespeare drew much more on his experience of the world around him than people without a knowledge of that world realise. Even some scholars well read in the literature of the age are apt to think that he was above and beyond experience, 'transmuting' is their word for it – as if he missed out on experience! That way lies bardolatry – another way of being unintelligent about him, making him unreal, out of touch with the content of his time. The New Arden editor specifically says that previous views of the play have not realised 'the creative interplay between author and environment, the fact that the feelings of the author are a part of the climate of opinion in which he lives'.

There should be no difficulty about the dating of the play: it visibly comes between *Troilus* and *Measure for Measure*, and breathes the uneasy atmosphere of 1603, the Queen sickening to her death, people's nerves on edge, a new succession from which they knew not what to expect, the worst plague since the year 1593. Shakespeare certainly gave his public something new, with a cutting edge. There is the theme: an honest middle-class girl is in love with a spoiled young count, far above her station, and seeks to marry him, much against his will. We have come across that young aristocrat before: he is spirited, but petulant and wilful, he is full of aristocratic pride and refuses to be tied down in marriage. Still, very conscious of his nobility, he is respectful towards his mother, the Countess. We have met her before, too. Like the Countess of Rosillion in the play, Southampton's mother was kind and good, befriended and liked by the Queen, placed in grievous trouble by her wayward son. The upshot of the play is that he is made to do his duty and marry the girl. It would not be far off the mark to conjecture that the dowager Countess would have smiled on the poet's part, years before, in the campaign to get her son married – when he should have done, and in the right way.

There is a new tone, for Shakespeare, in the play. Earlier he had been glamourised by his admission into the world of the young Earl – understandably since he had learned so much and gained so much from it. Experience had taught him that its gilded denizens were no better than anyone else – some of them much greater fools than sensible middle-class persons, and the more blameable for their exaltation. He had always retained his own independence, himself on the margin of it, taking it all in. Here is the new note we have not had before:

> Honours thrive
> When rather from our acts we them derive
> Than our foregoers. The mere word's a slave,
> Debauched on every tomb, on every grave
> A lying trophy, and as oft is dumb. . . .

From the point of view of the theatre, we are given something new with the character of Parolles, the braggart coward of a soldier, and his merciless exposure. There is no joy in it, as with the reverberating discomfiture of Falstaff. Parolles – perhaps a kind of Captain Piers Edmonds – is cruelly unmasked. He is not created from within, like Falstaff; he is observed, and exposed, from without. He is really a Jonsonian type – tribute to the influence of the younger man upon the older, who had always been willing to learn from anyone. It makes no less effective theatre; the appreciative Charles I thought him the most memorable character of the play.

Parolles' words:

> Simply the thing I am
> Shall make me live . . .

echo as the message of the play. It is hardly surprising that it has never been popular.

Measure for Measure is a more satisfactory play, more moving emotionally; and that Shakespeare was more moved we can tell from the finer poetry it releases: no sense of a task carried through with little inspiration. We must not go into the play here, merely remark that the finest critical discussion of it is by Walter Pater, for there is a mind on a level with what it is discussing. Shakespeare got the story from Cinthio's collection of *novelle* and apparently looked up a play of his; he also read up Whetstone's versions of the story. What is interesting is the evidence here, as in other plays – *King Lear*, for instance – of his turning over a number of versions before deciding on the one that would make the best drama. He toned down several of the original Italian features to make it more presentable, where later dramatists of the Jacobean theatre in decadence would have heightened them, to achieve lurid melodrama.

The play bears evidence of having been written in 1604. Knowledge of the new King's dislike of crowds and popular clamour – such a contrast with the great actress who had had such a gift for playing to the gallery – was getting about and is commented on with sympathy. Performed at Court at Christmas 1604, actually on 26 December, these touches would have been grateful to James's ears. This play with its uncomfortable theme – the exposure of the lie in the soul – has never been a favourite; and there is a deal of sordid realism in the background, with a lot of talk about lechery and brothels and disease. 'What with the war, what with the sweat [i.e. plague], what with the gallows, and what with poverty, I am custom-shrunk,' says Mistress Overdone, giving her characteristic note to the play. Her name has a Jonsonian flavour about it, and the characters from low life are very convincing – Shakespeare knew them well enough, living on his own in London: Pompey, Mistress Overdone's pimp, Bernardine the condemned prisoner, Abhorson the executioner (horrifying, even played comically), Lucio the dissolute waster of a young gentleman – there were plenty of them about in Jacobean society. One cannot but notice the difference from the Boar's Head in East Cheap and the joyous bawdry around Falstaff: so short a time, and we are in a new world.

In this same year 1604 Shakespeare produced one of his most inspired works – *Othello, the Moor of Venice*. We know that there was a Court performance of it on Hallowmas Day, 1 November 1604, by the King's Men in the banqueting house at Whitehall – not the present Inigo Jones building, but the former wooden structure put up in Elizabeth's reign. Between Advent 1604 and Lent 1605 several of Shakespeare's earlier plays were revived at Court – *The Comedy of Errors, Love's Labour's Lost, The Merchant of Venice* – for the new King and Queen. Some have thought that the King's Men must have had a remarkable singing boy to take the parts, and sing the songs, of Ophelia and Desdemona in these years; but really they were well within an Elizabethan boy-actor's capacity.

The subject of *Othello*, innocent love injured and destroyed, inspired Shakespeare to one of his highest flights of imagination and poetry. This play is his most intensely concentrated, carried through with one breathless impulse of creation from beginning to end, no subsidiary interest whatever allowed to distract our attention from the tragedy. The poetry is equally inspired; the drama and passion of it produced some of his most wonderful passages:

> Not poppy, nor mandragora,
> Nor all the drowsy syrups of the world. . . .
>
> Put out the light, and then put out the light

– untranslatable into any foreign language, with its simple monosyllables suggesting echoing chambers of darkness and desolation. There is the finality and resignation of

> Speak of me as I am. Nothing extenuate,
> Nor set down aught in malice. . . .

The use of such a word as 'extenuate' reminds us of Shakespeare's lordliness about language. He needed such a range of words to express his ranging imagination; but from the first he had loved grand, echoing, eloquent words, with their Latinised endings. And, of course, we get the instinctive, sometimes half-hidden, alliteration that comes spontaneously to a true poet. Quite early on we have 'intermissive miseries', 'loathsome sequestration', 'particularities and petty sounds'; 'my words effectual', 'rehearse the method of my pen', 'and prove the period of their tyranny'; 'these eyes wax dim . . . as drawing to their exigent', 'just death with sweet enlargement doth dismiss me'. One can often recognise him, smiling and pleased, in his words and phrases – and how grandly they would resound on the lips of actors!

As with any great poet – compare Milton – the character of the verse registers subtle changes, not only in psychology, the response to subject, for example, but in the nature and age of the man. There is the bare bleak verse of *All's Well*, which did not inspire him, following upon the extraordinarily brilliant and richly Latinised verse of *Troilus and Cressida*, which evidently did compel him. Now there are the poetic depths and tender simplicities of *Othello*: his heart was affected, where *Troilus* had inspired his intellect.

From this time forward we note a new development in the metrical character of his verse. Even apart from prosody – if the two can be considered apart – his verse had already shown extraordinary range, flexibility and variety, the capacity to express everything (with the significant exception of religious emotion, like Spenser or Donne, or the philosophic *Angst* of *Dr Faustus*). There had been the simple descriptive verse of the early period, the end-stopped blank verse of *Henry VI*, along with the Marlovian rhetoric. Next the lyrical blank verse, with much rhyme, of *A Midsummer Night's Dream*, *Richard II* and *Romeo and Juliet*. Then the full capacity of maturity with the plays from *Henry IV* to *Twelfth Night*. The last reminds us of his continuous gift for writing songs in the musical measures usual for Elizabethan airs. While the verse, no less than the language, of *Hamlet* displays the ranging freedom, along with elliptical concentration at will, of the great tragedies: peak not only of his achievement but in the history of the language.

After the bareness of *All's Well* we note the growing tendency to depart from the line-unit to end sentences in the middle of the line. This must have satisfied some urge, with him probably conscious and unconscious working together, perhaps a response to some inscrutable psychological or even physical change. At forty, having gone through so much of life, he was in his rich, teeming autumn. After the early five-stress blank verse keeping the sense to the line, then the freer kind with the sense running on, we now have verse-paragraphs with frequent half-lines. It will be followed by a last period where the verse is irregular, sometimes incapable of exact scansion; we find strong rhythmic phrases of indeterminate length, a slackening of intellectual control in the interest of the elliptical, the suggestive, the echoing. It is like the impressionist brushwork of great painters in their last period, Titian or Rembrandt, the shorthand coming from the easy confidence of practised mastery, the slapdash not failing of its effect. While as to language, apart even from verse – if it is possible to disentangle then – we shall find with *Antony and Cleopatra* that no one has ever gone beyond it: it is impossible to do so. And he owed this power to drama, to the stage.

The increasing complexity of the verse made it difficult for the unofficial versions of the plays printed at the time, put together from memory, to be accurate. For example, the early quartos (bad) of *King Lear*, printed in 1607 and 1608, which have much mislineation, often unmetrical, passages of prose appearing as verse, and virtually no punctuation. They at any rate testify to a demand from the reading public for the work of the popular playwright. In the course of the year 1606, or at most 1605–6 – to the events of which there are, as ususal, references in the plays – he wrote *King Lear* and *Macbeth*, which are associated in more ways than one.

With these plays, and with *Cymbeline* later, Shakespeare enters new territory for his imagination to explore: legendary British history. Once more he resorted to Holinshed for a story; but, like the reading man he was, he looked up other sources, the antiquarians Camden and Richard Carew, the story as it appeared in *The Mirror for Magistrates* and in the *Faerie Queene*, which gave him the form of the name he preferred, Cordelia. He remembered the story of the blind king from Sidney's *Arcadia* for the blinding of Gloucester, and took the names of the fiends and other crazy touches from Samuel Harsnet's recent exposure of the claims of Catholic priests to exorcise demons from hysterical women.*

What is very odd is this. In the other versions of the old story the king does not go mad; but only a year or two before the play was written, Sir Brian Annesley – a gentleman-pensioner of the Queen whom Shakespeare could well have known – was certified as insane by two grasping elder daughters after his inheritance, while his youngest daughter, Cordell or Cordelia, tried to protect him. A year or two after the play, in 1608, it was this kind daughter

* For this, see my *The Elizabethan Renaissance: The Life of the Society*, pp. 264–72.

who married Southampton's young step-father, Sir William Harvey, after the death of the dowager Countess.

It is extraordinary how things come together, almost telepathically, in the psychic conditions that irradiate around genius. We have noticed before, after the Danvers–Long feud had erupted into murder in the Southampton circle, the playwright looking up a suitable story and writing *Romeo and Juliet*. Now there was an old play to hand in a *Leir*; it was on the basis of this that Shakespeare mainly shaped his play. It is interesting that it should have been in working upon an old play, as with both *Hamlet* and *King Lear*, that his genius should have so notably liberated itself: nothing could indicate more clearly his not caring where he got his plots from – it was only the dramatic possibilities he cared for, the conflict of character, the contrasting scenes he could execute, the passions display, the gamut of human nature in action.

Again, there is evidence of this overriding concern of the dramatist in his considering the various versions of the story and the alterations he made. In the earlier versions Lear did not die, but Cordelia killed herself from despair. Shakespeare transforms this, and in doing so elevates it to an altogether nobler level with the full implications of tragedy. With one hand he eradicated the sensationalism of suicide, giving Cordelia the strength of character to 'outfrown false Fortune's frown' to the last. On the other, with the aesthetic intransigence of genius, he saw that Lear, after such experiences, had to end tragically – anything else would be beneath the level of his agony.

Here we can only point to what is new in Shakespeare's development from *Hamlet* onwards, and true of all his greatest plays, not only the tragedies but the last romances. Their themes reach below the rational into the realm of the subconscious, into the primitive experiences which exist in the recesses of every human mind, though we are unwilling to acknowledge them. Whether it is the sensitive son's suspicion of the mother's falseness to the father; whether it is the mental torture of being in love with a girl he suspects of betraying him to his enemies; whether it is an ageing man's jealousy of an old friend over his wife and his final realisation of the wreck he has made of life and happiness; whether it is a soul sleep-walking in agony for the crime it has committed; whether it is ingratitude in its cruellest form, the ingratitude of children to father or mother; or the realisation that men kill what they love: all these things reach down to such depths in us that often a sensitive being can hardly bear to look at what is passing on the stage. It is his soul laid bare. Such is the power of the greatest of dramatists.

Merely on the intellectual level we now know that the successive stages of Leontes' jealousy exactly parallel Freud's analysis of the stages of psychotic jealousy, from the obsessional to the delusional. Hamlet's suspicions of his mother offer virtually a text-book case of the workings of the Oedipus complex; Macbeth the sleeplessness, the retribution of guilt. After the dreadful scene with Othello in which he reproaches Desdemona with being a whore, Emilia comes in with, 'How do you, my good lady?' Desdemona answers, surprisingly, 'Faith, half asleep' – but this is what is liable to happen when a woman has received a shock: she is really numbed. When Coriolanus's obsessive love for Rome is denied and himself rejected, he wants to set fire to it – this is a reaction well known in pathological psychology. Shakespeare knew, or intuited, it all; the miracle is that, by trusting his intuition, he found the appropriate images to express it: his genius found the language.

A perceptive critic today sees what Victorian-minded persons with their rationalist psychology found improbable or simply incomprehensible – Angelo's sudden conversion in *Measure for Measure* or the scales dropping from Leontes' eyes in *The Winter's Tale*, one of those scenes that so probe the heart. J. I. M. Stewart realises that Shakespeare is penetrating to our inmost nature and 'giving his fable something of the demonic quality of myth or folk-story, which is commonly nearer to the radical workings of the human mind than are later and rationalised versions. . . . Shakespeare clears away obvious motives for much the same reason as the psychologist: to give us some awareness of motives lying deeper down. . . . It is probable that the audience in some obscure way are brought to share his awareness, and so are not disconcerted by matters of which a conventional psychology and an unkindled reader will make little. What can powerfully affect us in the theatre is the perception – coming to us with something of the disguise and displacement characterising related disclosures in dreams – of types of conflict which consciousness normally declines to acknowledge. And the sovereign sway exerted over generations of spectators by tragic heroes possessed of a seemingly uncanny power to baffle rationalising commentary is the most striking intimation that this is so.'*

A further point that must be mentioned for what significance it had for Shakespeare the man – though one must not make a simple transference from the writer to the man – is his obsessive disgust with sex at this period, from *Hamlet* to *Troilus and Cressida*, from *Measure for Measure* to *King Lear*. It must indicate something in his state of mind, if not of body. 'Why would'st thou be a breeder of sinners? I am myself indifferent honest, but yet I could accuse me of such things that it were better my mother had not borne me.' It is like Swift: why breed at all? Lear's mind dwells on the subject, as Ophelia's had – and so does William Shakespeare's in every one of these plays.

> Adultery?
> Thou shalt not die: die for adultery! No.

– he was an adulterer himself. In *Othello* Emilia – with that name! – had no objection to it; Desdemona had, but it was the innocent who died. In the world,

> Behold yond simpering dame,
> Whose face between her forks presages snow;
> That minces virtue, and does shake the head
> To hear of pleasure's name;
> The fitchew, nor the soiled horse, goes to't
> With a more riotous appetite.
> Down from the waist they are Centaurs,
> Though women all above.

* J. I. M. Stewart, *Character and Motive in Shakespeare*, pp. 36–7.

Women are stripped of their pretences in these plays, one after the other; only the child-like and the innocent remain – and they are the victims.

There is not much difficulty in dating the play. 'These late eclipses of the sun and moon portend no good to us'; this refers to the eclipses of September and October 1605. Shakespeare's company had visited Dover in the autumn of 1604, so the celebrated description of Shakespeare's Cliff is in place. It is thought that the Weird Sisters may have been presented to Shakespeare's imagination by the Three Sibyls who appeared to greet James on his visit to Oxford in the summer of 1604. The play was performed 'before the King's Majesty at Whitehall upon St Stephen's night at Christmas last [i.e. 1606] by his Majesty's servants playing usually at the Globe on the Bankside'. A more unexpected performance far afield was that by Sir Richard Cholmeley's players up in Yorkshire, at Candlemas 1610, at Gowthwaite Hall, a nest of Catholic recusants. No Puritans, they were appreciators of Shakespeare. Apparently the version they acted was the shortened memorial reconstruction of the 1608 quarto.

That *Macbeth* followed *Lear* should be obvious from several touches reflecting Gunpowder Plot of November 1605, still more that it was written as a tribute to King James. His Majesty received a sharp shock with the revelation of this ingenious plot by a sworn knot of young Catholic malcontents, to blow him and his family, with all the lords spiritual and temporal and the Commons, at the opening of Parliament, sky high. A feeling of relief ran through the country at the royal family's deliverance – such was the contemporary feeling: for the first time there was a spontaneous sentiment towards the new dynasty. Ever responsive towards the public mood, Shakespeare was not likely to miss such an opportunity: his new play was to do honour to the Stuarts' legendary ancestor, Banquo. Tribute is paid to his 'royalty of nature', the 'dauntless temper of his mind', the 'wisdom that doth guide his valour' – all these to reflect honour upon James (with whom valour was not a noticeable characteristic, as Ralegh had the hardihood to point out).

Several times the prophecy is repeated:

Thou shalt get kings, though thou be none.

Banquo's putative descendant's special interest in witches and demonology – though a recessive curiosity which did not commend itself to the cultivated late Queen – was catered for by the Weird Sisters, who exert their influence upon the action. King James, who had much of the don in his composition, had written a book about demonology while in Scotland, to the atmosphere of which it was more appropriate. It was hardly likely to appeal to Shakespeare intellectually, whose own attitude was close to that of Reginald Scott's humane *Discovery of Witchcraft* (who did not believe in it), which we know Shakespeare read. However, needs must: a play is a play is a play; and there are further tributes to James's powers, as an anointed king, of healing the King's Evil – in which he took pride and was already exerting himself, where Elizabeth had taken this anthropological nonsense in her stride. It is hinted that His Majesty spoke with the power of inspiration, which he did not disclaim when put to him with theological unction by bishops with an eye to preferment. Lastly, his desire to bring about general peace and to be haled as *rex pacificus* throughout Europe – much the most respectable side to a not overly respectable monarch – is acclaimed.

Tactful William Shakespeare! one can hardly imagine Ben Jonson at it, for all his employment at Court. For Shakespeare, smooth as a glove, whose father was not a glover for nothing, no doubt it was all in the day's work.

A couple of passages refer to the trial of the Jesuit Provincial, Henry Garnet, in March 1606, which made a deplorable impression. Robert Cecil, who really ran the country, was determined to bring home to the Jesuits the consequences of their meddling in matters of state. The writings of such as Father Parsons inflamed young men like Anthony Babington and the desperadoes of Gunpowder Plot to criminal courses. After the scare of the Plot and the exposure of Garnet, Parsons, though an exile, was effectively silenced. For the Jesuit Provincial *had* known about the Plot – though his knowledge had come from confession. English law and public opinion did not admit the distinction: all they recognised was that he had known about it. Even the Catholic Northampton, who was a Privy Councillor, asked Garnet why he had not informed someone who could have put a stop to it, i.e. himself.

Popular hits were made by the ever-popular dramatist at the Jesuit doctrine of equivocation and that one need not tell the truth under examination, merely equivocate. What was an equivocator? One 'that could swear in both scales against either scale, who committed treason enough for God's sake, yet could not equivocate to heaven'. We are back with

> the fools of time,
> Which die for goodness, who have lived for crime.

Shakespeare always shares the normal sensible view – unlike a Shelley or a Milton; he was obviously taken with the word 'equivocator', so was the public. 'What is a traitor?' asks young Macduff. 'Why, one that swears and lies. . . . Everyone that does so is a traitor, and must be hanged.'

The play made an immediate impression, particularly the unnerving scene of the apparition of Banquo's ghost, which is referred to in *The Puritan* next year, 1607, and again in *The Knight of the Burning Pestle*. The play was probably one of those given at Court for the notorious visit of Queen Anne's brother, Christian IV: the Danish royal house, who were of course Germans, had German manners and made beasts of themselves with drink – a sad contrast with the sobriety and state of the late Queen. *Macbeth* was revised for performance during the festivities for Princess Elizabeth's wedding to the German Count Palatine, Frederick, from whom our present royal house descend. Unfortunately it is only the prompt-copy abridged for one or other of these performances that survives; so that the play as we have it is shorter than any except *The Comedy of Errors*. The fact that we have fuller and more eloquent stage-directions, and the book-keeper's own reminder to 'Ring the bell', though giving us a feeling of being in direct contact, are no consolation for such a loss. When Simon Forman saw the play at the Globe in 1611, he refers to Macbeth and Banquo riding through a wood, in an early scene which does not exist in our text. In any case, it was always a short play, of intense concentration, like a dark and sinister opera. And, like others of the tragedies, it has inspired composers of genius to make an opera of it – as Verdi did, no less than with *Othello* and *Falstaff*, though *King Lear* defeated both him and Debussy.

A mystifying story, which must relate to *Macbeth*, goes back to the seventeenth century. 'That most learned prince and great patron of learning, King James I, was pleased with his own hand to write an amicable letter to Mr Shakespeare. Which letter, though now lost, remained long in the hands of Sir William Davenant, as a credible person now living [1709] can testify.'* William Oldys, who was very knowledgeable about the early dramatists, repeats this. It would be very exceptional for a monarch to write such a letter; yet it is not impossible, especially for one who fancied himself as a writer, which James did – moreover, he was a generous man, and he had reason to be grateful for *Macbeth*. But it would seem that we have lost something of significance between William Shakespeare and Sir William Davenant.

Semper aliquid novi: always something new with Shakespeare; he was a 'ceaseless experimenter'. After these incursions into the Gothic world of northern Europe, back to the ancient world of Rome, from Holinshed to Plutarch for the next few plays. North's Plutarch was one of the books which the enterprising Richard Field took over from Vautrollier with his widow; he printed further additions to the Lives along with more issues in the early 1600s. (Something interesting in contacts between Shakespeare and his fellow Stratford schoolboy has also been lost, particularly in the early 1590s when the poet was in and out of the printer's shop in Blackfriars.) Shakespeare was thinking of *Antony and Cleopatra* before he had finished *Macbeth*; for Macbeth says of Banquo:

* Quoted in E. K. Chambers, *William Shakespeare, a Study of Facts and Problems*, II. 270.

under him
My genius is rebuked; as, it is said,
Mark Antony's was by Caesar

i.e. Octavius Caesar.

So again there is no difficulty about date: it followed straight on the heels of *Macbeth*, in 1607. In that year Samuel Daniel put out a revised edition of his *Cleopatra*, with alterations reflecting Shakespeare's play. We have already noticed that this admirable poet was noticeably susceptible to the dramatist's work; indeed, there was a certain kinship of spirit between them, an undoubted nobility of mind in Daniel, utter sincerity, an accomplished intellect that never fell for mere fashion, let alone the desire to shock of a Donne. A man of the people, he was as independent as he was cultivated and, as the brother-in-law of Florio, would have known Shakespeare. His affiliations, however, were with the Pembroke circle, with Philip Sidney's sister as his patron. Shakespeare had read the earlier version of Daniel's poem and probably the Countess's studio-play, after the classic manner of Garnier, *Antonius*. It is pleasant to observe these mutual influences of kindred spirits – Shakespeare-Daniel-Drayton – even though the busy theatre-man had no time for any literary life: he made time for a good deal of reading, all grist to the mill, and his plays bear evidence of it.

Once more, with *Antony and Cleopatra*, he produced something quite different, virtually unique. Though in a sense it is a continuation of *Julius Caesar*, the story of what happened afterwards, the new play is totally unlike that with its controlled, chaste classicism. *Antony and Cleopatra* is like Veronese in its rich colouring and its exotic trappings, and again, in a more subtle sense, in the suggestion that it is somehow in inverted commas: the world is not altogether well lost for love, there is an enigmatic smile that flits across the scene, but does not detract from its glow, like a Venetian sunset. If one did not know how little William Shakespeare cared for dull people's categories, one would call the play a romantic tragedy, it is so far away from its predecessor *Julius Caesar* and the classic play that was to follow, *Coriolanus*.

As always, Shakespeare was inspired by the theme of love; but again there is a difference – it is as if he had at last achieved detachment, there is an enigmatic smile upon the tragedy. And the last word is with the political type, Octavius Caesar. For all Shakespeare's endearing susceptibility, his intelligence had always understood that: do we not remember from the Sonnets –

> They that have power to hurt and will do none . . .
> Who, moving others, are themselves as stone,
> Unmovèd, cold, and to temptation slow . . .
> They are the lords and owners of their faces. . . .

There is Octavius, who became Augustus, ruler of the Roman world: these are they who inherit the earth, neither the meek, nor those who throw it away for love.

Now that we know more about the Elizabethan stage, we see how easy it was to carry the short changing scenes, shifting between Rome, Athens, Alexandria. Since there was little enough historical incident in the first half of the play, it is fascinating to watch with what acrobatic skill Shakespeare keeps the curiosity alert, interest aroused. And, since he knows next to nothing about Egypt, it is amusing to observe the old hand making the utmost of what he does know – he had always been a dab at that. There is the Nile, of course, its mysterious ebbing and flowing, the pyramids and crocodiles and the flies of Egypt (from the Bible). Occasionally he fills in with a magnificent roll-call of exotic Oriental names, to conjure up atmosphere:

> Bocchus, the king of Libya; Archelaus
> Of Cappadocia; Philadelphos, king
> Of Paphlagonia

– that name is from Sidney's *Arcadia* – and so on for a whole verse-paragraph, which would have rolled out well on an actor's lips, as from the Bible in church. From the literary point of view, we may note that this is a trick learned from Marlowe, to be handed on to Milton, the Bible their common denominator.

We must mention that in this play, more spectacularly than in any, the verse reaches heights not touched by his non-dramatic poetry: a scholar-friend of mine has well said that such passages as these are the *ne plus ultra* of the language:

> Burn the great sphere thou mov'st in! Darkling stand
> The varying shore of the world. . . .

(here is his imagination playing on the great Voyages we know he read). Or

> The odds is gone,
> And there is nothing left remarkable
> Beneath the visiting moon.

Impossible to analyse the psychological effects of such language – to those whose ear is attuned to English and its native rhythms, there is a suggestion of the illimitable and inexpressible, along with the falling cadence of pathos and farewell.

An inside knowledge of the faction-fighting upon the Elizabethan political scene has gone into *Antony and Cleopatra.* Ordinary appreciation of the play stops with the love; Shakespeare went beyond. As we have seen all along in this book, he was in a wonderful position – through his association with Southampton, through constant performances at Court – to observe the political stage as from a side-box, out of view. He understood it all, as well as Francis Bacon, who had a similarly *désabusé* point of view. Above all, there was the struggle for power, the partnerships made and broken, the ulcerated enmities, the friends deserting.

> The hearts
> That spanieled me at heels, to whom I gave
> Their wishes, do discandy, melt their sweets
> On blossoming Caesar. . . .

He had seen that, from close at hand, with Essex. Then, since these were Elizabethans, there is grief for the fallen enemy:

But yet let me lament
. . . that our stars,
Unreconciliable, should divide
Our equalness to this.

It is what Ralegh felt about his enemy Essex, as he watched his beheading from within the Tower, and wept. Who knew how soon it would become his turn?

Withdrawal was the dramatist's fortress, from which he could comment on what he saw:

I see men's judgments are
A parcel of their fortunes; and things outward
Do draw the inward quality after them,
To suffer all alike.

What he thinks of the people is what he has always thought:

our slippery people,
Whose love is never linked to the deserver
Till his deserts are past. . . .

When the story of Cleopatra and Antony is over, 'the quick comedians extemporally will stage us', and

mechanic slaves,
With greasy aprons, rules and hammers, shall
Uplift us to the view.

We are already in the atmosphere of his next play, *Coriolanus*.

It seems likely that he wrote this at home at Stratford, fairly clearly in 1608; for one thing, for a severe and classic drama, it is full of tell-tale country touches; for another, it has elaborate stage-directions, with notes for position, movements and even gestures, evidently for another to produce the play, with the author absent. We know that he went home to the country once a year, presumably in summer. On 5 June 1607 his daughter Susanna, the intelligent one who took after him, was married to her doctor-husband, Dr John Hall, a Cambridge man – her father would probably be there. Next summer, August 1608, he began suit in the borough court of record for a debt of £6 from John Addenbrooke. The jury gave its award to Shakespeare, with costs; but, since Addenbrooke could not be located, the gentleman of New Place – more careful about money than old John Shakespeare in Henley Street had been – sued Addenbrooke's surety in Stratford. Another suitor in the court that year had the romantic name of Florizel, which Shakespeare – with an ear for everything, an acute aural memory – would shortly make use of for the prince in *The Winter's Tale.*

In the month of September this year, 1608, his mother died and was buried at Stratford. In October he was godfather to the little son of Alderman Henry Walker, called William after him – but this might have been by proxy.

A good deal of quiet reading went into the play, besides North's translation of Plutarch, Shakespeare's stand-by in these years; characteristically, while reading up Coriolanus, he noticed Timon and kept him in mind for his next play. Whole passages of North's splendid prose could go straight into blank verse with little change; nevertheless, the play was carefully written, not carried through in one quick rush of inspiration: it is a pondered and thoughtful play. He looked up Philemon Holland's translation of Livy, and adapted a useful political fable from Camden's recent *Remains Concerning Britain*, which had come out in 1605. He also used hints from *Four Paradoxes or Politic Discourses*, propounding the martial virtues against the ill humours of peace, by Thomas and Dudley Digges. The latter was stepson of Shakespeare's friend and overseer of his will, Sir Thomas Russell, who lived out at Alderminster, a few miles from Stratford; his brother Leonard contributed verses to the First Folio. All probably acquaintances of the dramatist submerged in his work.

Again, there is no difficulty about the date of the play. 'The coal of fire upon the ice' refers back to his experience of the excessively cold winter of 1607–8, when the Thames froze over, for the first time since 1564–5, his first year: coals of fire were burned in the funfair upon the ice. The following year Ben Jonson scoffed, in his play *Epicoene*, at a rather silly line of the master's:

> He lurched all swords of the garland.

Ben improved on this: 'you have lurched your friends of the better half of the garland'. Surprisingly, there are endearing references back in the play to a wedding-night years before:

> more dances my rapt heart
> Than when I first my wedded mistress saw
> Bestride my threshold.

I have analysed *Coriolanus* in detail in my *William Shakespeare*; here we must concentrate on what is revealing of the author. With his mind ever on the look-out for something new, he produced a quite different kind of political tragedy from *Antony and Cleopatra*: that was luscious and romantic, *Coriolanus* is classical and stark, with a bitter taste. The story is the personal tragedy of a natural leader who loves his country, which needs above all the services he alone can render, but whose demagogic demands upon him he cannot accept. He is a man of uncompromising integrity: he will not stoop to talk the democratic humbug necessary to win their vote, but which he knows to be lies. The crux of his tragedy is that if he were not that kind of man he would not have been the saviour of his country. He is possessed by passionate love for Rome; when he is rejected, he turns his back on the city. He could have destroyed what he loved (as Othello did) but, by staying his hand, was himself destroyed.

Something of the social malaise of the time is reflected by its most sensitive register – with those elusive antennae – in this play. the achievements of the Elizabethan Age had been largely due to the unifying effect upon the nation of the long struggle with Spain; now that the pressure was removed, things were falling apart. Class-feeling was sharpened by the extravagance and ostentation of the Jacobean Court and aristocracy. The poor were no better off. May 1607 saw a threatened rising in the Midlands, which shook the complacency of the landowning class. The centre of the disturbance was Northamptonshire, the area most affected by enclosures of arable by the gentry (the Catholic Treshams having the worst record); but it spread to Warwickshire, where William Shakespeare, now a landed gentleman, was well aware of its dangers.

From Warwick William Combe reported the popular grievances to Salisbury this June 1608: 'the dearth of corn, the prices rising to some height, caused partly by some that are well stored refraining to bring the same to the market', i.e. holding out for higher prices. These, indeed, reached their highest this year. Then there was the issue of enclosure of arable for pasture, throwing the peasantry off the land. In his play Shakespeare concentrates on the issues of dearth of corn, class-conflict, the pros and cons of peace or war, all beating against the rock-like figure of a war-hero who cannot adapt himself to peace, let alone democracy and democratic humbug. *Some* humbug is a necessary element in a society, a kind of cement helping to keep it together; but if all is humbug – one thinks of the 1930s, before the war, and again ever since – society falls apart. Coriolanus was wrong not to accept the necessary modicum. His attitude to the people is not permissible, if understandable; he knows what idiots they always are, and is filled with contempt for them. But that is not a possible, or even proper, attitude for a politician seeking their votes – nor would such a one tell them what he thought. (In the interests of truth and instruction, a writer can and should.)

Since all writers give evidence of themselves in their writings, what can we descry of Shakespeare's personal attitude behind his repeated emphases, the changes he made from his sources to suit the drama and himself? In *Julius Caesar* he emphasised the dictator's personal weaknesses and gave an unflattering portrait – perhaps to keep some balance with the 'noble' silliness of the doctrinaire republican, Brutus, who in historic fact was less noble. Of Coriolanus Shakespeare gives us a more favourable picture than history warranted, and blackens the people of Rome, whose hostility had had more justification. Previously he had treated the mob with contemptuous good humour; now his attitude has hardened. Inconstant and variable as ever, there is now not a generous impulse in them; and, so far from being spirited, they are cowards too.

Coriolanus enforces that the people cannot operate without direction.

> where gentry, title, wisdom
> Cannot conclude but by the yea and no
> Of general ignorance, it must omit
> Real necessities, and give way the while
> To unstable slightness. Purpose so barred, it follows
> Nothing is done to purpose.

What could be more prophetic, what more exactly descriptive, of the last stage of democracy but that 'it must omit real necessities', that 'nothing is done to purpose'? We see the consequences in the state bereft

> Of that integrity which should become't,
> Not having the power to do the good it would,
> For the ill which doth control't.

It exactly describes the state of things today, when to call it in question is to be proscribed,

> And manhood is called foolery when it stands
> Against a falling fabric.

I wrote out these passages ten years ago, pointing out their aptness: since then everything has borne out their indelible truth, the scene worsened and darkened, the fabric of society falling apart.

Of course – when the whole intellectual leadership, at any rate all the half-baked intellectuals in control of the mass-media of democratic society, are bent on courses utterly contrary to honesty and common sense, contrary to the facts of human nature and society, victims of their own illusions and the propagators of lies. It is not true, and it never has been true, that men are essentially reasonable, non-violent, infinitely educable, and that they can be left to govern themselves by their own sweet will. The consequences of the inculcation of these delusions are to be seen on every hand in democratic society today. As if William Shakespeare, than whom no man has ever understood human nature more thoroughly, was wrong and superficial liberal intellectuals right!

In the play the idiot people are cock-a-hoop when the man who told them such home-truths is banished:

> The people's enemy is gone, is gone!
> Our enemy is banished! he is gone!
> Hoo-oo! [*they all shout, and throw up their caps*].

That great man, Oliver Cromwell – no Coriolanus – knew what to think of average humans: when the crowds turned out to cheer him off to fight the Scots, he said to his companion, 'Do not trust to that: these very persons would shout as much if you and I were going to be hanged.' Oliver Cromwell *knew* no less well than William Shakespeare; they were at opposite ends of the spectrum, but both men of imagination, in their different ways – both had their feet on the ground. Liberal intellectuals have neither: neither imagination, nor common sense. (If they had imagination, they would have more sense.)

The cult of the common man is the greatest enemy of incentive, quality, achievement; in itself it is a lie – as the people themselves well know – and its propagation eats away the heart-strings that hold society together. The age of Shakespeare was not afraid to face the truth about human nature and the human condition. We offer a fine contrast with the Elizabethan Age today.

CHAPTER 11

Blackfriars

THE year 1608 saw a decisive new development in the story of the King's Men and with it a new phase in the writing of their leading dramatist. Shakespeare's last plays, the group from *Cymbeline* to *The Tempest*, are different in type and character from what had gone before: they are often conveniently described as 'romances'. It has been usual to impute them to a new phase in their author's development, and this is not unlikely. But it is inadequate. With our realisation of how completely William Shakespeare was a man of the theatre, we perceive that the last phase in his dramaturgy was even more a response to the different demands upon him, with the take-over by the King's Men of the leading private theatre, the Blackfriars.

This was something exciting, experimental and very important in its consequences. 'No adult company in London had ever before performed regularly in a private theatre.'* We have seen that this move, which must have been considered for some time, had quite a story behind it. There was the long-established rivalry between the boys' companies and the men's companies, which came to a head in 1600–1. Ben Jonson's *Poetaster*, which had ridiculed some of the Chamberlain's Men, was performed by the boys at Blackfriars. Dekker's *Satiromastix*, which answered it, was played by Shakespeare's Company at the Globe in 1601. Three years later they simply annexed Marston's *Malcontent*, a Blackfriars boys' play, got John Webster to adapt it for the public theatre and acted it at the Globe. Now, by far the most prosperous and leading company, the King's Men, they were going to invade Blackfriars itself.

Actually the Burbages already owned it, but had been leasing it

* Bentley, *Shakespeare and His Theatre*, p. 69.

out. To take it over and operate it by the King's Men needed careful thought and planning for, if it succeeded, it offered the chance of a more select and expensive audience and larger profits. There was money in it – as the Philistine Edward VII observed to Sir Sidney Lee *à propos* of his *Shakespeare*. It was indeed the most profitable audience in London, upper class, ready to pay for something new, and apt to be connected with the Court. In theatre-terms it represented the increasing split in that integration of society which had made the greatness of the Elizabethan Age: it portended the widening division between upper and lower classes – select theatres for the former, the public theatres for the latter.

For the present, to those in theatre-business, it was the new opportunities to be taken advantage of that mattered. Indoor, more comfortable conditions, not open to the weather; evening performances by candle-light in winter; a smaller space and a more select audience demanded quieter, more intimate acting, with music and elaborated staging, the element of the masque – so popular at Court – to the fore. All this offered a challenge, particularly to the leading figure among the King's Men, at any rate the one concerned with more aspects of their work than any other. We have seen that all through his career he was always ready to tackle something new – Robert Greene had seen that from the first. Now the incentive was certainly there.

By this time the King's Men's profits from performances at Court amounted to four times as much as they had received, as the Chamberlain's Men, under the careful Elizabeth. By 1612 it was said that they were taking £1000 a winter more at Blackfriars than they had done formerly at the Globe.* By the end of James's reign the takings from the much smaller Blackfriars audience were more than twice as much for a bellowing performance at the Globe. By the reign of Charles I the King's Men were essentially connected in the public mind with the Blackfriars rather than the Globe. The last phase of Shakespeare's work reflects this transition and, in a sense,

* In these paragraphs I am indebted to G. E. Bentley, 'Shakespeare and the Blackfriars Theatre', *Shakespeare Survey*, *1*, pp. 38 ff.; and his *Shakespeare and His Theatre*, ch. IV.

is transitional in character. He himself had had his training and spent most of his life in the public theatre; all the same, frequent performances at Court, as well as productions for private occasions, gave him flexibility. The Blackfriars audience were always keen to have something new; the Globe, true to popular instincts, was faithful to old favourites. Shakespeare could appeal to both worlds; but in his last years the Blackfriars was becoming the more important concern to him and his fellows.

In the summer of 1608, special arrangements were entered into for the new venture. The Burbages said that their father had purchased the Blackfriars 'at extreme rates and made it into a playhouse with great charge and trouble'. It had been leased to Thomas Evans, who directed the Children of the Chapel there; 'the boys daily wearing out', some of them became King's Men. Now the Burbages bought the lease back, and to finance the venture they formed a group of seven men – themselves with Evans, and Shakespeare, Heming, Condell, William Sly. Each of them put down an unknown capital payment, and paid his share of the rent, £5 14*s* 4*d* a year. Five of these seven were King's Men, already 'house-keepers' at the Globe, so that 'the profits of the dramatic enterprise continued to stay almost entirely in the hands of the acting group'. We appreciate what exceptional incentive these men enjoyed, and what a close-knit fellowship the inner group formed.

Other steps were necessary to provide the kind of fare demanded by the venture; these were successful, for it prospered. Some five years later, in 1613, the dramatist bought himself a house in Blackfriars. This would be very convenient for winter performances, when he was now mainly based upon New Place, no longer a lodger about town. He paid £140 for the house, so it was another substantial investment: £80 down, £60 on a mortgage which was paid off at the date due. No trouble about cash now! His fellow-sureties – who sold the property for the family two years after his death – were John Heming, John Jackson, a well-to-do London citizen, and William Johnson. Now William Johnson was the host of the Mermaid Inn – another factual indication to corroborate a good old tradition.

It is Thomas Fuller of the *Worthies*, born in this year 1608, to whom we owe the information which tradition has fixed upon the Mermaid – we now see, probably enough. 'Many were the wit-combats between him and Ben Jonson: which two I behold like a Spanish great galleon and an English man-of-war. Master Jonson, like the former, was built far higher in learning; solid, but slow in his performances. Shakespeare, with the English man-of-war, lesser in bulk but lighter in sailing, could turn with all tides, tack about and take advantage of all winds, by the quickness of his wit and invention.'*

The well-known Mermaid tavern was in Bread Street, which ran from West Cheapside south to the river, whence a wherry would take one across to the theatres on Bankside. Bread Street east of St Paul's, Blackfriars just west, Silver Street not far to the north – it was a small world, dominated by the immense cliff of Old St Paul's, which had lost its soaring spire only a few years before Shakespeare's birth.

After his tiff with the Chamberlain's Men, Jonson wrote briefly for Philip Henslowe and his rival company, chiefly botching and mending, for he did not think any of it worth publishing subsequently. Soon he turned his hand to writing fashionable masques, for persons like Sir William Cornwallis and occasions such as the marriage of Lady Frances Howard and young Essex, so unfortunate in each other. With the *Masque of Blackness* in the winter of 1604–1605 Jonson inaugurated the series of brilliant Court masques which had such success that he was called on to continue them during practically the rest of the reign. His star was rising; already he had had considerable experience of writing for the boys at Blackfriars, and also of directing them. From his touching tribute to Solomon Pavy, who played old men's parts to perfection, his references to Nathan Field – one of the Blackfriars boys who became a King's Man – and from what people said about his relations with them, he was evidently closer to them than William Shakespeare was.

* Quoted in Chambers, *William Shakespeare*, II. 244.

With his good nature and his good business sense Shakespeare seems to have borne his quarrelsome junior no grudge. Just as he had given Ben his first opportunity with *Every Man in His Humour* and acted in it, so he had welcomed *Sejanus* and *Volpone* for the Globe. Show-business was more important than literary disputes. Jonson's work, with its appeal to more sophisticated audiences, both intellectual and at Court, would be particularly valuable for Blackfriars. He seems to have written his most amusing play, *Epicoene, or the Silent Woman*, for that audience; certainly *The Alchemist* was written for the King's Men. Henceforth he wrote nearly all his remaining plays for them, and during these years, from 1607 until he went abroad in 1612, he lived conveniently in Blackfriars.

Two dramatists of the younger generation, Ben's juniors and admirers, were also recruited to Blackfriars: their work was shaped admirably to the audience. These were Francis Beaumont and John Fletcher; thus was the future provided for: the longer-lived of the two, Fletcher, became Shakespeare's collaborator and eventual successor. Beaumont died, still a young man, in the same year as Shakespeare; but his intimate companion and survivor continued to dominate the stage at Blackfriars till his death, also early, in 1625. They made their name and fame together, the Castor and Pollux of the stage, or – as Ben Jonson called them – the Damon and Pythias. They were both gentlemen born: Beaumont of an old Leicestershire family, and an Oxford man; Fletcher, son of a handsome bishop, a favourite with Queen Elizabeth (until he married a second time). Aubrey tells us that they 'lived together on the Bankside, not far from the playhouse, both bachelors; lay together; had one wench in the house between them, which they did so admire; the same clothes and cloak, etc., between them'.

And thus did Jonson depict them in *Bartholomew Fair*, which, exceptionally, was not written for the King's Men: 'two faithful friends o' the Bankside', that 'have both but one drab', and enter with a gammon of bacon together under their cloak. During an absence in the country Beaumont wrote a verse-letter to Ben, two of their comedies 'then not finished, which deferred their merry meetings at the Mermaid'. In the sun of the countryside,

in this warm shine
I lie and dream of your full Mermaid wine.
O, we have water mixed with claret lees,
Drink apt to bring in drier heresies
Than beer, good only for the Sonnet's strain,
With fustian metaphors to stuff the brain.

There follows the famous tribute to the Mermaid and all the fun they had there:

What things have we seen,
Done at the Mermaid! heard words that have been
So nimble, and so full of subtle flame,
As if that every one from whence they came,
Had meant to put his whole wit in a jest . . .
when there hath been thrown
Wit able enough to justify the Town
For three days past, wit that might warrant be
For the whole City to talk foolishly. . . .

And so it goes on – another tribute to the tradition.

Beaumont and Fletcher's work was essentially geared to the private theatre, most of it to Blackfriars, for which their brilliant early plays, *The Knight of the Burning Pestle* and *The Faithful Shepherdess*, had been written already. At their first appearance these were not successful; but their next play, written for the new Blackfriars with the King's Men, *Philaster*, was a great hit and helped largely to settle the new direction. It was followed year after year by others, *The Maid's Tragedy*, *A King and No King*, *The Two Noble Kinsmen*, and so on. The large body of work accomplished by them, with Fletcher's after Beaumont's death, fixed their names inseparably in the public mind and carried forward into the future. After the barbarism of the Civil War, it was their work that appealed most, and suited the conditions best, of the Restoration stage. For the modern theatre from that time onwards followed the model of Blackfriars, not of the old Globe.

Once again, in 1608 plague came to disrupt conditions in the theatre world, as in 1603 and the longer visitation of 1592 and 1593 – with such consequences in Shakespeare's life. Now again the theatres were closed for most of 1608. Scholars do not sufficiently allow for the impact of these external circumstances; yet there is evidence of a hiatus in 1608 – Blackfriars does not seem to get going until 1609. And it looks as if Shakespeare's own work was interfered with. *Timon of Athens*, of this time, was never finished; *Pericles* offers a problem, but it seems fairly clear that Shakespeare completed someone else's first two acts with another three. Then in 1609, remarkable for the small number of plays published after a lean year for the stage, his Sonnets from years before were published. This is not without significance – just as they had been written in that earlier and more critical plague-period.

We must address ourselves to this period which other scholars have noticed to be problematical.

When Shakespeare was reading up North's Plutarch for *Coriolanus*, his eye lighted on the stories of Timon and Alcibiades which he decided to combine for his next play. Actually they had nothing to do with each other, and they are given only the loosest connection in the play as he left it. There is an indication of a sub-plot concerning Alcibiades and *his* grievance against Athens; but this would have been a repetition of Timon's, so it is left in the air. A Fool is introduced at one point, so that there was an alternative intention of a comic sub-plot, but it was not carried out. Nor had Shakespeare made up his mind about the characters – except for Timon and Apemantus, the cynical philosopher. The play is very short.

But it is all the more fascinating, for from it we have an authentic insight into how he worked. Even Greg waxes eloquent, observing that 'the drama has only half disengaged itself from the matrix of thought' – like the unfinished sculptures of Michelangelo still imprisoned in the stone from which they were being hewn. This play, arrested in the process of execution, entirely corroborates the modern perception that Shakespeare wrote scenes as he visualised them, not necessarily in the order of the play. He did not follow a unilateral development of plot, as a modern writer would. Thus he worked mainly on the first Act and the last two, leaving the middle in a sketched-out state, not filled in. Still, it is not chaotic or incoherent: the bones are there, unclothed with flesh.

A further consequence is still more enlightening, for it shows just how the bones were clothed, how the language came to him. When Ben Jonson wrote a poem, he wrote it in prose, then worked it up into verse. With Shakespeare things came more easily and naturally. In *Timon* there are chunks of prose intermingled with epigrammatic rhymed couplets, just as they occurred to him. Rhyme came easily to him – early or later there is always much more rhyme than non-poets notice, for it often comes spontaneously within the line rather than at the end: this is the way things come into the heads of natural poets. Though unfinished, *Timon* has a great deal of rhyme.

Why did he not finish this play?

It would seem that the subject did not satisfy him: it was not possible to make a hero like Lear or Macbeth, or even Coriolanus, out of Timon. Misanthropy did not come naturally to William Shakespeare: he was not a Swift – he really could not hate his fellow-man. The idea is expressed powerfully enough, and so are the things that help to justify it: hypocrisy, vanity, flattery, humbug, the sheer silliness of humans. They are all there in the play:

> Who dares, who dares,
> In purity of manhood stand upright,
> And say, 'This man's a flatterer?' If one be,
> So are they all . . .
> the learnèd pate
> Ducks to the golden fool

– i.e. dons sucked up to patrons, as today to press-lords or T.V. –

> All is oblique:
> There's nothing level in our cursèd natures
> But direct villainy.

Thus Timon, when the scales of illusion had dropped from his eyes: he went from one extreme to another. It is unlikely that that appealed to Shakespeare, with his catholic, essentially sound view of human nature, realising that, if there was bad, there was certainly far more good. The trouble with Timon is that he never engages our sympathy, as even Coriolanus does.

Again this play revealingly reflects the time, the nauseating aspects of Jacobean society, the vulgar ostentation, the insincerity in high places, the more sordid aspects of patronage, the pretences of society about art and letters, the humbug of those in the business about each other's work. A painter inquires touchingly of a poet: 'You are rapt, sir, in some work, some dedication to the great lord?' The poet replies, with the bogus modesty one knows so well – 'a thing slipped idly by me'. When he reciprocates with flattery of the painter's work, the painter modestly disclaims praise. The poet is moved to enthuse in verse:

> Admirable! How this grace
> Speaks his own standing! What a mental power
> This eye shoots forth! How big imagination
> Moves in this lip!

The painter yields: .. ..

> It is a pretty mocking of the life.
> Here is a touch. Is't good?

The poet goes one better:

> I will say of it,
> It tutors nature. Artificial strife
> Lives in these touches, livelier than life.

It might be a professional artistic circle any time, anywhere.

There is a direct reflection of the excitement over Virginia in these years in the themes so important in the play, the mania for gold – with Timon's set oration on it, like other orations in the plays to set the tone, Faulconbridge's on Commodity, for instance – and then at the end being reduced to digging for roots. In 1607

Jamestown was founded, the first permanent English settlement in America, for which the Elizabethans had fought so long. Immense enthusiasm was generated over it in the country, as we shall see. To encourage the enterprise, Shakespeare's friend Drayton wrote his splendid Ode:

> You brave heroic minds,
> Worthy your country's name. . . .

He bade them quickly aboard,

> And cheerfully at sea,
> Success you still entice,
>   To get the pearl and gold
>   And ours to hold –
> Virginia,
> Earth's only paradise.

The success was not equal to the poem. When the brave heroic minds got there, they fell victim to the mania for gold: the report came back, 'no talk, no hope, no work but to dig gold, wash gold, refine gold, load gold'. In fact, it was all an illusion, like Timon's and there was no gold. But this was how the colonists spent their time, instead of sowing the seed and laying the foundations of a subsistence agriculture. In the end they were reduced to digging for roots.

So far from William Shakespeare not being in touch with what was going on in the world around him, 'transcending' experience, it never was probable of so alert an intelligence. We have seen what an avid, if rapid, reader he was – it simply was that, overwhelmed with work, for the rest he kept to himself, as John Aubrey gathered later.

There was no time to attend to the printing of his plays, even if he had been interested in doing so. There is no sign that he was – the play was the thing: the play on the stage. His literary ambition was satisfied with recognition as a poet – to the Elizabethans that ranked higher; and he took his place along with the others, friend

Drayton and Daniel. He did not share Jonson's aggressive literary pretensions, and intellectuals rated Jonson more highly; from this time there are far more references to him. For one thing, he was a critic and discourser on literature, and that generates notice; for another, he had a following among the new literary generation, from Donne to Carew. Shakespeare was, above all, popular.

This is brought home to us in the case of his next play, *Pericles*, of which as usual he took no trouble to provide a text for any printer; a recent editor of the play makes the suggestion that the plague of 1608 may have disturbed printing conditions as it certainly did the stage. The result is a problem as to which there is no agreed solution. There is a consensus of opinion that the first two acts have only a few touches of Shakespeare, if at all; and that the last three acts are mainly his. If this is so, it would seem that he completed, or revised, a play begun by someone else; though this does not exclude the possibility that he might have suggested the lines for another to follow, in the first two acts. This, for some reason, we do not know – it could be absence from London on account of plague, or illness; at Stratford his mother died in September this year, 1608.

He had known the story of Antiochus from early days, but the form of the story comes from John Gower's *Confessio Amantis*. Gower is brought forward to play an important rôle as Chorus, very much as the Chorus is used in *Henry V* to suggest off-stage action, and to bridge space and time. This consideration inclines one to think that Shakespeare may have suggested the earlier part and completed the thing for himself. His hand in the second part is unmistakable; and perhaps no less in the over-all direction. For he characteristically played down the incestuous relations of Antiochus with his daughter, and made much more of the appealing part of chaste Marina.

Then, too, there are the brothel scenes, which the virtuous Victorians preferred to think of as not by Shakespeare: on the contrary, they are just like him – the bawdy is natural and would appeal to an Elizabethan audience, neither incestuous nor homosexual. Of Marina,

> Such a maidenhead were no cheap thing, if men were as they have been.
>
> There was a Spaniard's mouth so watered, that he went to bed to her very description.
>
> . . . your bride goes to that with shame which is her way to go with warrant.
> Faith, some do, and some do not.
>
> Fie, fie upon her! she's able to freeze the god
> Priapus, and undo a whole generation.
>
> Now the pox upon her green-sickness for me!
> 'Faith there's no way to be rid on't but by the way to the pox.

It is Shakespeare all through; the audience is titillated, then virtue triumphs – which is what it likes. A contemporary critic of perception has noticed 'the intense sexuality that is one of the enigmatic features of Shakespeare's last plays'.* True, it is there all right; but why enigmatic? It always had been there: at least, observable in his work from the time of his three narrative poems and his entry into the Southampton ambience – as an aristocratic society, more sophisticated and self-aware about sex and its cult.

Dramatically speaking, *Pericles*, for all the unsatisfactoriness of the literary form in which it has come down to us, inaugurated the last phase in Shakespeare's work. It is experimental, it offers novel situations and surprises – as *The Winter's Tale* does, paradoxically, with even more improbability and greater success. This was going to be the chief characteristic of the drama of Beaumont and Fletcher, which developed *along with* Shakespeare's new direction – no one has been able to establish which had priority, these young men or the older master. What we do know is that the master's work was ever present to their minds, most of all to Fletcher's: they sometimes achieved a play by reversing the situation in

* Leech, *John Fletcher Plays*, p. 165.

one of Shakespeare's, giving it a new twist or reversing the sexes. Their famous play *Philaster* seems to have taken *Hamlet* for its point of departure; *The Woman's Prize* may be seen as *The Taming of the Shrew* in reverse; *The Custom of the Country* a variation on *Measure for Measure.**

These evidences of his influence we cannot go into here: it offers a subject in itself. Professor Leech tells us, 'there is not, I think, a single play in the Beaumont and Fletcher Folios which does not display Shakespearean echoes'.†

Pericles was immensely popular. A pamphlet of 1609 testified to this:

> Amazed I stood to see a crowd
> Of civil throats stretched out so loud . . .
> So that I truly thought all these
> Came to see *Shore* or *Pericles*.

George Wilkins cashed in to publish a tale, *The Painful Adventures of Pericles, Prince of Tyre*, which is, however, based much more on Lawrence Twyne's *Painful Adventures*, though he knew the play. A surreptitious quarto of it, shockingly printed, went into some six editions up to 1635. It is curious to us that this play should have been so successful, as it was to Ben Jonson, who wrote grumpily:

> No doubt some mouldy tale
> Like *Pericles* . . .
> May keep up the Play-club.

Evidently it did, when his grand *Sejanus* or *Catiline* would not.

For our purpose all we need say is that this period, these years, set a bound between the previous works, the great tragedies, and the romances; and that this play announces new themes, a new vision. We are not at liberty to speculate on what these might mean in his own personal life; we must not make a direct transference. But real writers write out of the experience of their hearts, not

* Leech, *John Fletcher Plays*, pp. 52, 58, 84. † Ibid. p. 162.

merely from the arid intellect – as Proust so profoundly understood – and the themes of these last plays are reunion after long division, reconciliation, forgiveness. They are about children lost and found, bringing together divided parents; innocence threatened and retrieved from the fire; wife rejected and ill-used, then restored, as if from the grave. After storm and stress – the storms of *Pericles* and *The Tempest* – after all the evils encountered, the ills endured, a haven is found at last: the haven of home. For all their happy endings, these plays have an atmosphere full of suggestion and symbol, suffused with tears.

What can it have meant in his life?

The New Arden editor of *Pericles* has perceptively observed that at this time, after a plague-year, 'one would expect to find not merely a number of plays rushed to the printers by needy playwrights, but also much irregular printing: for the temptation of piracy must have been especially great. . . . The plague must have affected the printing trade too.'* Among the books brought forth in this year 1609 was *Shakespeare's Sonnets: Never Before Imprinted*, published by Thomas Thorpe, who had somehow got the manuscript – for which we are eternally grateful.

Thorpe was not a pirate, but a perfectly respectable publisher, who was a friend of Marlowe's friend and publisher, Edward Blount. It was through Blount's good offices that Thorpe had got the manuscript of Marlowe's translation of the First Book of Lucan's *Pharsalia*, which Thorpe published with an arch and idiosyncratic dedication to Blount. Thorpe wrote a number of such dedications, which have been described as 'bombastic'; but this is too crude a word: they are, rather, flowery and self-conscious, apt to be obsequious in a lower-class manner (he was the son of an inn-keeper). In the very next year he addressed another dedication, in somewhat extravagant terms, to the Earl of Pembroke, to whom he proffered another dedicatory epistle in 1616.

Thorpe had literary pretentions; but he also had literary tastes. In

* *Pericles*, ed. F. D. Hoeniger, New Arden Shakespeare, p. xxv.

1610 he dedicated a translation of Epictetus to John Florio. He is a curious figure, for he seems to have been more interested in the literary than the business side of publishing. He was exceptional in having no fixed premises; the manuscripts he got hold of he had printed for him by one stationer and sold by another. But what is remarkable is the quality of the manuscripts he procured and managed to publish. The year before he got the *Sonnets,* he published Chapman's *Biron* and Ben Jonson's masques of Blackness and Beauty. Altogether his sparse but distinguished list of publications included a work of Marlowe, three works of Chapman, four of Ben Jonson, including *Sejanus,* besides Shakespeare's *Sonnets.*

It is simply the flowery terms in which Thorpe gratefully dedicated the *Sonnets* to 'Mr W. H.', who had got the manuscript, that have led to so much unnecessary confusion: Thorpe called him 'the only begetter' ,which has led imperceptive people – including some eminent scholars – into confusing him with Shakespeare's young Lord. No lord could ever be addressed as Mr, as they should have known; it is also a not very obscure piece of knowledge that Elizabethans regularly referred to knights as Mr – Sir Francis Bacon is regularly Master Bacon; the Countess of Southampton always refers to her second husband, Sir Thomas Heneage, as Master Heneage. So 'Mr W. H.' cannot be a lord; he can be a knight.

Thorpe dedicated the *Sonnets* in his usual amateurish, overwritten fashion:

> To the only begetter of these ensuing sonnets Mr W. H. all happiness and that eternity promised by our ever-living poet wisheth the well-wishing adventurer in setting forth T. T.

The Countess had died two years before, in 1607, leaving all her household goods and chattels to her third husband, Sir William Harvey. Harvey was a young man, and next year, 1608, he married a young wife, Cordelia Annesley. This is why in 1609 Thorpe is wishing him 'all happiness', and 'that eternity promised by our ever-living poet' is the eternity that Shakespeare had promised Southampton years before, if he would marry and carry on the family to posterity. 'The well-wishing adventurer in setting forth' is a reference to the Virginia adventure, the second charter in which everybody was taking up shares, the great venture set forth in 1609.

That Thorpe got the *Sonnets* from the Southampton *cache* is corroborated by the fact that he published along with them Shakespeare's prentice-poem, 'A Lover's Complaint', of which the hero is the youth of the Sonnets – long, hanging curls, hardly any hair as yet upon his chin, rather ambivalent:

> His qualities were beauteous as his form,
> For maiden-tongued he was, and thereof free . . .
>
> That he did in the general bosom reign
> Of young, of old; and sexes both enchanted. . . .

We are back in those years that enshrined the decisive experiences of the poet's life, that had shaped his future. So much had happened in the years since: Southampton's disastrous following of his leader, Essex, at sea, into Ireland and rebellion; his narrow escape from the scaffold upon which Essex died; the two years in the Tower. There followed deliverance and favour with the new King; the delayed adolescent settled into an exceptionally happy family-life. In 1608 his second son Thomas was born, who succeeded as fourth Earl; so that the family was continued until the Restoration. Upon his death male issue failed, and the great inheritance, which would by then have purchased a dukedom, was split up among co-heiresses, and came ultimately to the Dukes of Portland, Bedford and Buccleuch. The poet's prophecy of immortality through his verse proved more lasting.

One thing about Thorpe's publication of the *Sonnets* we must not say – namely, that Shakespeare had nothing to do with it; for we do not know. He made no protest, as he had done over Chettle's publication of Greene's attack, and over Jaggard's putting his name on the title-page of *The Passionate Pilgrim*. Heywood tells us, 'so the author I know much offended that, altogether unknown to him, presumed to make so bold with his name'. Heywood added, 'he to do himself right hath since published them in his own name'. What are we to infer from this? It would not be far-fetched to say that any poet would be glad to see his sonnets ultimately in print. The coast was clear: it had all happened long before; Southampton was happily immersed in family life and public business, his problems over; his mother was now dead. Emilia and her husband had disappeared, almost certainly dead – I have never come across any reference to them after Forman's last notice in 1600. Not only was the old Lord Chamberlain Hunsdon dead, but his son and successor too.

With the return to normal conditions, in this year 1609 Shakespeare produced his next play, *Cymbeline*. It has been noticed that this play is exceptionally full of reminiscences of his earlier work, but the significance of this has been missed: in the interval he had been reading his early poems. The motivation that sets going *Cymbeline* is that of *The Rape of Lucrece:* the wager taken by a husband as to his wife's chastity during his absence. Situation and language are similar. When, in the play, Iachimo invades Imogen's bedroom, the room is similarly described and the former scene recalled:

> Our Tarquin thus
> Did softly press the rushes, ere he wakened
> The chastity he wounded.

Imogen is then described in language that recalls *Venus and Adonis*; while

> She hath been reading late
> The tale of Tereus; here the leaf's turned down
> Where Philomel gave up.

This goes back to *Titus Andronicus*, while she is described also as the rare Arabian bird of 'The Phoenix and the Turtle'.

There are not only verbal reminiscences but repetitions of situation: the circumstances of foreign invasion are very like those of *Lear* but, since it is Roman, Julius Caesar is recalled. The patriotic motive is altogether less convincing than in *Richard II* and *King*

John – naturally enough, since the circumstances were altered, the war over; and the language is constricted and elliptical, altogether less effective.

What is the reason of it all? The play is somewhat halting, its language long-winded and parenthetical; it is too long – for successful production it needs cutting. In a way it is experimental, like its immediate predecessors, *Timon of Athens* and *Pericles*. Even the unimaginative Chambers postulated a breakdown of health at this time. There is nothing improbable in that, after such years of passionate intensity and overwork. I have myself detected symptoms of nervous fatigue in the stuttering parentheses in the play's language, and in its *longueurs*. But, as to the fact, we have no information. We only know that for a subject Shakespeare went back again to his earliest favourite, Holinshed, and filled it out with other early reading, *The Mirror for Magistrates* and a tale from Boccaccio.

Perhaps more important, with our new emphasis on theatre conditions, is its experimental nature. Shakespeare may have had both Blackfriars and the Globe in view, somewhat undecided. The play does provide something new – the surprises, the improbable turns, the scenic spectacles, the atmosphere of fantasy. The old master labours hard to give it to them, with a masque thrown in, Jupiter on an eagle descending in thunder and lightning, with the apparitions of the dead falling on their knees. It was the changes and chances, the coincidences and improbabilities, that attracted that ardent playgoer, Simon Forman, when he saw the play – and, incidentally, preserved the original form of the heroine's name, Innogen.

With his next two plays, *The Winter's Tale* and *The Tempest*, the experimental period is over: Shakespeare achieved not one but two exquisite masterpieces. *The Winter's Tale* was almost certainly written at home at Stratford, in the winter and spring of 1610–11; it is full – more so than any of his plays since *A Midsummer Night's Dream* – of country atmosphere, of flowers and meads, country characters and junketings, a sheep-shearing feast with folk-songs, the pedlar songs of Autolycus: a marvellous late creation from Cotswold life to set beside those earlier bucolics, Bottom and his companions.

It has been common for the academic – even such eminent Victorians as 'Q' (Quiller-Couch) and Robert Bridges – to criticise the motivation of *The Winter's Tale*, Leontes' jealousy, as unconvincing and inadequate. But they were wrong. We now realise that Leontes' jealousy was a psychosis, and follows precisely the pattern analysed by Freud. It had been unconsciously smouldering, was somehow entangled with Leontes' earlier emotional feelings about his friend, and suddenly burst forth. The suddenness is not only highly dramatic, but psychologically exact: this is what happens in such cases. It is only one more example, but a striking one, of Shakespeare's intuitive knowledge of human nature foreshadowing the findings of modern psychology. As if he had not a deeper understanding of it, and its darker recesses, than my old acquaintances Q and Robert Bridges – neither of whom, as eminently respectable Victorians, liked to contemplate the uglier facts of life. Here, incidentally, is one of the profound contrasts between Victorian and Elizabethan literature.

Others – even such a grandee as Dr Johnson, whose own genius was not for drama – have thought the play insufficiently dramatic. That mistake is apt to come from reading the plays instead of seeing them. Anyone who saw Gielgud's production of *The Winter's Tale*, inspired by an inner understanding of Shakespeare's intentions and the genius to realise them, will know that the play is beyond belief moving. The reason is that the myth is archetypal: it lays its fingers on our hearts and searches into its recesses, in a way that the merely cerebral never can. Shakespeare 'preferred men to monsters quite as much as Ben Jonson did [that essentially cerebral man], but had a deeper intuition than Jonson of the monster that can lurk in the man.'* As for dramatic technique, 'Shakespeare clears away obvious motives for much the same reason as the psychologist: to give us some awareness of motives lying deeper down.'

* Stewart, *Character and Motive in Shakespeare*, pp. 31, 36.

Here is the place to pay tribute to those Shakespearian actors of our time – Gielgud, Olivier, Edith Evans – who have, above all, subordinated themselves to realising Shakespeare's intentions and, in so doing, have achieved superlative re-creations on the stage. How much they have achieved for our understanding of the dramatist, and how much we owe, in turn, to the benefactions of their genius!

For his new play Shakespeare turned to an old and popular tale of Greene's, *Pandosto*. It is ironical that at the end of his career Shakespeare should have turned back to the man who had attacked him at its outset – and perhaps foresaw its eventual success. For, 'there are more verbal echoes from *Pandosto* than from any other novel used by Shakespeare as a source'. We see Shakespeare, having read the tale again and made the changes he intended in the plot – significantly, a happy ending with the survival of Hermione instead of her death – with *Pandosto* 'at his elbow as he wrote; and as he wrote from time to time turned to the book to refresh his memory, using it sometimes almost verbatim, sometimes with little change and sometimes with much . . . but finding there the constant source for most of his material'.*

He used not only Greene's tale but his cony-catching pamphlets, those realistic transcripts of low life – about pick-pockets, confidence tricksters, sharpers, rogues – which are the most memorable things among his variegated output. (Greene had known all about low life, for he lived it.) Other touches, too, come indirectly from Greene, along with names from Sidney's *Arcadia* and strokes from Ovid and Golding. Altogether, the play is backward-looking, in the sense that the reading for it goes back to Shakespeare's early days and favourites. The indebtedness to Greene reinforces my earlier comment that something significant between Greene and the up-and-coming actor has been lost. Even in the subsequent literary relations, it has been commented, 'the extent of Shakespeare's knowledge and use of Greene has not been fully explored'.

* *The Winter's Tale*, ed. J. H. P. Pafford, New Arden Shakespeare, pp. xxx, xxxi, xxxv.

They should be – a much more useful contribution than most contemporary 'criticism' in symbolic and theoretic terms of which the author was blissfully unaware.

The best modern criticism deals with these plays in the relevant terms – the dramatic. A Blackfriars audience demanded something new, like Fletcher's *Philaster*, which had a prodigious influence, with its pastoralism *à la* Guarini such as a sophisticated audience relished precisely because it was sophisticated – like Marie Antoinette going milk-maiding to the petit-Trianon. Such an audience prefers the fanciful to the realistic, poetry and song to prating and orating, dancing and an element of Court masque. Shakespeare was in origin a man of the public theatre and public acting – but of all kinds; we have seen how catholic and comprehensive his contacts were, with private theatricals as well as Court and university productions and Inns of Court performances, in addition to the Theatre, the Swan, the Globe, and touring around the country. So there is no wonder that his last plays also appealed to all tastes: he always had.

Simon Forman saw the play at the Globe on 15 May 1611, and was particularly interested, as usual, in the strange turns of fortune, the tricks played, the resort to the oracle of Apollo, the authority of prophecy, and the lessons to be learned. He was much taken with Autolycus: 'Remember also the rogue that came in all tattered like Col-pixy [a hobgoblin], how he feigned him sick and to have been robbed of all that he had, how he cozened the poor man of all his money. And after came to the sheep-shear[ing] with a pedlar's pack and there cozened them again of all their money. How he changed apparel with the King of Bohemia's son; then how he turned courtier etc. Beware of trusting feigned beggars or fawning fellows.'

Forman, as a practising astrologer, saw the play from this special angle; but this did not mean that he did not appreciate other aspects, of character, dramatic situation, etc. – he may have appreciated the poetry and music, for he was a versifier, though a poor one, himself. In any case, the ordinary Elizabethan's taste turned to doggerel, as the ordinary person's does at all times. So his reactions to the plays he saw give us valuable indications of what contemporary playgoers went to see, and appreciated. The play had a very different audience at Court on Gunpowder Day that year, 5 November 1611; and it was one of the several plays by its author presented during the festivities for Princess Elizabeth's wedding in February 1613.

Everyone notices the close similarity between *Pericles* and *The Winter's Tale* in plot, situations and themes: the *Tale*, too, has coincidences of situation and echoes of thought and language with *Cymbeline*. Only, what was unsatisfactory in *Pericles* and *Cymbeline* is carried forward to artistic triumph in *The Winter's Tale* and *The Tempest*. All these plays have the impressionist technique of the last phase of a master – not that Shakespeare's work has at any time a static or statuesque perfection, it is too full of life. His greatest critic, Dr Johnson, noticed – as Ben had before him – that Shakespeare was often careless and perfunctory, his plays presented occasional inconsistencies and loose ends he never bothered to ravel up, perhaps did not even notice. Dr Johnson thought that in particular the endings of his plays sometimes gave evidence of his being in a hurry to get on with the next. There could be no clearer indication of the pressure under which he worked, that the demands of the theatre came first and last with his plays.

Several times he wrote with deprecating affection of old fireside tales, such as he liked and the world with him; Ben Jonson not. He thought *Pericles* a mouldy tale, and had no high regard for 'tales' as a genre. These late tales, except for *The Tempest*, have little unity; they range over space and time, and even *The Tempest* assumes a period and events prior to the play. They open all the more range to our imagination; they are full, like Prospero's island, of echoes and suggestions.

From our point of view it is the themes that are most suggestive of this latest phase in Shakespeare's life: they suggest homecoming. They are essentially about parents and children; they are about happiness achieved through suffering; innocence tried by adversity, no 'fugitive and cloistered virtue'; estrangement and separation, then finding each other again. They are about forgiveness for wrong done, and reconciliation. Those who are justified in the plays are a wronged woman, like Hermione; or innocent girls put to the test, like Marina and Perdita – these are they who arouse their creator's imagination, not the young men: they do not suffer, and have little interest for us.

The country atmosphere of *The Winter's Tale* is poignantly nostalgic: the life of Arden and Cotswolds is given final expression here. The songs express it, being, as usual, entirely in keeping: in this play they are close to folk-songs, indeed Autolycus sings customary pedlar songs. We are reminded that in the Elizabethan age folks of all kinds offered their wares with songs, as in the Cries of London, upon which composers wrote fantasies or variations. Spring is in:

> When daffodils begin to peer,
> With hey! the doxy over the dale,
> Why, then comes in the sweet o' the year;
> For the red blood reigns in the winter's pale;

summer in:

> The lark that tirra-lirra chants,
> With hey! with hey! the thrush and the jay,
> Are summer songs for me and my aunts,
> While we lie tumbling in the hay.

So, too, with the pedlar's songs: they are such as any Elizabethan pedlar would sing in hawking his wares:

> Will you buy any tape,
> Or lace for your cape,
> My dainty duck, my dear-a?
> Any silk, any thread,
> Any toys for your head,
> Of the new'st and fin'st, fin'st wear-a?
> Come to the pedlar;
> Money's a meddler
> That doth utter all men's ware-a.

These songs are perfectly placed in their required setting, and remind us that this exquisite song-writer in an age when all could write songs always shaped his to the needs of the play. They reflect, too, its dominant tone, from the sprightliness of *The Two Gentlemen of Verona:*

> Who is Silvia? What is she
>   That all our swains commend her?

and the gaiety of *As You Like It*:

> It was a lover and his lass,
>   With a hey, and a ho, and a hey nonnino. . . .

We move on to the melancholy music of *Twelfth Night*:

> What is love? 'Tis not hereafter;

mingled with the drunken catches and snatches of contemporary ballads of Sir Toby Belch, and ending with folksong, that rounds off the play a little sadly:

> When that I was and a little tiny boy,
>   With hey, ho, the wind and the rain. . . .

And so to the moodiness of *Measure for Measure*, and the sadness of Mariana in the moated grange:

> Take, O, take those lips away,
>   That so sweetly were forsworn;
> And those eyes, the break of day,
>   Lights that do mislead the morn.

There are the heart-broken, and heart-breaking, songs of Ophelia gone mad:

> How should I your true love know
>   From another one?

and the desolation of Desdemona, realising that she is forsaken, singing the Willow Song:

The poor soul sat sighing by a sycamore tree.

Cymbeline has a couple of exquisite songs:

Hark, hark! the lark at heaven's gate sings;

and, most moving of them all:

Fear no more the heat o' the sun,
  Nor the furious winter's rages;
Thou thy worldly task hast done,
  Home art gone, and ta'en thy wages.

Even yet there are Ariel's songs to come in *The Tempest*, very much in character for a sprite:

Where the bee sucks, there suck I:
In a cowslip's bell I lie;

and

Come unto these yellow sands,
  And then take hands:
Curtsied when you have and kissed,
  The wild waves whist. . . .

'The wild waves whist' is a phrase of Marlowe's, held in mind through all the years – one more indication of how important that influence, and the experience that went with it, had been. In the last play of all, *Henry VIII*, Queen Catherine in her trouble has a song sung to her,

Orpheus with his lute made trees,
And the mountain tops that freeze,
  Bow themselves when he did sing;

with its tribute to the power of music:

> In sweet music is such art,
> Killing care and grief of heart
> Fall asleep or hearing die.

No writer has ever witnessed more to its power, or been more responsive to the spell of music in its varying moods. To him music was the accompaniment of love:

> If music be the food of love

– as of course it was –

> play on;
> Give me excess of it.

This is immediately followed by an address to the spirit of love. There is no subject in the whole of Shakespeare on which he wrote more, to which he devoted more words than love – more even than to life and death. So love was at the centre of the universe for him, and he meant chiefly the love of men and women. We have seen him standing beside his Dark Lady, whom we now know to have been of a family of Court musicians, while she played on the virginals:

> Give me some music; music, moody food
> Of us that trade in love.

When Romeo and Juliet look forward to consummating their bliss,

> let rich music's tongue
> Unfold the imagined happiness. . . .

Music has many moods, capable of accompanying all the moods in life: martial, alarming, fearful; apprehensive, ominous, threatening; mysterious, inspiring, religious, mystical; pathetic, or consoling; humorous, comic, ridiculous. Bottom the Weaver considered that he had 'a reasonable good ear in music: let's have the tongs and the bones'. Richard II, in despair, felt

> How sour sweet music is
> When time is broke and no proportion kept!
> So is it in the music of men's lives.

And then,

> This music mads me. Let it sound no more.

Yet, even so, in him who gave it, it was a sign of love.

In *Measure for Measure* the attention is called to the ambivalence of its powers:

> music oft hath such a charm
> To make bad good, and good provoke to harm

– a characteristic double thought. We recall his condemnation, however, of

> The man that hath no music in himself,
> Nor is not moved with concord of sweet sounds,
> Is fit for treasons, stratagems, and spoils. . . .
> Let no such man be trusted.

In this same play, *The Merchant of Venice*, which is full of music, as so many appropriately are – not, on the whole, the history plays or classical plays like *Julius Caesar* and *Coriolanus* – there is a profound phrase:

> I am never merry when I hear sweet music.

This again is psychologically right: to the person who really understands and responds to music, it reaches depths beyond mere pleasure; it is beyond common experience.

In the public life of the time there was a mounting interest in Virginia – the Elizabethan name for all North America – and the planting of English stock there. After all, this was one of the main objectives for which the English had fought Spain for twenty years – the open door to the New World. The Elizabethans were not unaware that the future of the English stock and their language were involved in this historic opening; as the perceptive Daniel wrote,

> And who in time knows whither we may vent
> The treasure of our tongue, to what strange shores
> This gain of our best glory shall be sent? . . .

At that time no foreigner needed to know English; the Elizabethans could not know that it would become a world-language, or that their popular dramatist would be a grand instrument in its dissemination.

Immediately upon the conclusion of peace in 1604, two representative companies were founded, a London Company and a Plymouth one, to promote the planting of colonies on the southern and northern coasts of North America. Southampton's interest went back to his years in the Tower: in 1602 he backed a voyage to explore what became the New England coast for a suitable settlement. In 1605 he fitted out another voyage for those climes; later he became deeply concerned in the southern area, as Treasurer of the London Company. Hampton River and Hampton Roads, the original Southampton Hundred, were all named for him. In 1607 Jamestown was founded; in 1609 the second Charter drummed up a host of investors in the plantation – we have a list of nearly 600, with Southampton and Pembroke in the lead. The prudent investor in Stratford lands and tithes was not among them. They all lost their money.

In May 1609 there set sail the first large expedition, a little fleet with 600 colonists on board, the fruit of all this effort; it has been described as 'the true beginning of one of the great folk movements of history'.* But they ran into, what few English can have experienced before, not just a storm but a tropical tornado. Sir George

* W. F. Craven, *The Southern Colonies in the Seventeenth Century*, p. 96.

Somers' flagship, the *Sea Venture*, ran on the rocks of Bermuda and broke up, though not a life was lost. There on the uninhabited island the colonists remained for some ten months, until they had constructed pinnaces in which they reached Virginia in the spring. There was enough to eat, wild hogs and game and fish; but the island was supposed to be haunted, it was full of noises, which the people attributed to spirits and devils. And there were attempts at mutiny, groups of men withdrawing into the woods; one serious conspiracy against the life of the governor was unveiled and the author hanged.

It is not without significance that the plays of the most imaginative register of the time, from *Pericles* (1608) onward, are full of voyages, and sea-surges, storms and wrecks. Shakespeare's imagination was touched by the voyages; he read not only Hakluyt but Richard Eden,* and he did not fail to be caught by the exciting story of Bermuda. A ballad and a pamphlet describing the experience came out in 1610, but Shakespeare's direct source was the manuscript news-letter which William Strachey, who had gone out as secretary to the colony – a job poor John Donne wanted – sent home, before returning himself late in 1611.

Strachey was a man with literary associations; he had contributed a sonnet to Jonson's *Sejanus* on publication; he was a shareholder in the Children of the Revels, and was regularly in and out of Blackfriars. Other acquaintances of Shakespeare besides Southampton were interested in Virginia, particularly Sir Dudley Digges, whose brother Leonard wrote commendatory verses for the publication of the Plays. Sir Dudley was a friend and neighbour of John Heming and Henry Condell; Digges's stepfather, Sir Thomas Russell, lived out at leafy Alderminster, not far from Stratford: Shakespeare asked him to become overseer of his will. Digges's own father had written books on military discipline; one of these books, edited by his son in 1604, *Four Paradoxes of Politic Discourses*, Shakespeare read before writing *Coriolanus*. Sir Dudley possessed a portrait of the

* The editor of the New Arden edition of *The Tempest* calls this well-known man, inaccurately, Robert Eden.

astronomer, Tycho Brahe, with the names of his ancestors, including Rosenkrantz and Guildenstern – names taken up into *Hamlet.*

We see more and more clearly the background to the dramatist's life; everything was grist to his mill, every hint picked up.

Besides the general situation Shakespeare adopted details from Strachey, the curious phenomenon of St Elmo's Fire running down the rigging, for example, which he attributes to Ariel, his creation in the play. Strachey mentions the first description of the Islands by Oviedo, whose first names, Gonzalo and Ferdinando, are seized on for characters. The name of the heroine, Miranda, is symbolic, as usual in the romances, like Marina and Perdita. As with Autolycus in *The Winter's Tale*, it is Shakespeare's own invention, the unique character of Caliban, that holds the mind. It arose from his reflection on primitive society, as revealed in the Voyages; we know that he read Ralegh's *Guiana*, and the name, of course, is a play on cannibal. For Shakespeare had none of the illusions of Montaigne's cult of the primitive, sick as he was of the savagery of the French Wars of Religion. Shakespeare knew that savages could be as savage as the so-called civilised, that blacks are no better than whites.

He had read Montaigne's essay on Cannibals, in Florio's translation of the *Essays*, which Edward Blount had published in 1603 – it was to have another edition in 1613. From this source came Gonzalo's description of a communist commonwealth, without property or use of money, trade or government, force or laws:

> All things in common nature should produce
> Without sweat or endeavour. . . .

Shakespeare, whom no amount of imagination could seduce from common sense, knew that this was nonsense. Indeed, it is precisely the man of imagination who knows how untrue the theorising of the intellect is to the real condition of humanity. Shakespeare's comment on utopianism is brief and to the point: communism of women as well as property and work?

> No marrying 'mong his subjects?

Answer:

> None, man; all idle: whores and knaves.

The play was written probably in the summer of 1611, for Simon Forman did not see it along with *Cymbeline* and *The Winter's Tale* in April and May; it has been thought, at home in the country, from the full stage-directions, more elaborate than for any other play, except his last, *Henry VIII* – as if for others to produce. It was performed on Hallowmas Night, 1 November 1611, at Whitehall 'before the King's Majesty'. It found favour with the public, as usual – as Ben Jonson's *Catiline* failed to do that same year. He remembered this three years later, and wrote grumpily in the Induction to *Bartholomew Fair*, 'if there be never a servant-monster [i.e. Caliban] in the Fair, who can help it, nor a nest of antics? He [Ben] is loth to make Nature afraid in his plays, like those that beget *Tales*, *Tempests*, and such-like drolleries.' Though testy, Ben was not really ill-humoured; perhaps it was a kind of game with him, not without a little mutual advertisement.

I have given an account of the play elsewhere;* here what is relevant to our purpose is to notice the atmosphere of farewell, Prospero's renunciation of his magic, the withdrawal from the practice of his art. With our fuller knowledge of the writer now, it is not possible that he had not himself in mind, as he had with Berowne earlier. He is saying good-bye:

> Our revels now are ended. These our actors,
> As I foretold you, were all spirits and
> Are melted into air, into thin air:
> And, like the baseless fabric of this vision,
> The cloud-capped towers, the gorgeous palaces,

* See my *William Shakespeare*, pp. 430–7.

The solemn temples, the great globe itself,
Yea, all which it inherit, shall dissolve
And, like this insubstantial pageant faded,
Leave not a rack behind.

With this double-minded man, so given to the double-talk of the imagination, there is a secondary suggestion of the Globe here. Oddly enough, in the way nature has of imitating art, or with the prognostic gift of poets (the only true prophets), the Globe did dissolve, in a couple of years, by fire.

CHAPTER 12

'Home Art Gone'

WHAT was Shakespeare doing in the year 1612, after he had written *The Tempest* the year before?

Here is a real gap in our knowledge of this busy, prudent, discreet man, no public figure – unlike Ben Jonson. We know that he was at Stratford in September 1611, and in London on 11 May 1612 when he gave evidence in the Mountjoy law-suit; he was expected to give further evidence on 19 June but did not appear – he had evidently gone back to Stratford as usual for the summer.

For some time now he had taken things easier, his rate of production slowing down to one play a year. The order seems clear: after leaving *Timon* unfinished and completing *Pericles*, he produced *Cymbeline* in 1609, *The Winter's Tale* in 1610, *The Tempest* in 1611. But there is no play for 1612, the first indication of a gap; earlier, he had no difficulty in producing two plays a year: in 1604, for example, *Measure for Measure* and *Othello*, in 1608 *Coriolanus* and the unfinished *Timon*.

His work was coming to an end. Meanwhile his junior, Ben Jonson, had been going from strength to strength, a play and sometimes two masques in a year; and critical opinion rated him higher than the popular, more modest actor and playwright.

Shakespeare continued in health and to move between Stratford and London, in accordance with the double demands upon him now of the theatre and the man of property and family at home. In September he contributed, as a leading townsman along with his cousin, the lawyer Thomas Greene – who occupied New Place for a time – towards the charges of procuring a bill in Parliament for the better repair of highways, a matter of interest to him who travelled them regularly. An early neighbour in Henley Street, Robert Johnson the vintner, who later kept the White Lion, leased a barn from the gentleman of New Place, at a goodly rent.* And in this year 1611 the vicar moved into the old priest's house in Chapel Yard, to become the poet's neighbour.

Schoolmaster Alexander Aspinall was a near neighbour, too, in the School Yard. Head of the Grammar School for over forty years, 1582–1624, he was a most familiar figure in the town. He had married the widow of a wool-trader, whose business he carried on, and became an active man on the town-council, like John Shakespeare before him: burgess, chamberlain, alderman. But he refused to become bailiff (i.e. mayor) and, resigning as alderman, was retained as council man 'for his continual advice and great experience in the borough affairs . . . and in regard he is an ancient Master of Arts and a man learned'.

It was not until 1613 that the master provided another play, *Henry VIII*. In a sense it was a return to the form, the chronicle-play, in which he first achieved success. For his source he returned also to his early favourite, Holinshed, whom he followed more closely even than usual, adding to it touches from Hall's Chronicle and Foxe's *Book of Martyrs* – most popular of Elizabethan best-sellers. In a deeper sense the play completes the arc of his achievement; for, with Cranmer's prophetic speech at the baptism of the Princess Elizabeth, Shakespeare was able to pay tribute to the triumph of her reign, the epoch that was to take her name, now that it was all over. Always a master of dramatic and artistic decorum, he must have intended the propriety of this: he was rounding his work off.

Once more he was responding to popular feeling. Here was another Princess Elizabeth, popular not only for her name but her out-going personality, who was making a popular Protestant marriage. (It is from her that our present royal family descend.) She was a god-daughter of the great Queen, whose memory the marriage

* Eccles, *Shakespeare in Warwickshire*, p. 133.

festivities renewed; there was a resurgence of national feeling such as had not been experienced under the Stuarts. Elizabethan memories came surging back, now seen in perspective as history; many history plays were reissued at the time. And Shakespeare made the most of the opportunity, for the last time, as he had been ready to do all along.

Once more, too, the old master offered something that was different. Henry VIII's successful reign did not offer one central issue upon which it could be pivoted; there was a succession of falls of great personages, Buckingham, Wolsey, Queen Catherine. So the play became a ceremonious piece, with a background of splendid pageantry, dumb shows, processions, a baptism, plenty of sennets and trumpets and even cannon shot off. To align it with the other late plays there is a Vision enacted, like a masque. Its atmosphere is in keeping with these, for the dominant mood is one of patience in adversity, compassion, acceptance of one's fate.

This is most remarkable, especially when one considers the Protestant partisanship of Tudor historical writing, in the treatment of Cardinal Wolsey and Queen Catherine. No one had had a good word to say for Wolsey, for Catholic tradition – which made a hero of More – was almost as unfriendly as the Protestant was hostile. Shakespeare read the biography of the Cardinal by the man who knew him most intimately, George Cavendish, his confidential attendant; it is just like Shakespeare's magnanimity of mind to have given a more sympathetic portrait of Wolsey than any – far more so than Holinshed's, from whom he departed on this matter. It is yet one more index of his human understanding (as with Henry VIII's great-uncle, Richard III, we may add).

The most sympathetic character of all is the ill-treated Queen Catherine, who thus takes her place along with Marina and Hermione. This, too, offered another example of the dramatist's breadth of sympathies, for Catherine of Aragon was no heroine to a Protestant England, whose martyr was Elizabeth's mother. William Shakespeare was above this littleness of mind, as he was above sectarian quarrels and pointless disputes about religion. The dramatist reaped his reward; the play offered two exceptionally fine parts for actors, in Queen Catherine and Wolsey, and has always been successful.

For all its sympathy for these two Catholic characters – demanded by the drama, apart from personal feelings – the play is strongly Elizabethan in tone and in its upshot. Now that the reign had passed into history, he took that opportunity to pay tribute to it, which he had not done at the moment of the Queen's passing, so shortly after her execution of Essex and condemnation of Southampton. He could now sum up her achievement in the form of prophecy:

> She shall be . . .
> A pattern to all princes living with her,
> And all that shall succeed. . . .
> She shall be loved and feared; her own shall bless her;
> Her foes shake like a field of beaten corn. . . .
> In her days every man shall eat in safety,
> Under his own vine, what he plants; and sing
> The merry songs of peace to all his neighbours.

This speech follows the form of Biblical prophecy, and reflects the language and imagery of the Bible, heard Sunday by Sunday in church.

A few personal touches bespeak his own past. There is the 'soft cheveril' of his father's shop, the deerskin from which the finest gloves were made. Bardolph of *Henry IV* comes alive again among the jostling crowd attending the infant Elizabeth's christening: 'there is a fellow somewhat near the door: he should be a brazier by his face, or, o' my conscience, twenty of the dog-days now reign in's nose'. There is very little bawdy, but that the old hand has not lost its cunning, with a new inflexion, of the voyages and Virginia colonisation, we are given: 'have we some strange Indian with the great tool come to Court, the women so besiege us? Bless me, what a fry of fornication is at door! On my Christian conscience, this one christening will beget a thousand.'

The play was carefully written and subtly organised, with contrasts of scene and pace, the crowd and processional scenes, grand personages in their splendour, and then revealed as souls alone with themselves at their end. None of the rapid scamping he had sometimes been reduced to in the rush of the theatre: he had time now. We have a good text of the play.

Once more he addresses the audience in his own person in the Prologue, in the courteous tone he had adopted from the beginning:

> I come no more to make you laugh; things now
> That bear a weighty and a serious brow,
> Sad, high and working, full of state and woe . . .
> We now present.

But there is something, if not for everybody, at any rate for a variety of people:

> Those that can pity, here
> May, if they think it well, let fall a tear:
> The subject will deserve it. Such as give
> Their money out of hope they may believe
> May here find truth too.

There was something also for the lighter-hearted who only wanted to see a show:

> Those that come to see
> Only a show or two, and so agree
> The play may pass, if they be still and willing,
> I'll undertake may see away their shilling
> Richly in two short hours.

There we have the 'two hours' traffic' of a Shakespearian play, with its uninterrupted speed in performance.

The Epilogue, too, concludes with its recognisable note:

> 'Tis ten to one this play can never please
> All that are here. Some come to take their ease,
> And sleep an act or two; but those, we fear,
> We have frightened with our trumpets; so, 'tis clear
> They'll say 'tis naught. . . .

Then there come those

> others to hear the City
> Abused extremely, and to cry 'That's witty!'
> Which we have not done neither. . . .

Perhaps that is a glance at the private theatres, which made a feature of mocking the bourgeois – as Jonson and his like did – on the part of the older master who had made his career with the public theatre and on the public stage. He ends, as he had done before, with an appeal to the women to applaud his play: then 'all the best men are ours'. Insinuating, courteous, almost obsequious – 'Let me be obsequious in thy heart' – this concludes his lifelong love-affair with his audience, like Dickens' with his readers.

At a performance of *Henry VIII* on 29 July 1613, which may have been the first, the Globe was burnt down. It seems that the play was produced, as the elaborate stage-directions indicate, with pomp and circumstance. Cannon were shot off at King Henry's entry for the masque at the Cardinal's, and a spark caught the thatch afire. People were so 'attentive to the show' that they took no notice of the smoke, so that the fire ran right round the circle of the building and consumed it to the ground. There must have been some losses of theatre-properties – perhaps some manuscripts; it might be due to this that we have not got the Burbage theatre-papers, as we have Henslowe's. Ben Jonson recorded the event in verse:

> Against the Globe, the glory of the Bank . . .
> Flanked with a ditch and forced out of a marish,
> I saw with two poor chambers taken in
> And razed, ere thought could urge this might have been!
> See the World's ruins! Nothing but the piles
> Left.

Nothing from Shakespeare, to whom it mattered more – no insurance in those days, and he was a sharer.

However, the theatre was rebuilt, finer than before, with no thatch to its roof, while the King's Men went off on tour. It is unlikely that Shakespeare accompanied them as in old days: more and more Stratford called. His brother Richard died there in February this year 1613 – brother Gilbert, whom we have seen taking seizin of the land purchased by William, had died the year before. In July 1613 daughter Susanna, who had married Dr John Hall in 1607, brought suit for defamation against a slanderous young gentleman, John Lane, of the family who lived not far out along the meadows at Alveston. This young spark had said that Mistress Hall had 'the running of the reins and had been naught with Ralph Smith'. For this Master Lane was excommunicated; but it is likely enough that Susanna had the running of the reins – she was the clever woman of the family. One hears nothing of her mother; evidently there was nothing to be said.

In London this year Shakespeare bought the house in Blackfriars, and supplied the words for Rutland's *impresa*. Sir Henry Wotton reported that at the tilt some of the mottoes were so 'dark that their meaning is not yet understood – unless perchance that were their meaning, not to be understood'. Was Shakespeare and Burbage's one of them?

Shakespeare also put his hand, gave several touches, to Beaumont and Fletcher's play, *The Two Noble Kinsmen.* A few passages are recognisably Shakespeare's; we do not know whether he had any further part in outlining the plot, as he may have done with *Pericles.* When his faithful colleagues, Heming and Condell, did their best and brought together his plays after his death – from the manuscripts and prompt-copies which were the property of the Company – they did not include these two plays.

Shakespeare himself did nothing to publish his work, but this was the normal attitude of contemporary dramatists. It was his junior, Jonson, who was the exception and in 1616 published a folio of his plays as a first volume of his Works – to some people's irritation at his egoism. But we have reason to be grateful for it – if only William Shakespeare had been a bit more egotistical about his output of plays! Proust understood that 'human altruism without an element of egotism is sterile', and that all creativity comes out of the ego, is an extension of it. Shakespeare's ego was satisfied by recognition as gentleman and poet; being an actor and writing plays came somewhat lower in his scale of values.

With our proper emphasis on the man of the theatre we appreciate now that there is no mystery in the matter; as with Heywood, a fellow actor-dramatist who specifically expressed it, the 'act of creation reached its fulfilment when his actors presented his play before an audience'.* The plays belonged to the Company, and were for them to deal with. After Shakespeare's death they did, to the best of their ability, though it was a difficult and burdensome business getting together such a mass of material, securing a decent text for some of the plays, organising it, arranging with a consortium of publishers to back it, getting it printed, and then getting it sold. Never had there been such an undertaking before, thirty-six plays in one volume by one man – Ben Jonson's folio of 1616 was nothing to it, though he was there to see to it himself.

The venture presented great difficulties and took several years to bring off. We can read the apprehensiveness of Heming and Condell whether the big Folio would sell in their appeal 'to the Great Variety of Readers'. 'Well, it is now public and you will stand for your privileges we know: to read, and censure. Do so, but buy it first. . . . Judge your six penn'orth, your shilling's worth, your five shillings' worth at a time, or higher, so you rise to the just rates – and welcome! But, whatever you do, Buy. Censure will not drive a trade, or make the jack go.' Censure meant Criticism; here the old actors fell back defensively on the plea that, however critical play-goers and readers might be, 'Know, these plays have had their trial already and stood out all appeals' – they did not need any critical commendation.

So, 'the collected edition they sponsored was very much a memorial to an actor-dramatist by his actor friends',* as they said, 'only to keep the memory of so worthy a Friend and Fellow alive as was our Shakespeare'. They very properly dedicated the volume to the brothers, the Earls of Pembroke and Montgomery: the former was now Lord Chamberlain, the latter shortly to succeed him in the

* Bentley, *Shakespeare: a Biographical Handbook*, p. 184.

office, with its supervision of the stage. Montgomery was to show himself even more interested in the well-being of the King's Men than his brother; but both of them had 'prosecuted both them [the Plays] and their Author living with so much favour, we hope that they outliving him, and he not having the fate, common with some, to be executor to his own writings – you will use the like indulgence toward them you have done unto their parent'. Since their lordships had so much liked the plays when acted, 'the Volume asked to be yours'.

Finally, underlining the theatrical origin of the venture, 'comes a most unusual feature, one never found before in an English collection and seldom since'.* It is a list of 'the Names of the Principal Actors in All these Plays'. There they are gathered together, many of them familiar to us in the course of this book. Twenty-six are named, beginning with Shakespeare himself, followed by Burbage; then Heming, Phillips, Will Kemp, Pope, Bryan, Condell; other familiars are Sly, Cowley, Robert Armin – who took Kemp's place and played the parts of Feste and the Fool in *Lear* – and Nathan Field (the son of a Puritan!), John Underwood and William Ostler, who had been boy-actors before becoming King's Men.

Very interesting commendatory verses were arranged for, to speed the bulky ship with its precious cargo on the way – without the labours of his loyal Fellows half of Shakespeare's plays would not have come down to us – and the verses have a representative spread. Two of the authors were Oxford men. Leonard Digges, Sir Dudley's brother, was a literary scholar, one of whose translations was published by Edward Blount. His verses paid tribute to Shakespeare's 'pious Fellows' who, at length, 'give the world thy works'. Actually Digges wrote far more informative verses for the publication of Shakespeare's *Poems* in 1640. In these he points to the dramatist's facility, no labour to him to contrive a play, 'art without art unparalleled', and the naturalness of it all, not translated or plagiarised from others, the originality and fertility of invention. An ardent playgoer, he had often seen the audience ravished at the

* Ibid., p. 188.

appearance of Caesar, or Brutus and Cassius half-drawing their swords on each other, when they would not brook a line of tedious *Catiline*; while *Sejanus* too was irksome. Yet let Falstaff, Hal and the rest come – you scarce shall have room, the theatre was so crowded, as for Beatrice and Benedick or Malvolio:

> The cockpit, galleries, boxes, all are full.

Another literary Oxford Fellow, James Mabbe of Magdalen, who did the admirable translation of the famous Spanish novel, *The Rogue*, lamented Shakespeare's early death;

> We wondered, Shakespeare, that thou went'st so soon
> From the world's stage to the grave's tiring-room.

Mabbe knew Florio, for a book of whom he had provided verses; so he probably knew the dramatist. Cambridge was represented by Hugh Holland, a Fellow of Trinity and a Welshman of literary interests, who knew Ben Jonson and, like him, had been educated at Westminster under Camden. Most important, representing both the stage and literature, was Ben Jonson's magnificent tribute

> To the memory of my beloved, the Author.

In the unparalleled generosity of this long comprehensive summing-up all minor reservations or minimal criticisms are drossed away. Jonson was a critic of principle, who possessed justice of mind; and how concisely he summed up Shakespeare's development:

> I should commit thee surely with thy peers,
> And tell how far thou didst our Lyly outshine,
> Or sporting Kyd, or Marlowe's mighty line.

The player-poet had paced himself beside each in turn – and then gone beyond them all; though he knew no Greek, his peers were

Aeschylus, Sophocles, Euripides. The most popular of playwrights –

Soul of the Age!
The applause, delight, the wonder of our stage!

– whose matter came from Nature itself in rich profusion, nevertheless his work owed as much to Art.

For a good poet's made as well as born.

In this, his most considered judgment, Ben Jonson estimated Shakespeare as much for his art as he did for his native genius.

There were people – chiefly the young intellectuals of Ben's tribe – who admired him more; Jonson himself knew better.

It is to be observed here that Shakespeare's real fame was made, not by people at large, but by other men of genius; perhaps it is always so: they *know*. One of the most immediate indications is the enthusiasm of the young Milton, as early as 1630:

Dear son of memory, great heir of Fame.

Milton is the opposite pole in our literature – the universal scholar, the epic poet, the Puritan, the moral and political idealist, the doctrinaire intellectual with little knowledge of human beings – yet he loved Shakespeare. From Milton to Dryden, to Pope and Dr Johnson, who for all his classical principles and Augustan assumptions was the greatest of Shakespeare critics; from him to the Romantics, Hazlitt and Coleridge, to Keats, who lived within the shadow of Shakespeare, and Tennyson and Matthew Arnold. And so onward to eternity – or, more probably, the end of our civilisation, as we have known it since the Renaissance. This is apart from the fertilising influence of his genius, not only in literature but in the other arts, especially in music and painting, all over the world. A subject in itself, we cannot go into it here.* We may content ourselves with the insight of one who was outside the tradition of our

* Cf. my *The Elizabethan Renaissance: the Cultural Achievement*, pp. 345–6.

language, and from another art. Verdi called Shakespeare 'the greatest authority on the heart of man'. What a tribute from so great a man himself!

Ben Jonson also wrote the lines – he probably gave more help to Heming and Condell than we know – beneath the inadequate engraving from which we derive our portrait of Shakespeare. Nevertheless, the wide world knows well what he looked like: never was there such a dome of St Paul's of a cranium, except perhaps on the head of Walter Scott or Henry James.

What was he doing in these last two years, 1614 and 1615? Evidently enjoying a measure of well-earned retirement and his status as the gentleman of New Place. He continued to journey between Stratford and London; for in October 1614 he was at home, while on 17 November Thomas Greene wrote of 'my cousin Shakespeare coming yesterday to town' with his son-in-law, Dr John Hall. He remained away over Christmas, the season for Court performances, presumably living in his newly acquired house in Blackfriars.

In the summer of 1614, in July while Shakespeare was in residence, a raging fire devastated the thatched houses of Stratford. It did immense damage and affected its prosperity for a number of years; but it did not touch the fine stone house of New Place. In these years there was some trouble over enclosures out at Welcombe, where Anthony Nash managed Shakespeare's holding; one of his friends, Thomas Combe, was involved. Shakespeare does not seem to have been much concerned in, or about, the matter, though the town-council wrote him letters and his lawyer-cousin Greene kept him informed. Shakespeare looked on from a distance, too busy still to bother, if we may judge from Greene's memorandum of September 1615: 'W. Shakespeare's telling J. Greene that I was not able to bear [bar?] the enclosing of Welcombe.' It would be like him to accept what could not be helped.

In his later years there was intelligent companionship in his family-circle, with his daughter Susanna, 'witty above her sex . . . something of Shakespeare was in that', and her husband, Dr Hall. Eight years older than Susanna, Hall was only eleven years younger than her father – in whose later plays several doctors appear, perhaps a close acquaintance new to his experience. Hall was a Cambridge man, a successful practitioner with a large practice in Stratford and among the gentry of the surrounding countryside.* The most interesting of these to us are the Rainsfords, just out across the meadows at Clifford Chambers. They were friends and patrons of the poet Drayton, who spent his summers there with them, and whom Dr Hall treated for a tertian ague.

Susanna and Hall had an only daughter, Elizabeth, born in 1608, the plague-year. Aged eight at the time of her grandfather's death, he intended to provide a dowry for her and then cancelled it as she was yet so young. At eighteen she was married to the lawyer Thomas Nash, of thirty-three, son of Anthony Nash. Upon his death she married Sir John Barnard of Abington near Northampton, and died there, leaving money to her poor relations, the Hathaways at Stratford; while Sir John ordered the 'old goods and lumber' in the house there to be disposed of or burnt. Lady Barnard was Shakespeare's only grandchild; with her his direct family came to an end.

Shakespeare's widow lived on for another seven years after him, though over eight years his senior; she died in the year that the First Folio of his works came out, 1623. An old sexton said that 'she did earnestly desire to be laid in the same grave with him', but no one durst touch his gravestone for fear of the curse inscribed in his lines thereon. Hall died in 1635, Susanna in 1649. There they all are gathered together before the altar within the sanctuary of the church.

In February 1616 a marriage was found for the younger daughter, Judith, who evidently took after her mother – she couldn't write. The happy husband, Thomas Quiney, was a vintner and son of Shakespeare's old friend, Richard Quiney, the well-educated alderman and bailiff of the borough. The couple had a boy, baptised Shakespeare, who shortly died: nothing in the family way seemed

* See Harriet Joseph, *John Hall. Man and Physician.*

able to keep the name going. Her father's will, made on Ladyday, 25 March 1616, provided for Judith: £100 dowry and £50 more if she gave up her claim to the cottage in Chapel Lane; another £150 for her children, provided her husband settled an equal sum on her and them. Her father left her also his large silver-gilt bowl.

When he made his will that March day – it was a Monday and was written by lawyer Francis Collins – he was 'in perfect health and memory, God be praised'. It is a very characteristic document, generous and neighbourly. All his lands and houses were entailed upon Susanna and her heirs, and in default upon Judith and hers; there was the intention he had always had, of founding a family – though frustrated of its being carried in his name by the death of Hamnet, twenty years before. To his sister, Joan Hart, he left the old home in Henley Street, which she occupied, for her life, £20, all his clothes, with £5 apiece to her three sons. He left his widow to her daughter's care, who looked after everything, though he reserved for Anne the next-best bed – the big double-bed would be needed by Susanna and John. They were to be executors. Little Elizabeth was to have all his plate.

A number of friends in and about Stratford were remembered with bequests – we cannot specify them all. 'I do entreat' – a characteristic word – Thomas Russell and Francis Collins to be overseers of the will, with £5 to the first and 20 marks to the second. He left his sword to Thomas Combe of Welcombe, where their interests neighboured. 'I give and bequeath to the poor of Stratford £10 . . . to Hamnet Sadler 26*s* 8*d* to buy him a ring, to William Reynolds gent. 26*s* 8*d* to buy him a ring, to my godson William Walker 20*s* in gold, to Anthony Nash gent. 26*s* 8*d*, and to Mr John Nash 26*s* 8*d*; and to my Fellows, John Heming, Richard Burbage and Henry Condell 26*s* 8*d* apiece to buy them rings.'

A generation after, the vicar of Stratford recorded the tradition that Shakespeare had a merry meeting with Drayton and Ben Jonson, drank too hard and died of a fever there contracted. Nothing improbable in that; certainly the illness was sudden, for when he made his will he was 'in perfect health and memory', a month later he was dead: he died on 23 April, St George's Day. He died, as he had lived, a conforming member of the Church of England. His will makes that perfectly clear – in fact, puts it beyond dispute, for it is the regular Protestant formula: 'I commend my soul into the hands of God my Creator, hoping and assured by believing through the only merits of Jesus Christ, my Saviour, to be made partaker of life everlasting.'

As he lay in the house dying, the Chapel bell across the way knelling for the passing soul, as was the custom, what memories must have flitted in and out the chambers of his mind: so many triumphs at the Globe going back to its opening, with himself as Chorus in *Henry V*; performances at Court before James and Anne, or the more resplendent Queen, whose expressed wish was a command to present Falstaff in love; the writing of *The Merry Wives* in consequence, in a great hurry for the Garter festivities at Windsor; Essex's tragedy, in which Southampton was so deeply involved; the early days of friendship, the happiness and good fortune of finding such a patron in the golden youth at such a time, the equivocations and ambivalences of love; the brilliance and daring of Marlowe, the 'dead shepherd', the flame so early extinguished; the rivalry and admiration, so much learned from him; the passion and torments of love, Emilia at the virginals, himself standing beside her; the spell, the torment of desire, the disenchantment. And so back to earlier scenes, the pretty country folks in the acres of rye on the way to Shottery, bringing a bride in over the threshold of the crowded old home in Henley Street; the schoolboy with his satchel making his way down the dark winter streets, the Chapel bell ringing as now, but not to school:

> No longer mourn for me when I am dead
> Than you shall hear the surly sullen bell
> Give warning to the world that I am fled. . . .

Comparative Chronology

		1557	John Shakespeare marries Mary Arden		
1558	Elizabeth I becomes Queen				
		1564	Christopher Marlowe born Plague at Stratford	1564	William Shakespeare born
1569	Northern Rebellion	1569	John Shakespeare Bailiff of Stratford		
		c.1570	Emilia Bassano born		
		1572	Ben Jonson born		
		1573	William Lanier born Southampton born		
1575	Queen's visit to Kenilworth				
		1579	Spenser's *Shepherd's Calendar* North's Plutarch		
				1582	Shakespeare marries Anne Hathaway
1583	Queen's Company formed			1583	Daughter Susanna born
		1584	Lyly's *Campaspe*		
1585	1st Lord Hunsdon becomes Lord Chamberlain			1585	Twins Hamnet and Judith born
		1587	Holinshed's *Chronicles*, 2nd ed. Marlowe's *1 Tamburlaine* Kyd's *Spanish Tragedy*	1587	Shakespeare witnesses deed at Stratford
				1587–90	Shakespeare acting and touring
1588	Spanish Armada Leicester dies	1588	Marlowe's *2 Tamburlaine* Sidney's *Arcadia*		
		1590	Spenser's *Faerie Queene*		
				1590–1	*2 and 3 Henry VI*

1591	Essex expedition to Normandy	1591	Southampton in Normandy Sidney's sonnets published	1591	*1 Henry VI* *Titus Andronicus* 'A Lover's Complaint'
1592	Plague	1592	Daniel's sonnets published Thomas Watson dies Robert Greene dies Marlowe's *Edward II*	1592	Sonnets begin Robert Greene's attack published *The Comedy of Errors*
				1592–3	*The Taming of the Shrew*
1593	Plague	1593	Marlowe dies Emilia Bassano marries William Lanier	1593	*Love's Labour's Lost* *Richard III* *Venus and Adonis* published Sonnets continue
		1593–4	Thomas Kyd dies		
		1594	Countess of Southampton marries Sir Thomas Heneage Lord Chamberlain's Company formed Daniel's *Civil Wars*	1594	*A Midsummer Night's Dream* *The Rape of Lucrece* published *Romeo and Juliet* Sonnets continue
				1595	Sonnets end *Richard II*
1596	Capture of Cadiz	1596	Lord Chamberlain Hunsdon dies Lord Cobham becomes Lord Chamberlain Hamnet Shakespeare dies John Shakespeare takes out coat-of-arms	1596	*King John* *The Merchant of Venice* Shakespeare coat-of-arms granted
1597	Islands Voyage	1597	Southampton on Islands Voyage 2nd Lord Hunsdon becomes Lord Chamberlain	1597	*1 and 2 Henry IV* Shakespeare buys New Place
1598	Irish Rebellion begins	1598	Marlowe's *Hero and Leander* published Jonson's *Every Man in His Humour* Southampton marries Elizabeth Vernon	1598	*As You Like It* *Much Ado about Nothing*

1599	Essex in Ireland	1599	Southampton in Ireland	1599	*Henry V*
					Julius Caesar
		1600	Jonson's *Poetaster*	1600	*Twelfth Night*
			Dekker's rejoinder, *Satiromastix*		
				1600–1	*Hamlet*
1601	Essex rebels, is executed	1601	Southampton in Tower	1601	?*The Merry Wives of Windsor*
			John Shakespeare dies		'The Phoenix and the Turtle'
				1601–2	*Troilus and Cressida*
		1602	Southampton in Tower	1602	Shakespeare buys land at Stratford
1603	Elizabeth I dies	1603	Southampton released	1603	*All's Well That Ends Well*
	James I succeeds		Chamberlain's Men become King's Men		Shakespeare and Fellows become Grooms of the Chamber
	Plague		Jonson's *Sejanus*		
				1604	*Measure for Measure*
					Othello
1605	Gunpowder Plot			1605	*King Lear*
					Shakespeare invests in Stratford tithes
		1606	Jonson's *Volpone*	1606	*Macbeth*
		1607	Daughter Susanna marries Dr John Hall	1607	*Antony and Cleopatra*
			Southampton's mother dies		
			Edmund Shakespeare dies		
1608	Plague	1608	Sir William Hervey marries Cordelia Annesley	1608	*Coriolanus*
					Timon of Athens (unfinished)
			King's Men acquire Blackfriars		
			Granddaughter Elizabeth Hall born		
			Shakespeare's mother dies		
1609	The Virginia Adventure. Wreck of the *Sea Venture*	1609	Jonson's *Epicoene*	1609	*Pericles* completed
			Beaumont and Fletcher's *Philaster*		Sonnets and 'A Lover's Complaint' published
				1609–10	*Cymbeline*

		1610	Jonson's *The Alchemist*		
		1611	Jonson's *Catiline*	1611	Shakespeare contributes to Highways Bill *The Winter's Tale*
		1612	Gilbert Shakespeare dies	1612	Shakespeare testifies in Mountjoy suit *The Tempest*
1613	Princess Elizabeth's wedding	1613	The Globe burns down Richard Shakespeare dies	1613	*Henry VIII* Shakespeare buys house in Blackfriars Shakespeare writes Rutland's *impresa*
		1614	Great Fire at Stratford Enclosure at Welcombe		
		1616	Daughter Judith marries Thomas Quiney Jonson's *Works* published	1616	Shakespeare dies
		1623	Shakespeare's widow dies	1623	First Folio published

INDEX